FEB 2 5 2013

Additional Praise for The Golden Shore

"The Golden Shore *is about more than one man's love affair with California's iconic coast. It's the history of an environmental consciousness that has been impressed upon people around the globe. This is a vital story that will help inform future generations of how and why we work so diligently to protect and preserve California's majestic coast. I applaud David Helvarg for this great work.*"

—*John Laird, chair of the California Ocean Protection Council*

"*Having lived in California for forty-four years, I was surprised by how much I learned from David Helvarg's book* The Golden Shore. *It blew my mind. If you have the same love affair for the beautiful California coast and ocean as I do, this marvelous and compelling book is a must-read.*"

—*Jean-Michel Cousteau, explorer, founder, and president of Ocean Futures Society*

"*Boy, I loved this book. As a Californian who's spent much of his life talking about and fighting for more protection for our oceans, I really enjoyed reading about my fellow Golden Staters' multifaceted saltwater passion. David Helvarg captures, in a really readable way, the insane, quirky, and head-over-heels love we have for our seas.*" —*Ted Danson*

"*As geography, history, and myth, the power of California as place, society, and dream is best encountered on its shoreline. In 'Facing West from California Shores,' Walt Whitman bore witness to this drama. In the decades that followed, writers such as Mary Austin, J. Smeaton Chase, Robinson Jeffers, and John Steinbeck each encountered the California shore as fact and symbol. And now David Helvarg embarks upon an odyssey up the coast of dreams, asking the question: what is contemporary California telling itself about itself—and what does this mean for the nation?*" —*Kevin Starr, author of* California: A History

The GOLDEN
SHORE

The GOLDEN SHORE

California's Love Affair
with the Sea

DAVID HELVARG

Thomas Dunne Books

St. Martin's Press ☒ New York

All photos are courtesy of the author (pp. 1, 113, 164, 244, 268, and 292) except for the National Oceanographic and Atmospheric Administration (pp. 15 and 217), the Ocean Institute (p. 35), the Monterey Bay Aquarium (p. 62), the U.S. Navy (p. 138), and those courtesy of Kyle Thiermann (p. 88) and Jesse Alstatt (p. 190).

THOMAS DUNNE BOOKS.
An imprint of St. Martin's Press.

www.thomasdunnebooks.com
www.stmartins.com

Library of Congress Cataloging-in-Publication Data

Helvarg, David, 1951–
    The golden shore : California's love affair with the sea / David Helvarg.
    p. cm.
    Includes bibliographical references and index.
    ISBN 978-0-312-66496-1 (hardcover)
    ISBN 978-1-250-02752-8 (e-book)
  1. Pacific Coast (Calif.)—History. 2. Pacific Coast (Calif.)—Environmental aspects.
3. Pacific Coast (Calif.)—Economic aspects. 4. Pacific Ocean—Environmental conditions.
5. California—Description and travel. I. Title.
    F868.P33H45 2013
    917.94—dc23

                            2012041968

St. Martin's Press books may be purchased for educational, business, or promotional use. For information on bulk purchases, please contact Macmillan Corporate and Premium Sales Department at 1-800-221-7945 extension 5442 or write specialmarket@macmillan.com.

First Edition: February 2013

10 9 8 7 6 5 4 3 2 1

To Richard Henry Dana Jr.
For describing it

To Ed Ricketts
For making it fun

To Peter Douglas
For protecting it

And to Sylvia Earle
For your energy

Contents

HOME WATERS

I get up at 4:00 A.M. and meet my friend Dave Schwartz in Tiburon. We chase some raccoons off his dock before he motors his sixteen-foot Boston Whaler across Richardson Bay to Sausalito, where I meet him at the boat ramp with the towing trailer. By 7:00 A.M. we're twenty-nine miles down the coast at the Pillar Point ramp in Half Moon Bay going through a safety inspection with the Coast Guard Auxiliary. It's Mavericks's big-wave contest and thousands of people are converging on this famed surf spot along a stretch of coastline between San Francisco and Santa Cruz, hoping to see the world's top big-wave surfers ride what everyone agrees is one of the epic breaks of the century.

We meet our friend June and a short time later head out the harbor entrance. With a strong flood tide, big swells, and shifting wind chop, we're battered and soaked as soon as we clear the channel. After ten minutes of testing the boat's rough-water capabilities, we turn around and head back to wait for the tide to crest. While we're kicking back watching the Jumbo-Tron next to the Jim Beam stand, waiting for the first contest heat to begin, a sleeper wave washes over the crowded beach down the bluffs from us, knocking people off their feet and off the seawall. From our boat we can see a big tournament tent, metal scaffolding, speakers, an empty skiff, and half a dozen people wash out into the harbor, immediately followed by other folks in kayaks going to their rescue. The people in the water are quickly recovered, but thirteen others, mostly on the beach, are injured according to news reports.

With the high tide laying down, we head back out the harbor entry just after 10:30 A.M. and manage to surf and slide over the swells a few miles inside the reef before rounding back up toward the breaking surf line half a mile offshore where monster waves are crashing with the deep *ka-booming* resonance of calving glaciers. Here we join a flotilla of forty camera boats, observers, and PWCs or personal watercraft with floating "drags," light sleds used to rescue surfers from the impact zone after they wipe out. There's also a buoy with big replacement surfboards tied to it, including one that's already been snapped in two like a dry twig by the force of a breaker. Two camera helicopters and an orange Coast Guard Dolphin rescue helicopter circle overhead.

I've seen big-wave contests on the North Shore of Oahu and they're impressive, but these icy-cold apartment-building-sized giants thundering through sharky seas into the infamous "boneyards" rock pile and exposed coastal bluff beyond seem way more challenging. Thousands of people now line the cliff top, waiting to see epic rides but also epic wipeouts. This is nature's NASCAR, the site where big-wave surfer Mark Foo died in 1994 and fellow pro surfer Sion Milosky wiped out and drowned in 2011. From where we are, a few hundred feet away, the surfers look like they're sliding down moving gray-green mountains, chased by white avalanches where the lips of the waves reach out and then break to gravity, trailing twenty-foot rooster tails of mist behind them that set off fractured rainbow shimmers.

"It's hard to explain how much water was moving around out there," contest winner Chris Bertish of South Africa later says. "I took the worst beating of my life out there."

"We set a new bar. No one ever paddle-surfed waves that big for a contest. But we train for this and we have the equipment to prevent drowning most of the time," adds second-place winner, Shane Desmond of Santa Cruz.

We motor behind the shoulders of the waves for a quick lunch in the longer swells farther out, where we spot some gulls, some cormorants, and the rolling back and tail of a California gray whale, one of more than twenty thousand who migrate past the golden shore every year.

Back at the break, the giant waves are still going off like howitzers at ten-second intervals. We watch heart-stopping drops and people making impossibly steep lines down nearly vertical walls of water and several scary wipeouts with ten-foot boards flying and surfers skipping like stones down the face of the waves before hitting the trough and being swallowed up in body-munching cataracts that thunder down on them like Thor's hammer. One surfer thinks he's made his ride but fails to see the Mack Truck's weight of white water suddenly coming up behind him. "Dude, that lip just swallowed him," someone notes with awe. We see Shane Desmond take some perilous drops and make it through the boom and reverb on a wave seven times his height. A local who isn't wearing a brightly colored rash guard, which contestants wear over their wet suits so judges ashore can figure out who's who, takes a really steep drop and then pops back up through a bottom tube about the size of the Devil's Slide auto tunnel they're drilling through the mountains just north on Highway 1. He makes it out the other side to wild cheering. Shane and another contestant paddle over to congratulate him.

As the contest comes down to its final heat the top guys hang farther out waiting for something bigger than the fifty-foot waves that have been showing up throughout the day. Those few observers who aren't taking pictures or trying to avoid collisions with other observers' boats just shake their heads in disbelief until the final air horn signals that the biggest wave contest in history is officially over.

Back at the boat ramp, Dave goes to get the car and trailer while June hits the restroom. When I turn my back, a seagull steals a bag of fresh bread from among our stuff on the boat. It flies a few yards away before settling on the water. I'm shouting at it to let go of the plastic bag, which can choke and kill birds, turtles, and other sea life. Desmond, who's just been towed in to the ramp, jumps on his board and paddles over to take the bag away from the bird. I toss the gull the now soggy bread and congratulate Shane on his second-place finish. It turns out the forty-year-old father of two works for Whole Foods in Santa Cruz and is also concerned about plastic pollution of the seas, so we discuss the merits of charging a fee for single-use plastic bags versus banning them outright, and I realize he's both a regular nice guy, just another Californian who loves and cares about the ocean, and at the same time a metahuman, one of a handful of our species who can ride moving mountains of water five and six stories high and not only survive but also make it look sweet.

So what is it about California, the most populous of the United States, and the Pacific Ocean, the world's largest body of water, covering one-third of the planet, that creates such a powerful crosscurrent of culture, risk and reward, history, economy, and mythology? That's what we're going to investigate. There's the recreational aspect, of course, with year-round access, including more than a hundred million day visits a year to Southern California's beaches, also the transportation element, the kite surfers, sailboats, ferries, tankers, and container ships that make San Francisco Bay a maritime ballet by the Golden Gate, and that draws day sailors to Avalon and Two Harbors on Catalina or inspires dive boats to drop anchor off the Channel Islands. There are the fishing boats working rough seas outside Morro Bay, Half Moon Bay, Bodega Bay, Fort Bragg, and Crescent City hauling in still wild and wildly delicious salmon and Dungeness crab, rockfish, black cod, and spiny urchin for export to Asia. There's the coastal and global trade going back to shell beads and cow hides that now includes the nation's two biggest ports, Los Angeles and Long Beach, which together make up a single sixteen-square-mile megaport, the Western Hemisphere's largest and the gateway to Asia and the Pacific. If you buy anything that says "Made in China" it probably came across these docks or through Oakland.

There's also the restored marine wildlife of a still vital and productive sea, the "Serengeti of the ocean," with pods of dolphins, whales, elephant seals, sea lions, harbor seals, sea turtles, sea otters, pelicans, albatross, and white sharks, called "the man in the gray suit," although the females are bigger, up to twenty-one feet long.

There's offshore energy, both clean and dirty, with the memory of the 1969 Santa Barbara oil spill always lingering; navy towns and training ranges for securing the seas; San Diego's aircraft carriers and submarines; Coronado, with its SEAL contingent and the Pacific Fleet docked at 32nd Street; also San Clemente and San Nicholas islands; Point Magu and Port Hueneme; thirty-five miles of air force coastline at Vandenberg, and the marines at Camp Pendleton with their seventeen miles of coastline, including one of the state's best surf beaches, Trestles, which is still open to the public.

There's the cutting-edge marine science practiced at Scripps, U.C. Santa Barbara, around Monterey Bay, at U.C. Davis's lab in Bodega Bay, and Humboldt State's at Trinidad, plus the awe and wonder you can feel surfing, sailing, diving, paddling, walking the beach at sunset, or just drinking your margarita at a waterfront bar in Laguna Beach or above Big Sur, waiting for the green flash on a calm, flat day as the sun sinks in the western sea.

California's shoreline is where U.S. westward expansion ended but the promise never did, where the frontier turned to liquid and a gold rush and a world war transformed the golden shore. This is where half a million Chinese, Japanese, Filipino, and other Pacific Rim immigrants whose landfall was not on Ellis Island but on Angel Island in San Francisco Bay, came to vie for power with a Eurocentric eastern establishment. This is where environmental engagement and the frontier mentality forged a new dialectic of nature along Highway 1, the most scenic coastal road in America.

It remains a challenge even to express what it is that links the innovative, entrepreneurial, and risk-taking spirit of Californians who've built the eighth largest economy on earth to the ocean that borders their state and state of consciousness, infusing both with a sense of tidal flux, a belief that change is the only constant and if you can just catch that next wave you'll be sitting on top of the world. Today about half the world's population lives within 150 miles of a coastline. In California that figure is closer to 90 percent within fifty miles. Seventy percent live in its twenty coastal counties. Most of the state's gross domestic product of almost $2 trillion is generated in this coastal zone that accounts for fourteen of the state's nineteen million jobs. Though mostly unstated, it's understood that California, stretched between arid Southern deserts and damp Northern forests would, without the Pacific Ocean, be little more than a long skinny clone of Nevada.

On a per capita basis, California's more than thirty-seven million people can claim less than two inches of coastline each, not even a thumb's length of sand and rock overwashed by salt water. Yet what a glory that 1,100 miles of urban ocean and hidden wilderness coves, precipitous coastal cliffs, sea stacks, and wild beaches offer up. Along with the nation's biggest ports, most gnarly waves, and striking underwater wonders—including vast kelp forests and a submarine canyon larger than the Grand Canyon— there are also the largest concentrations of white sharks and blue whales in the world. What a bounty of maritime history and ongoing conflicts up and down its famed waterfront from Oregon to the Mexican border, from Crescent City, which was battered by a tsunami in 1964 and again in 2006 and 2011, to Point Reyes, where the ground split in the 1906 earthquake (and shook again in 1989) to Southern California's Huntington Beach, "Surf City, U.S.A.," and points south to where California becomes Baja California.

It's a sometimes seamless-seeming ride through time and salt water from "Sea Dog" Francis Drake's pursuit of Spanish galleons off the north coast to today's U.S. Coast Guard chasing Mexican "pangas," small boats smuggling drugs and migrants, off the southern coast now that the land border has tightened up. It's a wild ride along an ocean no less epic for its having been discovered and rediscovered by generations of California watermen and women seeking both predictable wonders and unknowable truths while living on the edge.

In telling an epic tale like that of *The Odyssey* or California's tumultuous love affair with the sea, form suggests one start with a scene of domesticity. After all, it is only logical that every journey starts from home, so let's start with mine.

I live on the edge of San Francisco Bay in an early 1990s marina town house development in the East Bay community of Richmond. My home is adjacent to the San Francisco Bay Trail and a sailboat marina just past which I can see Brooks Island, Angel Island, and the south tower of the Golden Gate Bridge on days when the marine layer's not too thick. Many of the themes I came to explore while writing this book are re-created on a local scale here in my home waters.

A short jog around the marina and I can enjoy the cityscapes of San Francisco, Berkeley, and Oakland, along with views of the cargo ships and giant gantry cranes at the Port of Oakland. Looking to the west, I can see a World War II Victory ship tied up at the commercial Port of Richmond, both reminders of the vital role that maritime trade and warfare have played in California's history.

However, the earliest human impacts on California would have to begin with the coast's first people, some of who lived and worked less than half a mile offshore from where I now live. Here on the 373 barren acres of Brooks Island, a thin green gloss of plant life buds every winter. Ohlone Indians lived on and around this island for some three thousand years and other people passed through the neighborhood ten thousand years earlier. It is 159 feet at its peak and has colonies of Caspian terns and California gulls. Its early native settlers left behind shell mounds and kitchen "middens" (food dumps) that in some areas also became burial mounds. When I drive to the movies in nearby Emeryville, I travel on Shellmound Street near where they left one of the largest middens—more than sixty feet high and 350 feet in diameter—which later became the location of an amusement park and still later a contaminated industrial site.

When the Spanish arrived in the late 1700s, there were some fifty Ohlone communities of roughly two hundred people each living between San Francisco Bay and Monterey Bay to the south. They ate abalone and mussels, ducks and other waterfowl, as well as venison, acorn, nuts, and berries. They slept in tule reed and redwood bark huts and got around in tule reed boats using double-bladed paddles. Like other coastal tribes, they had a rich culture focused on dance, body adornment, basket weaving, and spiritual storytelling, including an origin tale in which the world began as water. Like most tribes, they were decimated by the European conquest.

The story of California's coastal tribes is more than just a historic tale however. Today the Ohlone, the Chumash, the Yurok, Tolowa, and many other people are reclaiming their heritage as part of a reignited movement of native people who value and depend on the ocean for their sustenance and way of life.

For a time European settlers used Brooks Island for grazing and rock quarrying, calling it Sheep Island. Still later in the 1960s and '70s, Bing Crosby and his Hollywood pals leased it for the "Sheep Island Hunting Club," where they shot exotic game birds. Today it's managed by the East Bay Regional Park District and includes a ranger's house and landing dock along its otherwise empty shore.

Scooting past it on a daily basis, often launching from the edge of the bay trail, is a different kind of tribe—dedicated kite surfers and occasional old-school windsurfers who take advantage of the bay's challenging breezes that can quickly turn to gale-force winds in order to find their "stoke" (surfer idiom describing a sense of awe and adrenaline-fueled wonder). Kite surfing is one of the more recent among many derivatives of board surfing that makes up one of California's major recreational activities and cultural influences.

Years ago, after an accident where I caught a surfboard to my throat at Stinson Beach, my East Coast cousin asked, "Aren't you a little old to be surfing?" A middle-aged man splinting his shins jogging around the Central Park reservoir in Manhattan or along the Cedar River in Cedar Rapids, Iowa, is considered sensible, taking care of his health, avoiding the risk of diabetes or heart attack even if he gets shredded by a Doberman or run over by an SUV. Find your pleasure bodysurfing in the ocean off Northern California where a few big sharks feed and you're suspected of being an arrested adolescent, of taking needless risks. "Guilty as charged," many Californians might respond. It's the integration of work and play along the shore that they could argue has helped spark the imaginative leaps of creativity—that balance of structured thought and limitless horizons—that have turned California into a world leader in the computational, high-tech, biotech, and biomedical fields even as its geographic and climatic diversity provided opportunity for it to become a global nexus of ocean trade and agriculture. As one of the nation's last terrestrial and maritime frontiers, California's golden shore has attracted those willing to uproot themselves for a new life, generations of greenhorn adventurers and others with a high propensity for what behavioral science literature calls sensation-seeking behavior. Not surprisingly those ranking highest on the Sensation Seeking Scale (SSS) tend to be young, male, and single, a demographic that defines California's three major waves of immigration to date, including the gold rush, World War II (young soldiers and war factory workers who later settled), and first-wave twentieth-century migrant Latinos, including young men from Mexico separated from their families who picked the crops and sent their money home as part of the Bracero guest-worker program of the 1940s, '50s, and '60s. That's the same demographic as surfing when it went huge in the 1950s and '60s, although over time surfers have aged and surfing has attracted a larger cohort of women.

Watching the windsurfers launch from Vincent Park, I can look across a dredged channel at the two gantry cranes in the Port of Richmond, the state's sixth largest, and the quay where a big Honda car ship stops by every week or so. (Just out of sight is Chevron's Long Wharf, where much of Northern California's oil is offloaded and refined.) Maritime trade has been a driver of California's development and culture going back centuries from soapstone bowls and sea otter skins to cow hides to today's consumer electronics, clothing, and furniture imports from China offloaded at city-sized port terminals in Oakland, L.A., and Long Beach.

In 2012 the MSC *Fabiola,* a 1,201-foot-long container ship able to carry 12,500 twenty-foot shipping containers, sailed into San Francisco Bay, becoming the largest vessel to date ever to dock in North America. California today is responsible for more than 40 percent of the nation's seagoing trade. That's why you can't talk about California without talking about its ports, as we will. War has been the other major driver of the state's development, from the navy's 1846 seizure of Mexican California's capital at Monterey through today's major military bases, defense contractors, and training exercises in and around Southern California.

Coincidentally, my neighborhood is part of the Rosie the Riveter National Historical Park, which includes a memorial walk alongside the marina that was once Kaiser Shipyard Number Two. Richmond's Kaiser shipyards built 737 Liberty ships and ten later-model Victory ships during World War II, employing more than ninety thousand workers and transforming a small industrial swamp town into a bustling multiracial boomtown. By the end of the war, the yards were turning out a ship every four or five days while additional freighters, oil tankers, submarines, and destroyers were produced at other sites around the bay. The clinic for the Kaiser shipyard workers later became the Kaiser Permanente health care system.

While Northern California produced ships for the war, Southern California assembled thousands of fighter planes, bombers, and C-47 (DC-3) transport planes in its aircraft factories, establishing the region as a center for aviation and later home to much of the U.S. defense and aerospace industry.

With so many white males drafted out of the workforce, women, African American and Mexican American workers were finally allowed to work in the state's shipyards and defense factories, including a large influx of African American laborers from the South. Their hardhat labor helped save democracy while also advancing the nation's slow march toward equal rights. In Richmond women made up about 25 percent of the workforce while in some war factories 80 percent of the workers were female. At the tip of my neighborhood memorial, where a prowlike deck hangs over the water, is a plaque with an inscribed quote from one of our local "Rosies." It reads: "You must tell your children, putting modesty aside, that without us, without women, there would have been no spring in 1945."

My eighty-five-year-old neighbor Lou Berg, a World War II torpedo plane gunner, gives me a tour of the restored *Red Oak* Victory ship that's berthed at the old Shipyard Number Three off Canal Boulevard, just past a four-acre car lot where the Japanese-made Hondas are offloaded.

He shows me the gray deck guns and cargo winches that still work and takes me up and down ladders belowdecks, despite his two metal knees, and shows me the crew bays with their canvas "racks" (bunks), where Richmond middle-school kids can now stay for a week at a time learning how to tie knots, read navigation charts, and make griddle cakes.

"Bill Jackson, the chief engineer, he's ninety-two, African American, and served in four wars. He can handle the kids," Lou explains with a grin. Since World War II Richmond has remained largely African American, and more recently Hispanic, but mostly low-income given that the industrial waterfront jobs that left in 1945 never returned.

The 455-foot ammo ship *Red Oak* Victory was christened on November 9, 1944. It was one of seven hundred ships waiting at Ulithi Atoll in Micronesia for the invasion of Japan when the United States dropped atomic bombs on Hiroshima and Nagasaki, ending the Pacific war in the fall of '45.

After the war *Red Oak* Victory became a merchant vessel hauling ammo from California to Korea and Vietnam before it was retired to the ghost fleet of surplus vessels in Suisun Bay (northeast of San Francisco Bay), where it was rediscovered and restored in the late 1990s.

Near the old ammo ship I recognize the decaying wooden form of the 204-foot steam schooner *Wapama,* which used to be dry-docked in Sausalito when I lived there. Although the schooner was designated a historic landmark in 1984, no one's been able to raise the funds to restore it. *Wapama* is the last of 225 timber ships that used to haul redwood and Douglas fir logs down from Eureka on Humboldt Bay to the Bay Area or San Pedro and San Diego in Southern California in the late nineteenth and early twentieth centuries. Much of California's trade, settlement, and transportation was carried out by sea well into the twentieth century.

California redwoods helped rebuild San Francisco after the 1906 earthquake. Sometimes the *Wapama* would stop in Bodega Bay to pick up potatoes as deck cargo but often lost them overboard in the rough waters of Four Fathom Shoals just north of the Golden Gate. That's how this still-infamous stretch of turbulent water came to be known as the Potato Patch.

While many people have a movie- and media-fed impression that the coast of California is an undifferentiated extension of the Southern California bight below Point Conception with its usually quiet blue waters and wide flat sandy (and sunny) beaches at Santa Barbara, Malibu, and San Diego, most of the state's coast north of the point is wild, steep, and rocky, plus frequently impacted by the even wilder North Pacific. This is the fetch of dangerous storm-tossed waters that early European explorers, brigands, and treasure galleons had to master. It's never stopped being a challenge whether for an early nineteenth-century sailor and scholar like Richard Henry Dana Jr., whom you'll shortly get to meet, or recreational sailors, surfers, divers, and swimmers still lost to these cold dark seas on an all too regular basis.

While willing to take individual risks to claim the pleasures of the sea, Californians have learned from their past mistakes and are today helping restore and protect marine wildlife and shore environments up and down the coast.

San Francisco Bay, for example, has been dramatically altered over time—first by geological forces, particularly during the last ice age, then over the last 150 years by more rapid anthropogenic (human-driven) changes. These include the infill of the bay during the gold rush initially by abandoned ships as the forty-niners headed for the hills, and then by much more monumental sediment runoff from hydraulic mining of the mountains between the 1850s and 1880s, which filled up and obscured the bay's waters. Only now is the bay beginning to regain its pre–gold rush clarity. The bay was also filled in, fished out, constricted, and polluted throughout the 1940s, '50s, and '60s. During the early 1960s, however, people began to mobilize to turn things around, which they did beyond their own wildest, most hopeful expectations.

Of course new and disturbing challenges remain—both natural (the state's major coastal cities were built up around some of its major earthquake faults) and natural seeming (sea level rise and ocean acidification linked to the burning of fossil fuels).

Yet even today, living on the bay, the second largest estuary on the West Coast, I'm amazed how, after centuries and millennia of human impact, habitation, and dumb decisions there remains a wealth of wildlife on and off the water. This shallow bay includes a broad delta to the north where the freshwater of the Sacramento River meets the salty tidal surge from the Golden Gate's deep narrow opening halfway down the bay below its famous Depression-era bridge. This interaction has created a natural brackish nursery for crabs and fish, including spawning herring that draw hungry seabirds and other predators like big sevengill sharks that haunt the deep channel between the Golden Gate and Alcatraz Island.

In 2011, with one of the largest herring runs in years under way, I watched tens of thousands of full-bellied gulls floating and swooping around Point Richmond in the East Bay like so many flapping white carnations with black cormorants mixing in among them, along with more than a dozen big raucous sea lions. The herring, making up the largest urban fishery in America, had already topped out that year's catch quota for the commercial boats that regularly pull their nets within a stone's throw of the tourists on the Sausalito waterfront and were now providing a smorgasbord for seabirds.

The bay's southern mudflats and fringing tidal marshes offer easy forage for a range of other critters, including wading shorebirds, raccoons, snakes, frogs, and bobcats.

Jogging around the Richmond Marina I've seen birds and animals both native and exotic, including Canada geese, wild turkeys, coots, egrets, hawks, cormorants, great blue herons, night herons, avocets, curlews, ducks, loons, bat rays, harbor seals, sea lions, jacksmelt, sea nettles, ground squirrels, feral cats, a skunk, and even a wild salmon one time up our plastic strewn Meeker Creek, where we hold an annual shoreline cleanup.

Other occasional visitors to the bay include white sharks, gray whales, a few famous humpback whales—Humphrey, Delta, and Dawn, who wandered up the Sacramento Delta before being herded back out to sea—and a lone sea otter I saw bobbing along on its back off Alcatraz Island in the middle of a 2007 oil spill (he survived). In many ways the bay shoreline is a miniature of the state's coastline. It is also where the state's coastal protection movement got its start.

Yet as safe and satisfying as it often feels inside this most protected of natural harbors, there's nothing like heading out the Golden Gate past Point Bonita on a freshening day knowing that while you could go straight on past the Farallon Islands and over the horizon to Hawaii, Asia, and beyond, turning right or left, starboard or port, can offer equally great maritime adventures along the ancient yet ever-changing coast of California.

NATIVE TIDES

Before the people there was only water.

—MIWOK CREATION TALE

The Miwoks had it right. Before California there was the miles-deep ocean. The geological assembling of California would take uncounted millennia of tectonic plates surfing the liquid magma of the planet's heart and riding up on one another. These collisions, marked by tens of thousands of massive earthquakes, moved rocks and minerals around the planetary orb like sand grains in a breaking wave.

Of course the very concept of plate tectonics, the idea that coastal California, with its diversity of steep mountains, terraced marine bluffs, and wide, flat, sandy beaches, is a product of millions of years of collision and grinding between the North American and Pacific plates, was considered scientific heresy until relatively recent times. In the 1950s and '60s, work on Atlantic seafloor spreading, and the mapping of midoceanic ridges and magnetic fields by Walter Pittman, Bruce Heezen, cartographer Marie Tharp, and others, confirmed the theory of plate tectonics or continental drift. This theory made sense and also explained what most curious schoolchildren had already figured out: That Africa, South America, and the other continents seemed to fit together like so many jigsaw pieces because they did. Over millions of years, they'd all drifted apart from a single supercontinent, Pangaea.

The Atlantic's volcanic ridges and ranges and the Pacific's still highly active volcanic ring of fire, along with earthquakes, climate and temperature variations, ice ages and carbon-linked warmings, have also had huge impacts on the rise and fall of sea levels in different ocean basins, particularly in recent millennia.

Some twelve thousand years ago during the early Holocene, a Paleo-Indian hunting party might have set off through a grassy river valley passing between a pair of high bluffs topped by live oak, Pacific madrone, and bay laurel. Those bluffs marked an opening between the wide valley and an otherwise contiguous range of low green mountains adorned with majestic pines and three hundred-foot-tall arrow-straight redwood trees. They'd hike another twenty-seven miles across golden meadows of rye grass, and white, yellow, and pink trillium, tree tobacco and fireweed, and through pine, sycamore, and cypress groves past grazing herds of mule deer and big elk too skittish to approach and then, near a coastal swale, give wide berth to a wary grizzly and her two young cubs feeding on the carcass of a dead fur seal. Overhead in cerulean blue skies California condors with ten-foot wingspans circled, waiting for their chance to feed.

Soon the hunting party reached a rocky headland with several craggy granite peaks where thousands of cormorants, puffins, and gulls roosted, whitening the rocky pinnacles with their guano. A few miles beyond, on a wide beach, they cautiously snuck up on a mob of Steller sea lions and elephant seals much larger than themselves. Then, in a quick rush of adrenaline and bravado, they targeted a single large animal, administering a lethal clubbing to the beast, marine mammals being one of their key sources of protein. Next, using sharp stones and obsidian blades they would have begun the slow process of butchering their kill.

During this last major ice age, with the sea level more than three hundred feet lower than it is today, it was possible for hunters to travel by foot through what is now not a river valley but the waters of San Francisco Bay and on through the naturally formed Golden Gate bluffs across what is today open Pacific waters to California's own Galapagos, the craggy Farallon Islands twenty-seven miles off San Francisco. These islands are famous not only for their still abundant bird life but also for the visiting white sharks that cross a nearby marine abyss to feed on young elephant seals and other marine mammals that continue to congregate there.

Farther south, the Channel Islands off Santa Barbara were at the time one large near-shore island called Santarosae, which was settled by California's earliest native people using tule canoes constructed of bundled tule reeds common along the marshy coast. Even farther south, the grass and brush-covered islands of Cortes off San Diego would later sink beneath the waves to become the Cortes Bank submarine mountaintops.

Archaeological digs on what are now the Channel Islands of Santa Cruz, Santa Rosa, and San Miguel have found ancient Indian artifacts and food middens that indicate they feasted well off marine mammals, waterfowl, urchins, mussels, and abalone, later using the abalone's mollusk shell for fishhooks that made shiny lures. The ability to fish expanded their diet to include finfish, lobster, shark, and moray eel. At night and during foggy days they could warm themselves with mesquite, cypress, and pine fires and wrap themselves for comfort in thick otter fur robes.

The Chumash tribe's origin tale may reflect an original settlement on the island of Santarosae that became less tenable as the sea channel to the mainland expanded with glacial meltwater toward the end of the ice age. With sea levels rising at more than a meter a century, foraging trips to the mainland would have become more difficult over time.

In the Chumash story the island population became too crowded and so the creator gave the people a rainbow bridge to cross to the mainland but warned them not to look down. Those who did fell from the rainbow into the ocean, but taking pity on the drowning people, the creator turned them into dolphins. Anytime I sail through the Santa Barbara Channel or head out to Catalina from Long Beach, spotting hundreds of white-sided and common dolphins leaping in great schools through the sea, I can't help wondering who they are.

It was the late glaciated ice age some fifteen thousand years ago that brought the first small bands of humans to California's shores from Siberia across the Bering land bridge and adjacent rocky ice fields but also, according to newer research, along the Aleutian Islands and West Coast in skin boats and other small watercraft.

They initially settled in the warmer south until, over several thousand years, from about 10,000 to 6,000 B.C., temperatures rose, and sea levels with them, creating more coastal estuaries, wetlands, lagoons, and tidal pools in Northern California that proved excellent habitat for hunting and foraging. Bands and clans of people migrated back north from Baja and Malibu to Elkhorn Slough by the Salinas River, to Half Moon, San Francisco, Bodega and Humboldt bays, as well as to the banks of the Carmel, Russian, Noyo, Mattole, Klamath, and Smith rivers just south of Oregon, where people are still somewhat hostile to bands of Californians moving north.

By 9,000 B.C. sea level rise had severed the Bering land bridge, separating Russia from Alaska and effectively stranding the native populations of California and the Americas. The Californians might have numbered in the high hundreds by then. By the time European explorers first caught sight of California around A.D. 1500, the natural wealth of the region had seen the native population expand to some three hundred thousand people living in culturally distinct tribal societies including the Tongva, Chumash, Esselen, Miwok, Pomo, Sinkyone, Yurok, Tolowa, and Shasta.

Native peoples' lives and livelihoods depended on California's bountiful shore and coastal range, as well as on the acorn flour–, duck-, salmon-, and venison-rich territories that extended inland to the great estuarine wetlands of the delta and central valley. Tribes also settled the region's northern temperate rainforest, southern high desert, and even the foothills of the Sierra with its stark granite mountains' range of light.

The biological abundance of the coast, however, allowed for cultural diversity unseen in the interior regions to the east and south. More than sixty languages based on twenty distinct linguistic groupings were spoken in California. Villages and towns of upward of one thousand people appeared in coastal regions rich in salmon, shellfish, acorns, rabbit, deer, and marine mammals, including seals and dolphins that could be trapped on or near the shore.

In the northern spruce and redwood forest between what's now Humboldt Bay and the Oregon border, the Tolowa, Yurok, Chilula, Bear River, Wiyot, Mattole and other tribes occupied coastal lagoons, bays, and riverbanks. Here they built wooden plank houses with round doors and sweat lodges for spiritual purposes and to help take the chill off. They built with redwood and cedar, including dugout canoes made from redwood logs worked with fire, adze, and elk horn wedges till they were as smooth, symmetrical, and polished as any Royal British launch. Some were two-person transports; some were seagoing trade and hunting craft more than forty feet long by eight feet wide that could hold crews of a dozen or more men. While runs of chinook and coho salmon, steelhead trout, smelt, and other fish were abundant almost year-round on the Klamath and other rivers, the big redwood dugouts were essential for launching the big-game sea lion hunts of late summer.

Before dawn on the day of a hunt, one of the canoe skippers would go down to the beach and listen to the sound of the waves to determine the size of the groundswell and conditions offshore. If he was satisfied and got the headman's agreement, his crew would then launch through the surf, paddling with all their strength. Once outside the break, they might travel twenty miles or more to the islands, promontories, and rock outcrops where Steller sea lion colonies had their rookeries. There they would drop off two-man hunter-killer teams.

With the close approach of these two-legged predators, a fifteen-hundred-pound male might rise up on its front flippers and draw back its head just before lunging at its attacker. Before it could, the point man would suddenly thrust a sharpened stick into its mouth to keep its head back and the second man would come up behind the animal and club it to death, trying to crack its skull with the first blow.

Having had similar-sized elephant seals rear up at me, I can imagine the desperate hunger that would compel a man to keep advancing in this situation. On slippery rocks and sea-flushed mats of giant kelp or pickleweed, amid mobs of large panicked, barking animals stampeding for the refuge of the sea, I'm sure more than just the pinnipeds met death and injury in these encounters.

Even after a successful kill, it was still a huge challenge to drag the animal's body into the surf and then tip the big canoe over into the water until the carcass could be rolled or pushed inside it. Then the crews, often with two or more dead animals aboard their vessels, certainly cold and wet to their skins, with the salty smell of blood and sea foam in their nostrils, perhaps seasick or carrying injured or dead hunters, would have to paddle hours back to the mainland through sea states that even today can make mariners nervous whenever they venture onto the North Pacific off of California.

About eight hundred miles to the south a different kind of maritime culture was evolving among California's first settlers, including the Chumash and dolphin-hunting Tongva (or Gabrielino), peoples living near or on the Channel Islands (San Miguel, Santa Rosa, Santa Cruz, San Nicolas, Santa Catalina, and San Clemente). Along the Southern California coast these people lived in conical homes made of tule grass, sometimes with whalebone rafters scavenged from beached whales.

With rising sea levels forcing them to navigate more open waters, the Chumash and their neighbors developed a new kind of boat, replacing or supplementing tule reed boats with more elegant, rugged, and seaworthy plank timber canoes known as tomols or in the case of the Tongvas, te'aat (tiat). These were ten to thirty feet in length and three to four feet wide. The Chumash called the tomol the "House of the Sea," for its reliability, and their crews used double-bladed kayaklike paddles to propel these lightweight seagoing canoes through the ocean.

California archaeologist Brian Fagan suggests the first plank boats might have appeared thousands of years ago on Catalina Island, where the Tongva quarried soapstone that could be worked into cooking pots, slabs, and other tools for trade with other tribes. This would have given them commercial incentive to build faster, more seaworthy boats that could haul hundreds and later thousands of pounds of cargo between the islands and the mainland and along the coast. He calls whoever developed these earliest plank boats that didn't get waterlogged like tule or tip over like redwood "the rocket scientists of their time."

By around A.D. 650 the tomol had become the centerpiece of Chumash culture, similar to the role the automobile now plays in Southern California. A secretive guild known as the Brotherhood of the Canoe was responsible for the construction of each new tomol, its boat-building knowledge handed down through the generations from senior craftsman to apprentice.

Redwood logs that drifted down the coast and washed ashore made the best construction material since old-growth redwood swells when it gets wet, making better seals. Uprooted pine trees that washed down area rivers during winter storms were also widely used. After splitting the logs with whalebone or antler wedges workers selected only straight-grained planks without any knots to guarantee no cracking or leaks over time. Planks were then trimmed and finished using various adzes including pismo clamshell. The brotherhood then sanded the hull boards with sharkskin before fitting them together. Small holes were bored in the planks with stone or bone awls, and the planks were laid edge to edge and fastened with milkweed fiber cords passed through the drill holes. Tule plant was then stuffed into the cracks as caulking. Additional caulking was done with yop, a mix of natural asphalt from local tar pits and pine pitch melted and boiled together in stone bowls, which was then poured along the edges of the planks and into the drill holes. A crossplank at midship both reinforced the boat and acted as a seat. Another coat of yop was used to waterproof the boat, which was then painted with red ochre, a fourth and final coat of sealant before the finished tomol was decorated with geometric shell designs.

Only male members of leading families were allowed to own tomols.

Grizzly or black bearskin capes identified the owners and masters of these boats that, carefully maintained, could last for decades to be passed down from one generation to the next.

Tomols allowed for a widespread trading network among various tribes who lived on Point Conception, Santa Monica Bay, and the Channel Islands. There were designated shipping routes, and signal fires on the islands were used as early aides to navigation. Interestingly, all this maritime trade took place within a day's paddle of what are now America's two largest trading ports, Los Angeles and Long Beach.

When Juan Rodriguez Cabrillo explored the California coast in 1542 he saw so many tomols hauled up at one obviously wealthy village he named it Pueblo de las Canoas, or "town of canoes." It was later renamed Malibu. Another explorer spotted the brotherhood doing their boat carpentry in another village and gave it a name that's stuck, Carpinteria. Today you can see the *Helek,* a replica tomol built by modern-day Chumash, at the Museum of Natural History located on a scenic hillside above the old mission town of Santa Barbara.

Partially intact tomols have also been found in ancient Channel Island middens along with dolphin bones; seal and fish bones; and abalone, clam, and limpet shells. Carefully studied by archaeologists and marine ecologists, these leftovers tell a tale of the ocean's abundance, overexploitation, and prey population crashes and rebounds over centuries as native people overfished what was locally available. When one food species disappeared the Indians either targeted new food species or moved their villages to locations where there was yet untapped abundance.

California's biological richness and diversity, a hallmark of its coast and climate, also meant that while its native peoples became accomplished boat builders and basket weavers, they didn't face the geographically and ecologically based food scarcity that drove other peoples to develop fixed agricultural systems and the social stratification and specialization needed to expand the crops, irrigation systems, roads, and granaries that go along with settled agriculture. California's coastal tribes didn't have the incentive to construct hierarchical corn- and potato-based city-states like the Aztecs,

Mayans, Incans, or Tiwanakans to their south. In those societies the emergence of surplus wealth generated priestly classes and god-kings who required tribute, both human and material, and the mining of gold and silver for urban centers of commerce and temple-based worship and sacrifice. These "cities of gold," in turn, inspired their own destruction as the conquistadores of Spain led by Hernán Cortés laid waste to whole civilizations using armor, swords, lances, horses, and later priests to subdue the defeated survivors who would then become the Indian vassals, slaves, silver miners, and neophytes of "New Spain."

For California's native people, the lack of gold- and silver-rich cities, and their distance from the new colonial power center of Mexico City, established in 1521, delayed but failed to prevent the devastation to come.

California's pre-Columbian population of some three hundred thousand people would, by 1900, plunge to some twenty thousand as a result of the guns, germs, and steel of European settlers and conquerors Spanish, Mexican, and Yankee. Most of this destruction occurred within a two-hundred-year period between the establishment of the California mission system and the gold rush era, a period that exemplifies the United Nations' definition of genocide, which addresses actions intended "to destroy, in whole or in part, a national, ethnical, racial or religious group." This period included the deaths of more than 20,000 native people during a single malaria epidemic in 1833, as well as the death of some 100,000 Spanish mission Indian slaves and neophytes through starvation, disease, and suicide. In addition there were some 100,000 additional murders, rapes, starvations, and suicides linked to the gold rush miners and death-squad militias such as the Humboldt Volunteers, Eel River Minutemen, Coast and Klamath Rangers, and Placer Blades.

In a not untypical incident in February 1860, the Humboldt Volunteers massacred as many as 250 elderly Wiyot men along with women and children on Tuluwat Island in Humboldt Bay and at several other locales while the tribe's able-bodied men were away gathering supplies for a celebration. Until that time there'd never been any conflict between the tribe and white settlers in the area, although a few members of a different tribe were suspected of stealing some dairy cows. The attackers used mostly hatchets, clubs, and knives so that people in the nearby town of Eureka a few hundred yards away wouldn't hear the sound of gunfire. Afterward the slaughter became known as the Indian Island or bloody island massacre, though the island itself officially became known as Gunther Island when Robert Gunther, a dairyman, acquired ownership that same year. Still, while several suspects were identified, no one was ever prosecuted for the killings. When writer Bret Harte, then working in the coastal town of Union (later Arcata) wrote an editorial in the *Northern Californian* condemning the killings shortly after they took place, his life was threatened and he was forced to flee to San Francisco.

Today the Wiyots lead an annual commemoration for the victims close to Indian Island that now holds some of the footings for the Route 255 bridge between Eureka and the Samoa peninsula. Driving over the bridge on a wet, foggy day, I can see Eureka's downtown waterfront just beyond the island's marshy landscape with its hammocks of trees where dozens of white egrets and herons flap and circle about their rookeries like ghostly apparitions.

Of course it's always been easier to colonize, massacre, and displace a people if you can first establish them as outside the realm of full personhood, as being other than human, an exclusionary role colonial racism and religion helped facilitate. Around 1825, Franciscan missionary Father Geronimo Boscana wrote:

> *The Indians of California may be compared to a species of monkey, for naught do they express interest, except in imitating the actions of others, and particularly in copying the ways of the "razon" or white men, whom they respect as being much superior to themselves: but in so doing, they are careful to select vice, in preference to virtue. This is the result, undoubtedly, of their corrupt, and natural disposition.*

Similar sentiments would later be expressed against California's Mexican land-grant holders, immigrant Chinese and Latin American miners,

Japanese fishermen and farmers, African American sailors, or anyone else it might prove profitable to displace or oppress for their land, timber, labor, or gold.

We go through a cattle gate on a wet, cloudy day and walk down a long partially flooded path past cattail ponds and creeklike back eddies of the Yontocket Slough. Just beyond the hillock of trees in front of us is Lake Earl, the largest coastal lagoon south of Alaska. Behind us are the mountains of far Northern California between the Klamath and Smith rivers and the Oregon border, also farm fields full of cows, some imported buffalo, and thousands of Aleutian geese spread across a floodplain that was once a redwood forest now reduced to several huge stumps too big to dynamite, scattered about farmhouse yards and pastureland. I look across the flooded green slough under a chalk-colored sky where several white egrets are standing staring back at me, one with a pair of frog legs hanging from its beak.

We climb the low hill to what was once a tree-sheltered village and is now the wooden fenced Yontocket Indian Village Memorial Cemetery, the site of a massacre of 450 Tolowa people in 1853. In the last few years the tribe and Tolowa Dunes State Park rangers have been concerned about grave robbers stealing and selling artifacts online and so are considering shutting down the trail. A marsh wren trills a reedy poignant birdsong.

"We're victims of massacres and genocide, and people as a group who suffer oppression that horrible will live with the effects for generations," says Sheryl Steinruck, a tribal member and a teacher at the Smith River Rancheria. Rancherias are small parcels of land given to California tribes in the twentieth century in lieu of eight million acres of reservation land they were supposed to get from treaties never ratified in the nineteenth century.

"I grew up in [the small Del Norte town of] Fort Dick by Military Road where they used to shoot any Indian who approached the fort and you didn't walk alone at night or you might not ever return," Sheryl tells me at the brown shingle tribal offices near where the cold clear waters of the Smith, the last major undammed river in the state, rush by. While white settlers didn't penetrate the "Redwood Curtain" of far Northern California until the 1820s, the aggressive frontier mentality they brought with them ("No law north of the Klamath") lasted longer than on other parts of the coast. The Tolowa called the whites Natlh-mii–t'i, which means "Knife Brandisher," and as late as 1895 there were government-sanctioned bounties for Indian scalps in Del Norte County.

"I'm an elder now." The middle-aged educator smiles. "When I was a kid we'd sit on the beach and no one was there. Now there's constant traffic and people on the beach. Still with all the new housing and stuff that the prison brought [the massive Pelican Bay Prison, which opened in 1989], we still need more jobs. We have 14 percent unemployment in the county." Sheryl has black hair, broad cheeks, lively brown eyes behind thin designer glasses, and a "111" Tolowa chin tattoo—three vertical black lines dropping from her lower lip to below her chin that traditionally signified a young girl's entry into womanhood. Banned by the government in the 1920s, Indian tattoos (her nephew Guylish Bommelyn brandishes an armful) are now part of a cultural reawakening that's taken place in Indian Country since the 1969 American Indian Movement seizure of Alcatraz Island in San Francisco Bay. The siege lasted eighteen months and involved more than five thousand native people. In California the revival takes different forms in different parts of the state and also reflects different levels of economic development between gaming and nongaming tribes since the federal Indian Gaming Regulatory Act of 1988 and state ballot initiatives in 1998 and 2000 that gave California's tribes wide latitude to run their own casinos. In Del Norte County on the Oregon border, the Tolowa and Elk Valley tribes have small reservation casinos whose income they've used to help buy back their lands. The Tolowa have expanded from 160 to 580 of their original seventeen-thousand-acre homeland. The Elk Valley Rancheria in Crescent City, with 94 members, a mix of both Tolowa and Yurok, has expanded their land base from one hundred acres to just over six hundred. The Yuroks, the largest tribe in the state with more than five thousand members but only a single gas-station casino, have still managed to expand their landholdings and sustain a resource-based economy built around salmon, timber, and tourism. More than ten thousand people visit their annual salmon festival each August.

In more urbanized Southern California, where tribes were driven to the brink of extinction, small bands like the Santa Ynez Chumash in Santa Barbara County have regained significant wealth running one of the largest casinos in the state. Along with individual payments to tribal members of more than $100,000 a year, part of their income has gone to restoring traditional practices including the construction of thirty-foot tomol canoes for tribal paddles from the mainland to the Channel Islands that can take up to ten hours. A few years ago tribal members completed a paddle in six hours accompanied by a pod of dolphins much of the way. Unfortunately, with gaming money has also come factionalism and fights over who is and is not an "enrolled" (federally recognized) member of the tribe. One of the Chumash spiritual leaders and "dolphin dancers" not from the Santa Ynez band is Mati Waiya, also the Ventura Waterkeeper, a member of the boat-based environmental group led by Robert Kennedy Jr. that targets polluters of all waters. Mati helped establish the Chumash Discovery Village at Nicholas Canyon Beach in Malibu that's described as "a living history museum."

For most of the tribes in Northern California, history is what one does every day since their livelihoods still depend on their ability to hunt, fish, harvest, and adapt to ongoing climatic and biological changes taking place in the state's coastal and marine ecosystem.

"When I was a kid there was a lot more rain. The rainforests held the moisture more—it rained more in the trees," Sheryl claims, despite a heavy winter of rains during my visit that has taken Del Norte's usual seventy-five inches annual rainfall to more than one hundred. "Also, since I was a child the smelt run has gone crazy," she says. "Those [1960s childhood years] were bumper years. You'd take these scoop nets down in the ocean gravel, this peasized gravel you look for where they go to spawn, and scoop up the fish and you'd need real muscles scooping all those fish and gravel. There'd be so many we'd have to say stop—enough—but no more. Plus, the razor clams we collected are all gone. Only the seaweed we harvest is still there."

She sounds like a lot of commercial fishermen I've talked to. Rich Young, the harbormaster in nearby Crescent City, fished commercially for more than twenty years before being forced out by newer boats and fewer fish. His dad and uncles were fishermen, and he lost a brother to a fishing accident in Eureka. He recalls the 1980s when federal subsidies helped overcapitalize the fishing fleet and everyone bought bigger boats with bigger engines and nets and fish-finding sonar. "It was a fisheries nightmare," he says. "We'd have one-hundred-thousand-pound trips of rockfish and we fished out the near shore and we'd go to two hundred fathoms and think that was deep, which it was at the time. When my dad and uncle fished they'd use lead line to find the bottom. Today with the electronics you can see the bottom and the fish. Fishermen up here went the way of the loggers [who clear-cut the forests]. Then it was like the stages of grief. First there's denial. 'There's as much fish as there ever was.' Then there's, 'A smart fisherman can still find fish,' which is true if you put bigger nets on the boats and bigger engines and rollers [that keep trawl nets from getting snagged] to go into rockier grounds because there are no fish left on the flats where we used to find them. And with the frustration you'd have fishermen attacking other fishermen saying the other guy was doing dirty fishing and I should have those fish. But in the end if there's no fish there's no fishermen."

Eventually the Pacific Fishery Management Council, which oversees federal waters off California, created an industry-funded buy-back program downsizing the groundfish fleet from 270 to 180 boats to help reduce the pressure on the resource. Today Crescent City is the largest fishing port in Northern California, thanks mainly to Dungeness crab. Crabs, squid, lobster, and sea urchin are now California's top-earning fisheries. In the past it was tuna, salmon, black cod, and other finfish, including sardine, which collapsed at the end of the 1940s. Scientists call this "fishing down the trophic levels" (down the food chain), although with sardines they were also targeting the forage fish, the small fish that the big fish feed on.

Almost all the coastal tribes used to camp out on the beaches during the summer to catch smelt and dry them for winter use. Now only the Tolowa have a regular camp on the Smith River in late summer where they wait for the smelt to return. "The Yuroks don't dry the fish anymore," Sheryl tells me.

"Some traditional fish for drying were the eulachon that came upriver [from the sea] but they have disappeared from the Klamath," Dave Hillemeier, program manager for the Yurok's fisheries, confirms. Eulachon is a kind of smelt also known as candlefish because it's so rich in fat that a spawning fish can be dried, strung on a wick, and burned for light. "In the 1970s they were caught with dip nets and they could fill up pickup trucks with them," Hillemeier says. "They were probably in decline even then but since have just disappeared. Last year we counted six in the river."

"Six individual fish?" I ask.

He nods.

At the Tolowa fish camp they collected thousands of fish for food and barter with other tribes. "Our camp has thirty to forty people at most, so it's not our population that's destroying the fishes' ecosystem," Sheryl insists. "If it is diminishing it's because of changes in the ocean. I think it's weather and pollution, and the decline of the smelt is really bad because they feed the whole food chain."

"We've been doing this for thousands of years," her nephew Guylish points out. "Now the Hmong [Laotian tribal refugees who forage along the state's beaches] leave nothing." It's true some Southeast Asian immigrants carry out systemic hunting and foraging along the coast. This has led both to confrontations with California Fish and Game wardens as well as to self-directed community education efforts.

"We try and watch the coastline and protect it," Sheryl says. "We have a renewal ceremony for the earth that we hold."

I suggest they consider holding it more often.

At their last fish camp tribal attendance was way down, along with the number of fish. There were just enough to eat but none left over for drying.

Along with the smelt, other threatened and endangered fish in far Northern California include two species of suckerfish or c'waam, also coho salmon, spring-run chinook salmon, and green sturgeon.

. . .

I visit the Yurok tribal headquarters off Highway 101 the day after they've acquired twenty-two thousand acres of land from Green Diamond Resource Company, a spin-off of Simpson Lumber. The more than thirty-four square miles of forest acquisition, a deal put together using almost $19 million from state clean-water funds, more than doubles the tribe's land base.

"I'm very happy with this. We need our land base for wildlife and culture and as a working forest and also for preservation," Tribal Chairman Tommy O'Rourke tells me, sipping from a big mug of coffee in his office. He's a short man with a neatly trimmed gray beard and mustache and big black cowboy (or in this case Indian) hat that is one of his sartorial trademarks whether on the reservation or lobbying to protect tribal fishing rights in Sacramento or Washington, D.C. "We still gather, harvest, and hunt in traditional ways and we've been at it for years," he says. "We want to return the land to a natural state and continue to claim more of our [estimated five-hundred-ninety-thousand-acre] homeland. It's hard to acquire this kind of land for a nongaming tribe [they actually run one small casino], even if you're the largest in California."

Before heading into a tribal council meeting, Tommy introduces me to Troy Fletcher, the tribe's policy analyst, who tells me the tribe had only six thousand acres in 1988 at the time of the federal Hoopa–Yurok Settlement Act that partitioned the two adjacent tribes' lands along the coastal river and set up a fund based on government timber sales that eventually brought the Yurok $90 million but only after twenty years of legal wrangling. This latest land purchase is a huge addition and benefit for the tribe, Troy explains. He notes that fish, particularly salmon, are central to their culture and identity. The tribe has seventeen fish biologists and thirty to forty technicians working for it, depending on the season. This fall's chinook salmon run is their healthiest, with about sixty-five thousand wild adult fish having returned from the ocean. The coho are the least healthy and are listed under the Endangered Species Act. They tend to hang out in the slack water around beaver-dammed ponds near the mouth of the Klamath. In the summer of 2011, a forty-five-foot mother grey whale and her calf also decided to spend several months cruising the Lower Klamath River until she accidentally beached herself and died. With the fall run of chinook, the tribe leaves the first thirty-five thousand fish alone to spawn and divides the rest up with 50 percent going to nontribal fishermen and 50 percent to the tribes for their own use. Of these, 80 percent go to the Yurok and 20 percent to the (upriver) Hoopa.

I ask Troy about the water fight over the river that took place in the early part of this century and resulted in the die-off of more than seventy thousand fish back in 2002. He says the conflict on the river that traumatized many tribal members also "helped galvanize our people."

In the spring of 2001 thousands of alfalfa, hay, and potato farmers marched through the streets of Klamath Falls, Oregon, and illegally opened canal headgates to protest a federal decision cutting their irrigation water in order to guarantee enough water remain in the river to protect endangered suckerfish and coho salmon.

Like the snail darter and spotted owl before it, the suckerfish quickly became the poster animal for right-wing critics of the Endangered Species Act, including Rush Limbaugh, Fox News, and the editorial writers at *The Wall Street Journal* who tried to frame the issue as "suckerfish versus farmers." What few of those promoting "suckerfish sandwiches" were willing to acknowledge was that the water crisis was precipitated by the worst drought to hit the Northwest in more than a century, a drought that, like the region's forty-six shrinking glaciers, is likely linked to climate change.

"Nineteen ninety-four was the last substantial rain we had," Ryan Kliewer, a young fourth-generation farmer who marched in the 2001 protests, told me. Winter rains in 2002 and 2003 finally relieved the "drought of the century" that then returned eight years later.

After the street protests, President George W. Bush's secretary of the interior Gale Norton, a veteran of the antienvironmental "Wise Use" movement of the 1990s, reversed course, slashing the river flow and returning much of the water to the irrigators. She did this despite federal scientists' reports that this would put the coho in serious jeopardy and a U.S. Geological

Survey report that showed keeping the water in the river would generate thirty times more economic benefit for downstream users in California. Six months after a ceremony at which Norton and Bush's secretary of agriculture Ann Veneman helped reopen the headgates, tens of thousands of salmon and suckerfish washed up dead along the banks of the now partially drained river. Only later did it come out that Vice President Dick Cheney and White House strategist Karl Rove had exerted personal behind-the-scenes pressure on agency scientists and managers to make sure the water went to the farmers in eastern Oregon rather than to where it was legally required to go. As Rove explained in a PowerPoint presentation to fifty top officials of the Department of Interior, they believed they still had a chance of winning Oregon for Bush in the 2004 presidential elections by "supporting our base," but had written off California.

"The administration needs to understand that federal agencies like the Interior Department are not a division of the Republican National Committee and at their disposal to give out political favors," complained Senator John Kerry of Massachusetts, who ran against Bush in 2004. Though Kerry lost the presidency, he won both Oregon and California.

Meanwhile Yuroks, Hoopas, commercial fishermen, and other angry downstream protestors dumped five hundred pounds of dead, rotting, Klamath salmon that had been FedExed from California onto the front steps of the Department of the Interior in Washington, D.C. The sudden decline of the Klamath salmon also led to wide-ranging restrictions on salmon fishing off California in 2007 out of fear that the last Klamath coho might be caught and killed.

Shortly thereafter, California's entire fall chinook salmon run collapsed: An estimated 1.5 million fish in 2005 dwindled to an estimated sixty thousand in 2008 before slowly bouncing back to a few hundred thousand in 2010 followed by more than one million the following year. This was due in part to seesawing oceanographic conditions tied to deepwater upwellings that saw the crash and recovery of krill and anchovy that salmon feed on. These changing offshore conditions, combined with agricultural water diversions in the Sacramento Delta that kill young fish, were the primary culprits responsible for the 2008 collapse, according to scientists and fishermen.

Recognizing how dependent we've all become on intact rivers, watersheds, and healthy ocean waters, the tribes, farmers, fishermen, environmentalists, government officials including the governors of California and Oregon, and the private power company PacifiCorp, reached an agreement in 2010 to take a more precautionary approach on the Klamath. It will see the removal of four marginally productive dams in order to restore historic water flows and fish runs along more than three hundred miles of the river that have been blocked off for sixty to one hundred years. Similar dam removals have had notable success in reviving coastal rivers in Washington State, Maine, and North Carolina.

I ask Troy Fletcher if the tribe is satisfied with the tentative 2020 date set for the dams' removals under the $1.4 billion project.

"With NEPA [the National Environmental Policy Act] and CEQA [the California Environmental Quality Act] and the other laws that have to be complied with, that's really not so long a time to wait," he claims. "All those analysis and permits, and working with the county and state and feds and everyone wanting their say—it's still years down the road, but we know this river can heal itself and we know it will."

At that point the Klamath will join the Smith twenty miles to its north as the second of California's great undammed coastal rivers, hopefully with restored and invigorated populations of California's iconic salmon. The Klamath was once the state's second most productive salmon river after the Sacramento with more than eight hundred thousand salmon coming home to its waters every year, along with steelhead trout, big seagoing sturgeon, and suckerfish that kept white settlers in Eastern Oregon alive during a nineteenth-century drought thanks to the c'waam being cooked and delivered to the starving farmers by their Indian neighbors.

I'm standing at an overlook above the mouth of the Klamath. I'm alone since I snuck by the road closure sign and drove around the landslide that's blocked most of Requa Road after a week of heavy rains. A sheriff's truck is the only other vehicle I've seen on the twisting cliff-side drive up here.

The big river's outlet to the sea runs far and fast below me, pushing a gravel-gray plume of riffling water one hundred feet wide a quarter mile out into the ocean on this side of a large boot-shaped sandbar that's formed below a forested hill, half of which looks to have been timbered sometime in the last forty or fifty years.

The view south from where I stand, with its gray sand beaches and granite bird rocks reminds me of the overview of the Waipio Valley on the Big Island of Hawaii, only much colder and on an even grander scale. I can't see any sign of people or their works for thirty or forty miles to where the low coastal mountain range is lost in blue haze somewhere shy of Trinidad Head, beyond which is Humboldt Bay and another fifty-six miles of largely inaccessible wilderness known as the Lost Coast, the longest stretch of unroaded oceanfront land in the United States outside Alaska. The funny thing is that this remote temperate rainforest is located on the northern edge of the most populous state in the nation. It makes me wonder how different what I'm seeing now is from what the first European explorers might have seen along this wild and dangerous stretch of the North Pacific.

THE AGE OF SAIL

*At length we began to heave-to after dark,
for fear of making the land at night on a coast
where there are no light-houses and but indifferent charts.*

—Richard Henry Dana Jr., *Two Years Before the Mast*

've sailed along much of the California coast and seen the same kind of wildlife: gray whales, sea lions, otters, albatross, common and white-sided dolphins, as well as some of the same rough seas and rugged coastline that would have greeted Sir Francis Drake in the 1570s, Richard Henry Dana in the 1830s, or the U.S. Navy when it seized California a decade later. California has been drawing sailors for centuries, whether they sought land, treasure, a new start in life, or the America's Cup.

The first Californians were a race of black Amazons riding not ships but griffins (winged lions) into battle against the Turks during the siege of Constantinople, or so Spanish author Garcia Ordóñez de Montalvo imagined in his 1510 novel *The Deeds of Esplandian.* The Californians were led by Queen Calafia, the largest and most beautiful of her people. California itself was "an island on the right hand of the Indies . . . very close to the side of the Terrestrial Paradise," a description some still take to be true.

In 1533 Hernán Cortés, having conquered Mexico and destroyed the Aztec empire, led an expedition across a narrow sea. They soon landed on what they thought was an island facing the Pacific Ocean, the new sea Balboa had claimed for Spain on a calm (hence Pacific) day twenty years earlier. By 1540 they realized the island was actually a peninsula, the Baja peninsula, and though it would take more than two hundred years before they began settling the lands to its north, the Spanish started calling it California after the mythical island of the Amazons.

In 1579 the English freebooter Francis Drake decided to name the forested coastal lands to the north Nova Albion, a Latinized version of New England, making a rather tenuous ownership claim for his queen and country given that his main purpose for sailing the California coast was to pirate Spanish treasure. The English, along with other mariners and mapmakers of the sixteenth, seventeenth, and eighteenth centuries, continued to draw maps of California as an island. In 1747 the king of Spain, in order to help facilitate his nation's territorial claims in the New World, issued a royal decree: "California is not an island." As it turned out he was right, although, like certain islands, such as Britain, Japan, and Australia, California's history has been a uniquely maritime one.

In 1542 Juan Rodriguez Cabrillo, a former conquistador who'd fought with Cortés and served in Cuba and Guatemala was commissioned to explore the uncharted waters north of Baja. He sailed out of "New Spain" (Mexico) on June 27 aboard the two-hundred-ton galleon *San Salvador* escorted by two caravels, small, maneuverable vessels with lateen sails that allowed them to sail windward (head upwind unlike square-sailed galleons that needed tailwinds for propulsion). On September 28 they landed in San Diego Bay, where they encountered local Indians who initially threw stones at them before there was a wary exchange of gifts. Cabrillo named the bay San Miguel. Despite his efforts at christening, none of his place-names stuck, though he would go on to explore the Channel Islands, including Catalina Island (which he named "San Salvador"), where a well-armed party of Tongva greeted them, also San Clemente, San Miguel, San Pedro, and Santa Monica Bay, where entrepreneurial Chumash in to-mol boats circled the ships offering to trade. Then he sailed on to Point Conception and as far north as Point Reyes and the Russian River, where rough seas and autumn storms forced the small fleet to turn around. Heading south, Cabrillo missed the entry to San Francisco Bay, setting a more than two-hundred-year precedent. The green masses of Angel Island and Alcatraz inside the bay may have helped camouflage the bay's narrow straits, giving its entry waters the appearance of an inlet or large cove at most. Plus, the heavy surf pounding what's now the Ocean Beach section of the city kept many sailors tacking southwest past Point Reyes, keeping a heading that would take them outside the Farallon Islands and well clear of the bay before turning back toward the coast. In fact, it would not be mariners but a land expedition in 1769 that finally discovered this grand estuary and the native people who lived on it. It would take another six years for Spanish sailors to discover "La Boca," or the mouth of the bay.

On his way south, Cabrillo encountered Monterey Bay, naming it "Bahia de los Pinos," Bay of Pines. Forced to anchor to avoid being blown ashore, he was astonished to discover he needed 270 feet of rope to hold the anchor. He had inadvertently found the rim of Monterey's submarine canyon that, bottoming out at nearly twelve thousand feet, is both deeper and wider than the Grand Canyon. The now battered fleet returned to San Miguel Island to overwinter, making repairs and hoping for peace with the local Indians. This was not to be. Fighting broke out just before Christmas when a landing party went ashore to collect water. According to one account, Cabrillo led a rescue party, slipping on the rocks and breaking his leg. Another version says he had already broken his arm near the shoulder earlier in the expedition. Whatever the cause, he developed gangrene and died on January 3, 1543, and was buried on the island with his sword.

His second in command continued exploring north, sailing to latitude 42 degrees, well offshore from what is now Crescent City by the Oregon border before turning back to Mexico, arriving with what was left of the expedition in April 1543. This was considered a successful venture at the time.

Today, along with a number of schools and streets named after him, there's also the Cabrillo National Monument on the tip of Point Loma in San Diego honoring this first European explorer of California. Though Cabrillo was long thought to be Portuguese, more recent historical reviews suggest he was probably of Spanish origin like those he served. His larger-than-life statue (donated by the Portuguese government) overlooks San Diego Harbor and the North Island Naval Air Station on one side of the point and tide pools and the Pacific Ocean on the other. It's a place I'd recommend to any tourist. If you look down the harbor channel to your left you'll see a fenced-in section of square white buildings with high-intensity lighting and guard towers on the edge of North Island's runways. That's the special weapons depot where the navy stores its nuclear warheads. During the Cold War the Soviets had eight nuclear weapons aimed at San Diego, enough to alter the geography of the bay Cabrillo had once visited.

By the 1560s Spain had colonized the Philippines from New Spain and began trading and collecting silk, spices, gold, and other treasures from across Asia. By the 1580s they'd discovered the best way to bring their treasure-laden galleons in from Manila to New Spain (for overland transport to Vera Cruz and shipment home across the Spanish main), was to follow the warm Japanese current that took them to California just off Cape Mendocino or points farther south if they were lucky. They would then sail down the coast past Baja to Acapulco. In 1582 the Manila galleon *Santa Marta* ran aground on Catalina Island, losing most of its treasure and becoming the first of thousands of shipwrecks that would occur off California in the centuries to come including clipper ships, steamships, fishing boats, warships, freighters, and tankers.

Another danger the big, poorly armed treasure galleons encountered were the armed representatives of their empire's rivals, including Francis Drake, who sailed out of Plymouth harbor in 1577, across the Atlantic, and around the Strait of Magellan before pillaging Valparaíso and other Spanish settlements along the west coast of Latin America. By the time he reached California two years later (in search of the Northwest Passage back to England) Drake had seized and plundered a number of Spanish ships but had also seen his own fleet reduced from five vessels to one, The *Golden Hinde*, a 120-foot-long three-hundred-ton armed galleon now carrying thirty tons of Spanish booty. In June he pulled into a protected harbor for repairs and traded with local Indians, possibly coastal Miwoks. His presumed landing place is today called Drake's Bay on the Point Reyes Peninsula (a great place to hike or kayak). Other possible sites where he may have made this stop have been identified from coastal Oregon to Santa Barbara. After Drake completed his repairs, and having failed to find the Northwest Passage, *The Golden Hinde* sailed on to Indonesia and around Africa's Cape of Good Hope before returning home in the fall of 1580, where Queen Elizabeth knighted Drake.

In 1595, after a rough Pacific crossing, the Manila galleon *San Augustin* made landfall near Trinidad Head in far Northern California. Under instructions from the viceroy of New Spain, its crew began surveying the coast for a safe harbor that might be suitable for future galleons' repair and resupply. While on this mission the battered ship grounded in a storm at Drake's Bay on Point Reyes. The galleon's surviving crew of seventy-six (plus a dog) took one of its launches and sailed back to Mexico but without their 150 tons of treasure. Coastal Miwoks soon began adorning themselves with shards of broken Chinese porcelain. Weekend treasure hunters with mail-order metal detectors continue to search for the remaining loot along the Point Reyes National Seashore, which is a treasure in itself. Other treasure galleons lost to the seas off California include the *Capitana, Nuestra Senora De Ayuda,* and *San Sebastian.*

In 1602 Sebastián Vizcaíno, a merchant and explorer, was ordered north from Acapulco to do a more systematic survey of the coast than Cabrillo's sixty years earlier. First he renamed the harbor of San Miguel, San Diego, and later named the channel near Point Conception, Santa Barbara. In December he rediscovered the "Bay of Pines" and knowing a good report might inspire a goodly reward, reported that this rugged surf-exposed crescent coast was, in fact, "the best port that could be desired, for besides being sheltered from all the winds, it has many pines for masts and yards and live oaks and white oaks, and water in great quantity, all near the shore." He then obsequiously named it after the viceroy who had sent him north, the Conde de Monterey. He continued to sail north out of Monterey, naming the Farallon Islands and Point Reyes and making it as far north as Cape Mendocino before stormy seas and the declining state of his crew's health (scurvy, hunger, hypothermia, festering sores—the usual) forced him back to Mexico.

Despite his overblown claims, it was decided California was too close to Mexico to deserve its own port but too far north to colonize. In 1606 further exploration was cancelled by royal decree and the northern frontier was left in the hands of the Catholic Order of Jesuits.

While the Jesuits built a mission system up and down the Baja peninsula over the next 150 years, it wasn't until the 1760s that Spain finally began moving its people farther north in response to increased maritime exploration by the British, French, and Russians, which posed a threat to Spain's claims of sovereignty in the New World.

As the Jesuits became more powerful within the Catholic Church they also came into conflict with the Spanish crown and in New Spain were replaced by Franciscans from Mexico City, including Father Junipero Serra. Serra, along with highly regarded military leader Captain Gaspar de Portola, led the first colonial "Sacred Expedition" north in 1769, which included three small ships and two land parties, more than three hundred men in all, headed from Baja to Alta (Upper) California. One ship sank and another's crew came down with scurvy. The land parties repeatedly lost their way, ran out of food and water, and fought off Indian attackers. Serra walked and stumbled along on a badly infected leg, possibly from a scorpion bite. By the time they reached San Diego half the expedition was dead. Serra immediately set about founding the first of what would be twenty-one Catholic missions each a day's walk from the other between San Diego and Sonoma (nine of these would be founded by Serra himself). Local Indians would burn his Mission San Diego de Alcala to the ground the following year.

Portola, with a party of sixty remaining able-bodied men, including Father Juan Crespi (but not Serra), continued on from San Diego to Monterey but upon arriving there on October 1 after many weeks of hard coastal hiking, couldn't believe the wind-blown rocky harbor they found was the same "best port," described in Vizcaíno's glowing account. Thinking they must not be there yet, and having faith in God, Portola and his men continued on. On November 1 a scouting party led by Sergeant Jose Ortega crested a hill and spotted a great bay. Father Crespi recalls their return to the main camp two days later:

About eight o'clock at night, the scouts who had been sent out came back from their exploring, firing off their guns as they arrived; and on reaching camp reported that they had come upon a great estuary or very broad arm of the sea extending many leagues inland.

After exploring the south bay, Portola led his men back from San Francisco to San Diego where two months later a relief ship arrived the day before the starving colony was to be abandoned and the survivors begin their long trek back to Baja.

By the time of the Boston Tea Party in 1773 there were fewer than one hundred Spanish living in Alta California. On August 5, 1775, with a new nation about to emerge far to the east, the first Spanish vessel, a small packet boat named the *San Carlos* managed to sail into San Francisco Bay. Despite an earlier one-man mutiny and a battle against outgoing tides, they were able to drop anchor late that night off Angel Island. On board was thirty-three-year-old Father Vicente Santa Maria who, upon landing the next day, recorded his first encounters with the local people.

> *As we came near the shore, we wondered much to see Indians, lords of these coasts, quite weaponless and obedient to our least sign to them to sit down, doing just as they were bid. . . . They were by no means filthy, and the best favored were models of perfection; among them was a boy whose exceeding beauty stole my heart. One alone of the young men had several dark blue lines painted from the lower lip to the waist and from the left shoulder to the right, in such a way as to form a perfect cross. God grant that we may see them worshiping so sovereign an emblem.*

Over the next sixty years Franciscan priests would, in the seeking and saving of savage souls, destabilize the California tribal cultures they encountered, baptizing 53,600 Indian "neophytes" while holding them and many more captive as mission workers and slaves, condoning the flogging and killing (by soldiers out of nearby presidios or forts) of thousands more who fought back, rebelled, or escaped. Tens of thousands of other Indians would die of the diseases introduced by these first European settlers.

Thin on the ground, the Spanish colonists and their higher-ups in New Spain kept a wary eye on other maritime explorers such as Commodore Jean-François de la Pérouse, who commanded a pair of five hundred-ton French naval frigates that visited California's new capital at Monterey in September 1786. La Pérouse wrote that California's soil was "inexpressibly fertile," that "no country is more abundant in fish and game of every description." He noted that the sea was covered with pelicans but complained about "the annoying stench" generated by the exhalations of the countless whales in the bay. "It is impossible to describe either the number of whales with which we were surrounded or their familiarity," he wrote. He also wondered at the lack of Spanish initiative in not killing and skinning for trade the many thousands of sea otters swarming in the kelp beds and wandering up onto the shore.

Six years later in 1792, the British navy ship *Discovery,* under the command of Captain George Vancouver, anchored in San Francisco Bay. Vancouver was impressed by the Spanish hospitality he received. He was more impressed if not astonished by the poor Spanish defenses, with only thirty-five troops and two old cannons protecting the bay. California, or Nova Albion, as Vancouver insisted on calling it, seemed ripe for the taking if too far from civilization ("the Christian world" as his sailors called it) to be worth the effort.

The first U.S. ship to visit California was the Boston-based *Otter,* which dropped anchor in Monterey Bay in 1796 seeking food and water. It had collected one thousand otter skins in the Northwest and was on its way to China via the Sandwich Islands (Hawaii). Ten years later the American-built but Russian-owned *Juno* sailed into San Francisco Bay under the command of Count Nikolai Petrovich Rezanov, a nobleman and founder of the Russian-American (fur-trading) Company. He and his scurvy-ridden crew were desperate for food and to secure supplies for their starvation-wracked Russian and native Aleut employees in New Archangel (Sitka), Alaska. The governor in Monterey, noting that Spain forbade its colonies from trading with foreign powers, was reluctant to sell him food for his colony. Rezanov, forty-two at the time, offered to marry the presidio captain's lovely fifteen-year-old daughter, Doña Concepcion, explaining that he would first have to go back to Russia to see if a Catholic wedding would be permissible to the Orthodox hierarchy. With potential bonds of marriage established, the *Juno* was allowed to load up on bread, dried meat, and other supplies and sail back to Sitka. The following year Count Rezanov died of fever while trekking across Siberia on his way home. His true intentions toward Concepcion would never be known. She didn't learn of his death for another thirty-four years but remained faithful to him, joining an order of nuns and becoming the first California woman to take the veil. Their romance would become the stuff of California ballads and novels.

At the time of Rezanov's visit, a third of San Francisco's mission Indians were dying in a measles epidemic that had no effect on the Europeans. Thousands of elk were swimming across the North Bay on their annual migration. The bay itself was full of giant twelve- to eighteen-foot sturgeon, seven-gill sharks, gray whales, seals, and sea otters, and its surface was covered by great flocks of pelicans and other seabirds. It was the otters, however, that would have the greatest impact on California's human history.

While famed explorer Captain James Cook never got as far south as California, reports of his early explorations across the Pacific sparked California's first commercial commodity boom. The treasure sought was not gold but fur from its resident otters or "sea beaver." With sixty thousand insulating hairs per square inch, sea otter fur is the plushest, most luxuriant on the planet and in the late eighteenth century became a fashionable style among China's Mandarin elite whose ladies favored capes made of the "royal fur." A few pelts Cook traded for in Nootka Sound, Alaska, in 1774 sold for $2,000 in Canton China, sparking a trading frenzy. Within twenty years the sound would be hunted out and more than one hundred thousand furs shipped to China.

The Russians had been trading for Alaskan otter skins since the 1740s. In 1799 Rezanov established his Russian-American Company. It was one of the earliest multinational corporations, hiring local Aleut converts to the Russian Orthodox faith to hunt the otter from their sealskin kayaks with slim but deadly bone harpoons slung with great accuracy from wrist launchers. Yankee merchant ships out of Boston were then hired to transport the furs to China. Yankee sailors also started hunting and trading on their own.

One hundred and eighty years later, in the 1980s, after hunters and fishermen had serially depleted California's sea otters, seals and sea lions, whales, sturgeon, abalone, and sardines, I got to witness another multinational hunting effort on the docks of Fort Bragg in Mendocino County. Local Anglo divers would bring heavy nets full of red and purple sea urchin ashore, where Mexican women in a dockside warehouse would chop out the urchin's orange gonads and shrink-wrap them on wooden sushi platters under the supervision of a Japanese manager. Refrigerator trucks would then rush pallet loads to San Francisco International Airport to be flown to Japan and served twenty-four hours later in Tokyo sushi bars. "It's an awesome operation," one longhaired diver with pirate tattoos told me. "The world's never seen anything like this before."

As the French and British joined in the North American otter trade, New Spain's own efforts to market "sea beaver" faltered. Vicente Vasadre y Vega, a Spanish businessman with more vision than diplomatic skill, proposed a new triangular trade that would move otter furs from California to China, where they would be traded for mercury that was needed for processing ore in the gold and silver mines of Mexico. In 1787 he shipped more than one thousand skins but managed to get into conflicts with officials in Mexico, Manila, and China. He abandoned the scheme a year later.

Because Spain prohibited trade with foreign vessels, Yankee otter hunters soon became engaged in illegal trade with California mission padres and Indians. In 1800 the *Betsy,* a 104-ton, two-masted brigantine out of Boston, stocked up on illegal furs on the California coast before making anchorage in San Diego claiming it had a load of Alaskan pelts bound for China. Three years later the *Alexander,* also out of Boston, smuggled 491 pelts aboard while its crew was being treated for scurvy in San Diego. Their illegal activity outraged the San Diego presidio's commander, Lt. Manuel Rodriguez. Only two weeks after that another Boston ship, the *Lelia Byrd,* commanded by William Shaler and Richard Cleveland, anchored in the harbor seeking supplies. The night before their scheduled departure, the Spanish guards placed on board saw them lowering launches and one later returning with a boatload of otter skins. Ashore, three of the *Lelia Byrd*'s crew were captured by Lieutenant Rodriguez and half a dozen of his horsemen while trading for a pile of skins with a corporal from the fort. Lieutenant Rodriguez chased the corporal back to the presido, leaving the Yankees under guard. At dawn, with one of his launches missing, Captain Cleveland ordered a reconnaissance of the shore. After finding out what was going on he disarmed the Spanish guards on his ship and made for the beach with four armed men where they got the drop on the other guards and recovered their three bound crewmen. With the first faint offshore breeze of the morning they raised their sails and slowly got under way. Shots rang out from presidio soldiers onshore and more shots were returned though no one was hit. Later the *Lelia Byrd* dropped its Spanish prisoners off on another beach. "The choice presented us was that of submission, indignant treatment, and plunder, or resistance and hazarding the consequences," Cleveland later claimed, ignoring who was plundering whom.

Meanwhile, the *Alexander* and another well-armed Yankee ship, the *Hazard*, were causing havoc in Monterey and San Francisco. Other Yankee boats employed in emptying out California's "otter grounds," included the *Derby, Peacock, Albatross, Isabella,* and *O'Cain.*

In 1809 the Russians led an expedition to Bodega Bay sixty-eight miles north of San Francisco where they killed and skinned 2,000 otters. The following year two U.S. vessels collected 7,000 pelts. In 1811 close to 10,000 were taken from California's waters.

In 1810 the Mexican Revolution broke out under the leadership of Father Miguel Hidalgo, though word of this would not reach California for another year. Between this new colonial war and Spain's struggle to repel Napoleon and his invading armies at home, the crown was unable to send any more supply ships to its distant California colony. It also did not help the situation when French pirates flying under the flag of the Republic of Buenos Aires sacked Monterey and several other settlements. Hungry soldiers from the presidios were soon begging food and clothing from the mission padres and their Indian workers. In this context, the willingness to ignore Spain's laws and trade otter furs for shipboard goods became almost universal.

In 1812 the Russians established another hunting camp at Bodega Bay and built a large agricultural settlement, Fort Ross, eighteen miles farther up the green and rugged coast to supply their Alaska colony. I recently visited the impressive reconstruction of this redwood stockade and compound, now a state historic park just off Highway 1, overlooking the sea. Some young Russian tourists were enjoying themselves, having a picnic by the fort with hardboiled eggs, smoked fish, tea, and soda, seemingly unaffected by the cold onshore winds.

Fort Ross was bigger and better armed than any of the Spanish presidios with a number of cannons, blockhouses, and a barracks inside the stockade walls as well as a twin-towered wooden chapel with a church bell cast in St. Petersburg whose clapper you can still clang.

This represented the most southern settlement of Russian America. Initially the fort and surrounding area was home to ninety-five Russians and eighty Aleut hunters. Fort Ross inaugurated California's first shipyard, built its first windmill, and produced California's first glass windows and metal stoves. Although they were asked to leave by local officials (at which point the Russians explained they didn't speak Spanish), Russian trade with Spanish California flourished.

The Russians took about two thousand otter pelts a year, but within five years had depleted Northern California's already heavily hunted waters. In 1819, in the wake of Yankee traders, they opened a sealing station on the Farallon Islands and tried to sell the rougher skins of fur seals to the Chinese, claiming they were otter pelts. With increased hunting pressure, California's northern fur seal population of more than two hundred thousand was soon gone. While they established good relations with the local Pomo and coastal Miwok Indians, the Russians also spread measles and smallpox that eventually wiped out those tribes in Napa and Sonoma. By 1841 the Russians had secured new food sources for their Alaska colonies through an agreement with the British-owned Hudson Bay Company. At that point they sold Fort Ross to John Sutter, an ambitious Mexican of Swiss origin who also owned an inland fort that later became the city of Sacramento and a sawmill on the American River where gold would be discovered seven years later.

By the 1830s California's sea otters were gone. The loss of this voracious marine weasel sparked a population boom of its favorite prey, sea urchin and abalone. Since urchins and abs feed on the underwater roots of kelp plants, California's giant kelp forests soon began to disappear as well, replaced by underwater "urchin barrens" and fields of abalone in a typical cascading ecological collapse that takes place wherever keystone predators are removed from their habitat, be they wolves in the forest, sharks on a reef, or cuddly-seeming sea otters from the kelp.

By 1911 when an international treaty banning the trade in sea otter skins was signed, there were fewer than two thousand left worldwide, and the California population was thought to be extinct.

In 1821 California became a part of the Republic of Mexico and following several Indian uprisings, Mexican authorities decided to split up the mission system, in part to break the power of the Franciscan priests who retained Spanish royalist sympathies. In their place civil authority was established with a secular "alcalde" system of mayors and judges, forts and small towns like Monterey, Los Angeles, and San Diego that remained isolated in a sea of vast family-owned land-grant rancheros (seized mission lands), on whose rolling golden hills huge herds of cattle, horses, sheep, mules, and goats grazed. Unfortunately, with the death of the fair-minded Governor José Figueroa in 1837 few Indian neophytes who'd worked for the missions got to inherit their lands that instead went to wealthy and influential Mexican families. Some Indians still hung around and became vaqueros, skilled horsemen and cowboys on the big rancheros. The mission buildings themselves quickly fell into disrepair.

By the 1830s California's non-Indian population had grown to more than five thousand Mexicans (known as Californios) and a few hundred newly arrived immigrants, including grizzled American mountain men who'd begun crossing the Sierra Nevada from the east and Yankee sailors and traders who were given an opportunity to prosper on this new coastal frontier provided they were willing to learn Spanish and convert to Catholicism.

A new trade was also emerging as dozens of vessels, including two-masted brigs out of Boston, arrived to sell finished goods to the Californios and buy their rancheros' cow hides and tallow (fat for candle- and soap-making). The Boston-based company Bryant and Sturgis offered $2 a hide, outbidding their Russian and British competitors and as a result one million California cowhides sold over the next two decades would be loaded onto Yankee ships by American sailors.

Richard Henry Dana Jr. was a student at Harvard when, following a bout of measles, his eyesight began failing. It was recommended he take a sea voyage to improve his vision and stamina. Rather than become a passenger on a tour of Europe, he decided to work on a western-bound Bryant and Sturgis brig, the *Pilgrim*, shipping out of Boston as a common seaman at the age of nineteen. Over the next two years, from 1834 to 1836 he rounded the cold storm-tossed waters of Cape Horn at the tip of South America before heading north to work off California emptying the ninety-foot brig of trade goods and reloading it with heavy hides.

With few good navigable ports, the young sailor often had to help anchor the vessel offshore and then wrestle the heavy hides onto launches in rough surf, "wading them up to our armpits," making sure the hides did not get wet and spoil. He traveled extensively along the thinly settled coast, seeing Monterey, Santa Barbara, San Diego, the wilds of San Francisco Bay, and the hide port of San Pedro. The aim was to collect forty thousand skins needed to make the voyage profitable. At the same time he kept a detailed journal.

Dana later sailed home to Boston aboard a second ship, the *Alert*, once again traversing the treacherous ice-fogged Straits of Magellan at Cape Horn, the wind this time blowing in all its full-force hurricane fury.

His eyesight and health restored, Dana returned to Harvard, entered law school, and organized his notes into a book, *Two Years Before the Mast*, published in 1840. His nonfiction narrative of life under sail, the hardships of the common sailor (including a captain who flogged his men when not working them to exhaustion) and the distant and exotic land of California quickly became a national bestseller. Among those strongly influenced by

Dana's book was his friend and fellow author Herman Melville, whose 1851 novel, *Moby Dick or the Whale* would become another classic, although not in Melville's lifetime.

Today a full-scale replica of the *Pilgrim* is home ported (along with twenty-four hundred recreational vessels) in the Orange County marina town of Dana Point, which is named after him.

Dana's descriptions of California before the gold rush, particularly his prose about its land and seascapes, helped define the rough-hewn romanticism often attached to this era although his initial take on arriving in January 1835 was hardly halcyon.

"The first impression which California had made upon us was very disagreeable. . . . [t]he open roadstead of Santa Barbara, anchoring three miles from the shore; running out to sea before every south-easter {storm}: landing in a high surf; with a little dark-looking town, a mile from the beach; and not a sound to be heard . . ."

He described the mission and town as lying on a low, flat plain

> but little above the level of the sea . . . The Mission stands a little back of the town, and is a large building, or rather collection of buildings, in the center of which is a high tower, with a belfry of five bells: The town lies a little nearer to the beach—and is composed of one story houses built of brown clay—some of them plastered—with red tiles on the roofs. I should judge that there were about a hundred of them: and in the midst of them stands the Presidio, or fort built of the same materials, and apparently but little stronger.

Later that month, having picked up their first load of hides, they sailed north to Monterey Bay.

> Here we could lie safe from the south-easters. We came to anchor within two cable lengths of the shore, and the town lay directly before us, making a very pretty appearance; its houses being plastered, which gives a much better effect than those of Santa Barbara, which are of a mud-

color. The red tiles, too, on the roofs, contrasted well with the white plastered sides and with the extreme greenness of the lawn upon which the houses—about an hundred in number—were dotted about, here and there, irregularly.

While generally disdainful of the Mexicans' pastoral lifestyle, dismissing the Californios as "an idle, thriftless people," he seemed rather taken by their horses.

The men in Monterey appeared to me to be always on horseback. Horses are as abundant here as dogs and chickens . . . they are allowed to run wild and graze wherever they please, being branded, and having long leather ropes, called "lassos," attached to their necks and dragging along behind them, by which they can be easily taken.

Along with riding horses, getting drunk, and chasing women, on his rare liberty days he also got to observe some of California's marine life including migrating whales. "For the first few days . . . we watched them with great interest—calling out 'there she blows!' every time we saw the spout of one breaking the surface of the water; but they soon became so common that we took little notice of them."

Most of his observations, however, concerned the backbreaking labor of collecting hides and the always challenging and dangerous work involved in sailing and anchoring off poorly charted coastlines.

Arriving off San Pedro, he described a desolate-looking place with a wide kelp- and seaweed-covered rocky shore at low tide, a low hill just past the shore, and empty vista beyond. San Pedro was, and still is, the port for the Pueblo de les Angelos (the town of Los Angeles) that was located thirty miles inland. A few days after arriving and sending their shipping agent to town, "large ox-carts, and droves of mules, loaded with hides, were seen coming over the flat country." The sailors offloaded their sales goods onto the rocky beach and waited for the oxcarts to come get them, "but the captain soon settled the matter by ordering us to carry them all up to the top, saying that, that was 'California fashion.' So what the oxen would not do, we were obliged to do." After hours of carrying heavy boxes and barrels up the hill they threw and slid the heavy hides back down.

South of San Pedro, San Diego with its well-protected harbor was a collection point for the hide boats to cure, sort, and stow their cargoes in large barnlike hide houses on a beach near the narrow harbor entry.

San Diego itself was brushy, treeless, and "not more than half as large as Monterey," with a quiet mission built around a hollow square and a presidio "in a most ruinous state" guarded by "twelve, half clothed, and half starved looking fellows." Its saving grace seemed to be its grogshop where the sailors gathered. "This was a small mud building, of one room in which were liquors, dry and West India goods, shoes, bread, fruits, and everything which is vendible in California. It was kept by a Yankee, a one-eyed man, who belonged formerly to Fall River (Massachusetts), came out to the Pacific in a whale-ship, left her at the Sandwich Islands and came to California." Even then California was attracting an eclectic mix of adventure seekers and entrepreneurs.

It was the least developed of California's bays that most impressed Dana, the one whose narrow entry the forty-niners would later christen the Golden Gate.

> We sailed down this magnificent bay with a light wind—the tide, which was running out, carrying us at the rate of four or five knots. It was a fine day; the first of entire sunshine we had had for more than a month. We passed directly under the high cliff on which the presidio is built and stood into the middle of the bay, from whence we could see small bays making up into the interior, large and beautifully wooded islands, and the mouths of several small rivers. If California ever becomes a prosperous country, this bay will be the center of its prosperity.

He noted that along with the mission and Presidio there was "a newly begun settlement, mostly of Yankee Californians, called Yerba Buena, which promised well."

Having just been staked out by an English whaler who'd deserted his ship, this handful of tents, shacks, and outhouses on the small cove at Yerba Buena would soon be transformed, in the glint of a nugget, into the roaring boomtown of San Francisco. When Dana's ship anchored there in December 1835 the only other ship in the harbor was a Russian brig wintering over from Sitka, Alaska. His visit would mark a pivotal moment in Californian, North American, and world history as the young sailor recorded the final bucolic time before an unpredictable storm of change, both political and demographic, washed over the golden shore.

Actually one change was predictable. United States expansionism, a.k.a. Manifest Destiny (a term coined in 1845), seemed bound to find its armed expression along California's thinly defended shoreline. Between 1841 and 1848 the number of foreigners, mostly Yankees, living in California grew from four hundred to seven thousand, including the first wagon-train settlers down from the Oregon Trail by way of the Humboldt River and others, including the ill-fated Donner Party of 1846, who tried to beat the winter snows over the Sierra Nevada. These newcomers soon outnumbered the Mexican Californios. In 1842 U.S. Navy Commodore Thomas ap Catesby Jones, having received a false report that the United States was at war with Mexico, sailed north from Latin America with two warships, seizing Monterey in October and accepting the governor's surrender before a local Yankee merchant (and future secret agent) Thomas Larkin convinced him there was no war. Embarrassed, he was forced to lower the Stars and Stripes from above the presidio, but the ease by which they had been hoisted was not lost on the other side of the continent.

In 1845 the United States annexed Texas, which had won its independence from Mexico nine years earlier. Mexico considered Texas a rebellious territory and its annexation an act of war. More than willing to oblige, the United States went to war with Mexico in 1846. U.S. forces eventually occupied the capital of Mexico City, forcing Mexico to "sell" Alta California and Nuevo Mexico—more than half its territory—for $18 million (including a debt rebate) under the Treaty of Guadalupe Hidalgo, which also established the Rio Grande as the new border between the countries. Domestic opposition to the war was widespread in the United States, particularly among Whigs and abolitionists. Many saw it as an attempt to spread slavery through the creation of new slave states (the Anglo-dominated Republic of Texas had legalized slavery after winning independence from Mexico). Among the antiwar dissidents were former president John Quincy Adams, future president Abraham Lincoln, and author Henry David Thoreau, who wrote his essay "Civil Disobedience" while in jail for refusing to pay his war taxes.

Ironically, a number of leading Californios, including Northern California commander General Mariano Guadalupe Vallejo, were prepared to integrate voluntarily into the United States, seeing it as California's best chance for development. However, advocates of Manifest Destiny such as President James K. Polk and Senator Thomas Hart Benton of Missouri were hell-bent on war as the surest means to spread the "Empire of Liberty" from "sea to shining sea." Benton's son-in-law, army captain and explorer John Charles Fremont—who'd opened the Oregon Trail—was instructed by President Polk to head to California with some sixty men including his murderous chief scout Kit Carson. There followed what California historian Kevin Starr describes as "an opera scene."

First Fremont threatened Monterey, then he retreated to Oregon. Then a U.S. marine lieutenant named Gillespie dropped off from a navy ship out of Hawaii arrived with secret instructions from the president for both Fremont and Thomas Larkin. A few dozen American settlers next seized General Vallejo and his garrison in Sonoma and declared the California Republic, raising a flag of a grizzly bear (now the state flag of California). The "bear flag revolt" would establish an independent republic that lasted some three weeks, with army captain Fremont and his crew joining it in week two. Around the same time the navy's Pacific fleet that had been patrolling between Hawaii and California arrived in force. Sailors and marines raised the Stars and Stripes over the presidios in Monterey and San Francisco.

The navy then ferried Fremont and his ragtag army of mountain men, volunteers, and Indian mercenaries along with more professional sailors and marines to San Diego, where they quickly moved north to capture Los Angeles. However, the subsequent misrule by the marine lieutenant and spy Archibald Gillespie (who'd since been promoted to captain) sparked a violent rebellion that led to several U.S. defeats and the deaths of scores of American marines and mule-mounted army dragoons (light cavalry) at the battles of Los Angeles and San Pasqual in San Diego. It would take a navy battalion of more than five hundred sailors and marines out of San Diego backed by army troops and volunteers to defeat the Californios and their skilled local horsemen in early January 1847. A final surrender was signed on January 13. Carson then spent three months on mule back carrying word of California's surrender back across the continent to Washington, D.C. When he arrived, President Polk wrote some new instructions and told Carson to turn his mule around and take them back to California.

Despite all the machinations of Fremont, Larkin, various spies and agents, and the Bear Republic rabble (who celebrated their early victory by getting drunk on General Vallejo's wine), it was U.S. naval power that proved decisive in the seizure of California.

Just over a year later and just two weeks before the end of the Mexican-American War with the signing of the Treaty of Guadalupe Hidalgo, on January 24, 1848, gold was discovered at John Sutter's sawmill on the American River.

The globe-spanning gold rush that followed transformed California in ways far greater than a mere change in political ownership. Between 1846 and 1853, California's non-Indian population grew from 14,000 to 300,000. In 1849 alone close to 100,000 prospectors or "forty-niners," mostly Americans but also Chinese, descended on California, headed to "Gold Mountain" along with gold diggers from Australia, Chile, Peru, France, Russia, England, the Sandwich Islands, and wherever young (and not-so-young) men dreamed of quick riches in distant lands. Two-thirds of them came by sea.

This risk-it-all mass migration (one in twelve would die) helped define California as a place where dreams and riches could easily be made or lost, where risk was the standard for doing business, and where the business of getting rich could also be rough, brutish, and racist.

Some one hundred thousand California Indians would die over the next twenty-five years. Along with Cholera, measles, displacement, beatings, rapes, and legal enslavement as indentured child servants, thousands were simply murdered outright. More than four hundred Pomos were massacred by the U.S. Army at Clear Lake in 1849, and 450 Tolowa were murdered by white "volunteers" near Crescent City in 1853—the first of a series of local killings of more than 1,000 people over three years. The Indian Island massacre off Eureka in 1860 took some 250 Wiyot women and children.

Mexican Californians and Latin American miners were targeted for beatings and lynching by mining camp vigilantes and San Francisco street gangs who later were given the appellation "hoodlums." Chinese were systematically excluded from the best mining sites and also targeted for vicious attacks. As a result many returned to San Francisco, where they opened laundries, restaurants, and founded their own "Chinatown."

Still, men of every race and nationality kept arriving. Women wouldn't reach ten percent of the population till 1855. Some of the first women to arrive were prostitutes who came by ship from Chile.

Most of the men arrived by clipper ship, sleek, three-masted vessels built for speed, cruising around Cape Horn from eastern port cities. This trip could take four to six months or longer. Cornelius Vanderbilt came up with a quicker method. His Accessory Transit Company began moving people by clippers, stagecoaches, and riverboats, cutting across the Central American isthmus at Nicaragua and reducing travel time to San Francisco and the gold fields from months to weeks. A similar route across Panama included the building of a railroad, the first step toward an eventual canal.

By 1850 California was admitted into the Union as a "free state," part of the Compromise of 1850 that attempted to delay the inevitable rupture between the free-labor and slave-holding systems of the north and south. By 1852 California was producing close to four million ounces of gold a year, and inland boomtowns and gold camps such as Sacramento, Nevada City, Marysville, and Amador had become major population centers lacking only in courts, judges, sheriffs, roads, sewers, safe drinking water, women who weren't prostitutes, and children.

In Southern California the pueblo of Los Angeles quickly grew from a collection of adobe huts to a brick town that sent its cattle north to feed the forty-niners. Its vineyards also produced half a million gallons of wine and its orchards hung heavy with olives, peaches, figs, and pears well irrigated by the Los Angeles River, which wandered across its sun-drenched open plain out to the sea. It was also experiencing a murder a day in its saloons and gambling halls. To counter this lawlessness a white vigilante band called the Los Angeles Rangers shot and hung some twenty (mostly Mexican) outlaws. The Rangers would eventually become the LAPD.

Back in San Francisco Bay, newly arriving sailors were abandoning their ships to join the gold seekers swarming the foothills, often not even waiting to offload passengers or cargo. By 1850, 635 vessels lay abandoned in the bay and along the waterfront. Many were hauled ashore to act as hotels, boardinghouses, bawdy houses (some 2,000 prostitutes had arrived by then) and saloons. Other ships became landfill as first Yerba Buena cove and than other waterfront wetlands and inlets were built over. At least one ship became a floating jail. There were plenty of rowdies to fill it.

These included a band of Australian criminals known as the Sydney Ducks (vigilantes would later hang four of them). Whenever a particularly gruesome crime was committed, word went out that "the Sydney Ducks are cackling in the pond." The waterfront area they congregated around by Broadway and Pacific up to Pacific Heights became known as Sydney Town and later the Barbary Coast (in honor of North African pirates and slave traders of an earlier era).

With whole crews of sailors abandoning their ships, it became increasingly difficult for captains to find able-bodied seamen for their outbound journeys. The grog shopkeepers and boardinghouse masters or "crimps" of the Barbary Coast quickly offered up a solution.

At the time there were no direct routes between San Francisco and the

Chinese port of Shanghai, and ships sometimes had to circle the globe to get there, so any long and arduous sea journey was said to be a "Shanghai Voyage." Sailors pressed into service against their wills were "being sent to Shanghai." By the time blind-drunk, drugged, and badly beaten sailors being provided as new crew had become a San Francisco industry, "Shanghaied" had become a verb.

The keeping of civil order in the early lawless years of the gold rush with its prostitution, booze, opium, gambling, robbery, murder, and graft was a challenge verging on a joke. One exception was the honorable work carried out by Capt. Alexander Fraser, head of the U.S. Revenue Cutter Service from 1843 to 1848. As commandant of a maritime law enforcement service originally created by Alexander Hamilton, he'd overseen the introduction of the first steam cutters, abolished shipboard slavery and flogging, fought corruption, and advocated unifying his service with the Lighthouse and Life-Saving services, an idea that would come to fruition ninety years later with the creation of the modern Coast Guard.

In 1848 Fraser, having completed his tour as commandant, was ordered to sail a revenue cutter, one of the service's fleet of small ships, around Cape Horn to San Francisco. He arrived eleven months later along with the first wave of "Argonauts" or forty-niners, at which point most of his crew deserted and headed up to the diggings. With a handful of new recruits he soon became a key enforcer of civil order on the bay, working to secure customs tariffs, enforce shipping laws, suppress mutinies, and arrest criminals, including boatmen employed by boardinghouse crimps who'd try to entice newly arriving sailors (sometimes at gunpoint) off the hundreds of ships jamming the harbor and into Barbary Coast boardinghouses where they could be more easily preyed upon. Fraser also worked with the harbor police who, along with their nightsticks and firearms, began carrying foot-long knives for self-defense.

The marine environment was another victim of the gold rush. To feed the tens of thousands of men massing in San Francisco a couple of enterprising fellows headed out to the Farallon Islands twenty-seven miles offshore where hundreds of thousands of common murres, a black-and-white seabird that lays a large egg, were nesting. They'd heard that the Russians had taken eggs off the main (southeast) island while seal hunting there. Now in the gold rush frenzy of '49 that first whaleboat load of three thousand eggs made it back ashore where each egg sold for a dollar. Soon hundreds of "eggers" were taking a million eggs a year from the island. By 1850 a small group had formed the Pacific Egg Company and begun fighting with freelancers who'd hit the islands with rappelling ropes and baskets to gather their own eggs off the steep crags and cliffs, stuffing them into the pockets of special egg vests. By 1855 the government had built a lighthouse on South Farallon Island and the lighthouse crew and the eggers began to fight. During the "egg war" of 1863, two men, a company man and an interloper, were killed in a shoot-out that left four others wounded. In 1881, with the seabird population in a state of collapse, U.S. marshals finally evicted the egg company from the federalized islands.

By 1855 the free-for-all era of the gold rush involving masses of men panning rivers for nuggets or digging mine shafts following shiny rich veins was coming to an end, but organized mining continued to expand thanks to a new industrial tool, the hydraulic cannon. Using gravity for its power, it took water diverted through ditches and wooden flumes high in the mountains and fed it into hoses and an iron-pipe "cannon" that produced a water jet with five thousand pounds of pressure at the nozzle.

By the 1860s "hydraulicking" was tearing apart and dissolving the foothills, running whole mountains through sluices in search of ancient gold-bearing gravel. This method generated eleven million ounces of new gold but at a huge cost. "Nature here reminds one of a princess fallen into the hands of robbers who cut off her fingers for the jewels she wears," wrote famed gold rush author and *New York Tribune* reporter Bayard Taylor.

Some 1.5 billion cubic yards of rock and earth (eight times the amount dug for the Panama Canal) was dumped down the canyons of the Western Sierra, burying California's salmon and steelhead trout rivers along with the wetlands and farmlands of the Central Valley until the practice was finally banned in the 1880s.

The impacts are still felt today in San Francisco Bay, whose waters have only begun to clear from the murky sediment runoff and debris fill generated in the mountains 150 years ago.

The rapidity of change wrought by the gold rush was also reflected in a postscript to *Two Years Before the Mast* written by Richard Henry Dana Jr. in 1859 when, as a well-established lawyer now known for defending sailors and escaped slaves, he revisited San Francisco Bay aboard the steamship *Golden Gate.* Where twenty-four years earlier there'd been a scenic wilderness outpost he found

> *a city of one hundred thousand inhabitants with its storehouses, towers and steeples; its court-houses, theaters, and hospitals; its daily journals; its well-filled learned professions; its fortresses and light-houses; its wharves and harbor, with their thousand-ton clipper ships, more in number than London or Liverpool.*

After putting up at the Oriental Hotel on the corner of Battery and Bush, he wandered around the town, eventually making his way to the docks where,

> *In one of my walks about the wharves, I found a pile of dry hides lying by the side of a vessel. . . . Meeting a respectable-looking citizen on the wharf, I inquired of him how the hide-trade was carried on. "O," said he, "there is very little of it, and that is all here."*
>
> *"The old business of trading up and down the coast and curing hides for cargoes is all over?"*
>
> *"O yes, sir" said he, "those old times of the* Pilgrim *and* Alert *and* California, *that we read about, are gone by."*

By now California's age of sail was giving way to steam-powered ships of wood and steel, harbingers of the industrial revolution. Even as the Civil War was brewing to the east a dynamic new American state was rising on the Pacific with the promise of new wealth from nature. It was to be gained not only from gold-bearing mountain streams and hillsides, forests, farms and mines, but also from its sparking waters, its deep blue sea.

Even as the riches of the gold rush transformed the state, other wealth was being extracted from its living seas. Where otters and seals had been extirpated, new markets emerged for the taking of "whale fish," abalone, and other marine life. While these creatures were slated to die in vast numbers, some would also return, even roaring back to life in the distant future we're now living in, not like Queen Calafia's winged griffins but like the phoenix rising from its own ashes.

GHOST FORESTS

All dripping in tangles green,
Cast up by a lonely sea,
If purer for that, O Weed,
Bitterer, too, are ye?
—Herman Melville

n the town of Richmond, where I live, you can still find the wooden pilings, rusted metal sheeting, and collapsed pier of America's last whaling station, run by Del Monte Fishing Company from 1956 till it shut down in 1971 just before passage of the Marine Mammal Protection Act that helped save the whales. From here they hunted an average 175 leviathans a year, including humpbacks, finbacks, and sperm whales—even an orca "that put up quite a tussle." The whales' oil was used for cosmetics and detergent and their meat sold for human consumption and, chicken feed, but used mostly for Calco dog food. It marked a tawdry end to a fierce but ultimately hopeful tale of California's evolving relationship with the sea.

Sixty miles south of Richmond, the small coastal town of Davenport in Santa Cruz County is named for John Pope Davenport, who founded California's first whaling station on Monterey Bay in 1854. They killed eighteen humpback and gray whales that year, collecting $500 to $1,000 each ($15,000 to $30,000 in today's dollars) for their oil, that was seen as essential for home lighting and as the lubricant of the machine age. While California's early whalers operated statewide, targeting migratory gray whales and other species, a larger slaughter was taking place to the south in the calving and breeding bays of Magdalena, San Ignacio, and Scammon's (now Ojo de Liebre) in Baja, California. Beginning in 1845, U.S. whalers would enter these warm, shallow estuaries and systematically empty them of the gray whales found there. Captain Charles Melville Scammon sailed the ship *Leonore* out of San Francisco Bay in 1855 to join in the "bonanza." Two years later, as Magdalena and San Ignacio bays were being depleted of "whale fish," he discovered another lagoon that was the last refuge of the grays, killing twenty that year and forty-seven the following. It was later named Scammon's in his honor.

At least eight thousand whales were killed in the Baja lagoons between 1846 and 1874—around the same time that millions of buffalo were being slaughtered on the Great Plains. As their numbers plummeted over the next seventy-five years, the last few hundred gray whales were granted an exemption from commercial hunting by the International Whaling Commission (IWC) in 1949. In 1972, they were given protection under the U.S. Marine Mammal Protection Act and, the following year, were covered by the Endangered Species Act. As a result, the Eastern Pacific population that migrates along the coast of California has rebounded dramatically to some twenty-two thousand individuals (they were taken off the Endangered Species list in 1995). The IWC and others have suggested this is close to their historic prewhaling numbers. But genetic studies done by Dr. Steve Palumbi, director of Stanford's Hopkins Marine Station in Monterey, has found that diversity and variation, inbreeding and mutation suggest their historic numbers in the Pacific were closer to one hundred thousand divided between Eastern and Western populations. Unfortunately the Western population never recovered from a continuous slaughter off of Russia and Japan, so that their number in the Western Pacific is now estimated at a critically endangered 130 individuals. On the long-fished waters off New England, the Atlantic gray whale had been exterminated by the 1700s.

Today, California gray whales that are baleen filter feeders, spend their summers gorging on amphipods and other tiny crustaceans on the muddy bottom of the Bering Sea, creating shallow pits or potholes in the process. By early fall, when Arctic sea ice expands (though not as much as it used to), they start their six-thousand-mile migration south, traveling some five miles an hour, twenty-four hours a day. By December they can be seen off California, although farther out than on their return trip. At this point the only threat they face is from overly eager whale watchers getting too close or cargo ships going too fast. By New Year's the first whales begin arriving at the calving lagoons of Baja. Here they will spend several months giving birth, rearing their young, finding mates, breeding in the shallow warm waters, and showing off their newborns to tourists watching from long wooden boats called pangas—proof to me that this is both a highly intelligent and overly forgiving species. On their spring migration north they travel closer to the land and are easily seen from Point Loma in San Diego, Point Lobos in Monterey, Point Reyes in Marin, Bodega Head in Sonoma, Point Arena in Mendocino, Shelter Cove on Humboldt's Lost Coast, Point St. George in Del Norte, and numerous other bluffs and promontories. Small pods including new mothers traveling with their calves may take this coast-hugging route to provide a small margin of protection from roving bands of pelagic (open-ocean) orcas who target their young as prey, one of nature's more horrific spectacles of bloody predation according to those who've witnessed the sometimes hours-long attacks.

In 1997 a fourteen-foot, eighteen-hundred-pound baby female gray dubbed J.J. was found alone near the coast of Los Angeles, perhaps having escaped such a threat. She was transported to SeaWorld in San Diego, and there nursed back to health over the next fourteen months. At the end of March 1998, having grown to thirty feet and almost twenty thousand pounds, she was released back into the ocean during the next northern migration. She managed to lose her radio tracking tags within a few days and return to the anonymity of the sea. Still, J.J.'s distress might have indicated a different, potentially larger threat to the whale population.

"In 1999 gray whales started washing up on shore thin and emaciated and their birth rates dropped and people were saying that's just what happens when a population reaches its carrying capacity," Steve Palumbi explains to me on a visit to his lab. "But if they're only at half their pre-whaling capacity [population number] and this is happening, then maybe the problem is not the whales but the carrying capacity of the ocean! The ocean may be changing with a warming climate. Their prey [cold-water-dependent amphipods] have been shown to be moving farther north from the Bering into the Beaufort and Chukchi seas, and so maybe they're having to travel farther—that additional one thousand miles to get their prey could be what's impacting the whales now."

At the same time, with decreased summer sea ice in the Arctic, gray whales have begun to linger longer while feeding in the north. Some are also feeding year-round off Kodiak Island, Alaska, behavior not observed in the past. So gray whales that can also feed in the water column and are far-ranging in their migratory pattern may prove to be an adaptable or "weedy" species better able to adjust to rapid environmental change than endemic or localized species such as the ice-dependent bowhead whale of the Arctic, whose survival is tied to a single at-risk habitat.

In other words, nothing in the ocean is as simple as it may appear, and even conservation victories such as the return of the California gray whales may be short-lived if not better understood and stewarded.

On a cool December evening in the year 2001, I attended a meeting of San Diego's Council of Divers being held at Scripps Institution of Oceanography in La Jolla.

Some thirty to forty burly recreational divers, men and women in denim, wool, and fleece, have gathered in Sumner Auditorium on Scripp's waterside campus to hear scientist Paul Dayton and see his slide show on marine protected areas (MPAs), including a network of no-take underwater state parks that California is supposed to establish this year (2001) based on its Marine Life Protection Act (MLPA) legislation of 1999. It will actually take another decade of contentious hearings, debates, and lawsuits to finalize the plan. Dayton, perhaps the world's leading authority on kelp ecology, wants to talk about what he calls the "Ghost Forest," California's kelp forests minus the giant black sea bass, big lobsters, moray eels, billfish, little fish, and abundant variety of abalone and otters that once thrived there.

Dayton shows a slide of a juvenile ab hiding under the spines of a big red urchin or "bomber," and the crowd "Awwws" its appreciation. Only divers could find a baby abalone cute, I think.

Other, older slides show black sea bass larger than the men who caught them, including a 628-pounder caught in La Jolla Cove in the 1960s and lifted off the beach by a tow truck. There are images of 1950s free divers holding lobsters the size of bulldogs, and an early-twentieth-century photo from Coronado Island of a man with a wheelbarrow standing atop four acres of spiny lobsters.

"Everything's changed in my lifespan," the sandy-gray-haired Dayton tells the divers. "I just don't see why there is such opposition to these reserves that enhance fishing and heritage values."

"If we establish them, will I be able to collect abs in my lifetime?" one diver wonders aloud.

"In your lifetime, probably not. I think it will be over fifty years before we see their recovery," Dayton admits.

I feel a slight twinge of guilt. I've never tasted passenger pigeon, but I've eaten wild abalone. When I first moved to San Diego in the 1970s, you could still free dive for a few remaining abs in the kelp beds off Point Loma, popping them off the rocks with a small knife or a pry bar. Abalone is a tasty single-shelled mollusk (pounded to soften the muscle, trimmed, lightly seasoned, and pan fried). Our cliff house on Ocean Front Street had abalone shells we'd found, displayed to show their silvery pink/green mother-of-pearl linings scattered about on various end tables and bedroom windowsills like so many decorative hubcaps, some up to a foot across and each with a string of puckered breathing holes. Abalone, more sweet than briny and with a texture like finely sliced pork, seemed as much a part of the California scene as surfing, beach volleyball, and avocados. Their shell imprints and shards have been found in one-hundred-million-year-old coastal rock formations and ten-thousand-year-old Indian middens.

Commercial abalone harvesting didn't get under way till the survivors of a flotilla of thirty-foot boats that crossed the Pacific from Guangdong Province, China, landed in Monterey in 1851. Within a few years the immigrants had established a small village that became known as China Point between what is now the Monterey Bay Aquarium and Hopkins Marine Station (look for all the harbor seals hauled up on the beach behind the fence). There they began drying shellfish and seaweed for sale and export back to China. They were soon joined by hundreds of Chinese men from San Francisco anxious to share in this new marine bonanza. With the decimation of the sea otters by Yankee hunters, the abalones, freed of their main predator, had expanded their range to the point that they literally pebbled the bottom of the region's rocky coastal coves and intertidal waters, clinging onto wave-washed rocks and clustering in tide pools. However, with the industrious efforts of these new hunters, the shoreline abalone population was all but wiped out between Monterey and San Diego by 1865. Like Western buffalo hunters turned "bone-pickers," who collected chuck wagons full of bison bones on the plains to ship east as fertilizer, some Chinese abalone hunters became pearl-button manufacturers, making their living off the mountains of iridescent mother-of-pearl-lined shells they'd earlier dumped along the shore. Others began shipping dried fish to China by steamer, including cod, halibut, rockfish, flounder, mackerel, and of course sardines, whose offshore abundance in the California Current would soon transform Monterey.

By now the Chinese had also introduced abalone into the California diet. Its culinary popularity started among poor young artists and bohemians in Carmel. It spread to their Bay Area friends, including author Jack London, and went mainstream after abalone steaks were served at the 1915 San Francisco World Fair. The Abalone Song, written by Carmel poet George Sterling in the early 1900s, reflects the high status the mollusk quickly attained.

Oh! Some folks boast
of quail on toast because they think it's tony
But I'm content to owe my rent and live on abalone.
Oh some like ham and some like jam,
And some like macaroni,
But our tomcat he lives on fat
And juicy abalone.

Friends would add verses as they hung out at each other's cottages pounding the abalones they'd caught to tenderize them, or at Monterey's Café Ernest sharing red wine, song, and poetry. One verse turned out to be a tragically mistaken biological assessment.

The more we take, the more they make,
In deep-sea matrimony.
Race suicide will ne'er betide
The fertile abalone.

Of course that also reflected a long-held belief among twentieth-century fisheries managers that you can't drive a fecund species of "broadcast spawners," like shrimp, squid, or abalone to extinction because they produce so many eggs. The only problem with that theory is it doesn't take into account the fact that abalone, unlike most Californians, tend not to move around once they've found a home to stick to. Unless there's another abalone of the opposite sex within a yard or so, they can puff all the eggs and sperm they want into the water column but they aren't going to produce any new larvae.

Still, the abs continued to thrive in offshore waters too deep to wade to and in inaccessible coves from Big Sur to Point Mendocino. In the 1920s and '30s, Japanese fishermen in metal dive helmets that fit over their heads connected to air hoses and wearing canvas suits and weighted shoes for bottom walking began collecting abs in the waters between San Pedro and Monterey. Roy Hattori was one of them. In the late 1930s a wave tossed him against an underwater rock so hard the impact cracked his helmet. Thinking fast, he grabbed an abalone from his collection basket and slapped it against the crack. It immediately glommed on, with its snail foot creating a waterproof seal till he was able to get pulled to the surface, saving him from drowning in his own hard hat.

It was the introduction of scuba—self-contained underwater breathing apparatus—in the 1950s and '60s that would reignite the fishery, overwhelming the abalones' last wild refuges. The new hunt expanded rapidly throughout the 1960s and '70s, as did record catches and the sense of limitless wealth that often accompanies economic bubbles. Famed *National Geographic* explorer and marine conservationist Sylvia Earle, who lives in Oakland, California, recalls working with Scripps scientists and students in the mid-1960s. "Abalone, oh my goodness," she recalls wistfully. "Grad students fed themselves on it till they were sick of eating. They'd fry and boil and sauté it and grind it up for bread. It was a grad students' staple diet."

At the same time it was becoming part of the diet of sea otters who were recolonizing the Central California coast around Monterey after a single surviving colony of "extinct" otters had been discovered below the steep cliffs of Big Sur in 1938, the year after Highway 1 was pushed through the isolated coastal mountain redoubt. Actually local naturalists had known about these otters for some time but had kept their existence a secret, fearing they might be hunted down and killed again, but this time, however, the marine weasels were protected.

Soon the mollusk population experienced a new collapse as divers and otters emptied out coastal coves and offshore rock formations and islands. As the population declined, previously unseen diseases such as withering foot syndrome also began to infect the mollusks. In the 1980s, as abalone became harder to find, many commercial divers switched over to sea urchin harvesting for the emerging Asian market, the latest fishing boom. By the late 1980s, a group of thirteen commercial divers had decided to target abalone in the cold, rough, white-shark-infested waters around the Farallon Islands, one of the last places where they could make a thousand dollars a day collecting the mollusk. They even supported the 1993 California White Shark Protection Act, figuring that would keep sport divers away from the islands. (Indeed, the only recreational divers who go there today are cage divers hoping to see a white shark). Other commercial fishermen supported the legislation in the hope the sharks would keep down the sea lion population that had rebounded with the Marine Mammal Protection Act and that competed with them for fish.

Soon the thirteen Farallon ab divers were down to a dozen after thirty-eight-year-old Mark Tisserand was bitten by a shark and forced to retire with a mangled leg. Joel Roberts, one of those who continued working after the attack, traded in his shotgun shell "bang stick," (Tisserand had been unable to release the safety pin on his quickly enough) for a Glock 9 mm pistol modified to shoot up to ten feet underwater. Still, Joel didn't feel very secure in one encounter where he ended up hugging the rocky bottom with his gun drawn as a sixteen-foot shark repeatedly cruised around him and as his compressed air dwindled to the last few hundred pounds. When the shark finally swam out of sight, Joel had to make a rapid ascent through fifty feet of murky green water to get back to his boat. "When I climbed on board I was so scared my mouth was literally foaming white," he later told me.

By then wild red, green, pink, and black abalone had largely disappeared from California waters. The white abalone, a particularly delicious deep-water variant, became the first shellfish to make it onto the federal endangered species list in 2001, followed by the black abalone in 2009. In 1972, the peak year of legal harvest, divers collected 143,000 pounds of white abalone off California's coast. When two scientists in a submersible surveyed the state's Central Coast twenty-five years later, they spotted only five abalone in 150 hours of underwater searching.

In 1998 commercial and recreational abalone fishing was banned in Southern California. Sport fishing of red abalone is still allowed in Northern California waters seven months a year but only by free-divers without scuba gear. They are allowed to take up to three legal-sized abs a day and no more than twenty-four a year.

The CO at the Coast Guard surf station in Fort Bragg, 164 miles north of San Francisco, knowing I'm looking for some search-and-rescue action, invites me to visit during abalone season. "That's a good time for rescues," he explains. Along with being a fun macho sport that results in about five drownings per year, plus a shark-related death every decade or so, abalone season also provides cover for illegal poachers, forcing California Department of Fish and Game (DFG) wardens to spend lots of time on cliff tops with binoculars doing surveillance. Numerous smuggling rings have been broken up, but with abalone prices at $60 a pound and more, abalone poaching continues to expand. "The profit from the illegal sale clearly outweighs the risks of getting caught," says DFG assistant chief Tony Warrington. In 2011, a thirty-one-year-old San Francisco man, Qiong Wang, was caught illegally taking abalone three times in three weeks by the Petaluma Police, Mendocino County Sheriffs, and the DFG. He was sentenced to a year in prison and fined $20,000.

Back at the 2001 Scripps meeting with Paul Dayton, a woman diver speaks of having grown up in Cardiff (in North County San Diego), where the beaches were covered in seashells when she was a child but are no longer.

After Dayton concludes his presentation, the president of the dive group (the only one wearing a sports jacket) encourages his members, representing some 1,500 local divers, to get involved in California's Marine Protected Area designation process, which is being strongly opposed by the recreational fishing industry.

A National Academy of Sciences report that year called for wilderness protection for 20 percent of America's coastal waters in order to sustain dwindling fisheries and wildlife populations. At the time, less than 1 percent of California's state waters were protected. That's why, in 1999, marine scientists, environmentalists, some fishermen, and some legislators worried about the impacts of overfishing and pollution had worked together to create and pass the state's Marine Life Protection Act.

"If we get reserves at the levels environmentalists want, you'll devastate opportunities for recreational fisheries and anglers," claims Bob Fletcher, the tall, trim, gray-eyed president of the Sportfishing Association of California, whom I interview the day after Dayton's meeting. "You have to balance the interests of the environmentalists with our right to make a living," Fletcher adds.

We're meeting amidst squawking gulls by the Sport Fishing Landing near Shelter Island on San Diego Bay. Here the docks are lined with dozens of fifty-five-foot and sixty-five-foot party boats: *Top Gun, Searcher, Prowler, Conquest,* and *Polaris Supreme,* along with one-hundred-foot-plus multi-day boats that head south of Baja in search of big tuna.

"I think reserves will decrease rather than increase yields," Fletcher tells me. "There will be more fish or whatever in the reserve, but for fisheries you lose more yield by taking habitat away [through protection].

"Let's not alienate everyone," he continues. "Let's start small, move them away from the coast, and document them over five to ten years."

He believes traditional fisheries management (for consumption) will restore the sea's living resources. Interestingly, it will be the recreational fishing industry that he represents, not commercial fishermen, who will prove most vocal in opposing California's plans for a network of marine protected areas. This could be because commercial fishermen play the role of top predator in the marine ecosystem and have witnessed how their own fishing power combined with other factors has led to the decline of many of their most profitable prey targets, including abalone, salmon, and rockfish.

"My best hunch is these [wilderness reserves] will have some useful benefits, but you still need fishing regulations and pollution controls outside these areas. You can't do whatever you please with the rest of the ocean," cautions Zeke Grader, head of the Pacific Coast Federation of Fishermen's

Associations, which today represents some seven hundred California commercial fishermen. "Some of our members say don't agree to anything, but I tell them that if we do right by the resource, we do right by our industry. If you get fishermen involved, they'll be the ones promoting these reserves and feeling the scientists and others are out there working for them."

By contrast, the state's recreational fishing industry is selling the "experience" of fishing, generating upwards of half a billion dollars a year in fishing-trip expenditures with many of their paying customers lacking the long-term perspective of professional fishermen and women. Today, California's recreational industry lists mackerel among its daily catches. When I moved to San Diego in the 1970s, mackerel were chopped up and used as bait to catch the big fish. Another popular catch today is Pacific barracuda, formerly known as "snot logs," and considered a nuisance catch.

I suggest that if environmentalists aren't satisfied with the Fish and Game Commission's final recommendations on marine protected areas they might sue, and if the Sportfishing Association isn't happy, they might sue, the result being years of additional delay as the promise of reserves gets tied up in court.

"I don't see that as such a bad thing." Fletcher grins. "I'm not against inaction."

Ten years later in 2011, with the process finally concluding and a network of protected areas covering 15 percent of state waters about to be established, Fletcher and two fishing groups file suit, claiming the Fish and Game Commission that oversaw the MLPA process had no legal authority and also failed to do a proper environmental review. A judge will quickly dismiss one of the suits.

That same year I attend the last of numerous MLPA public hearings. It is being held at the statehouse in Sacramento, where I again get to say hi to Bob, now retired from his post but still carrying on the fight as part of the Partnership for Sustainable Oceans an eco-sounding group opposed to MPA designations. The partnership includes the Sportfishing Association of California and fishing tackle manufacturers. Bob says the whole Marine Life Protection Act experience "has been a mockery of the open process. It's all about penalizing the fishermen. But what about the real threats from pollution?"

"We're conservation minded," John Rarson from the United Anglers of Southern California, another plaintiff, assures me. "We put [hatchery-reared] white sea bass back in the ocean. But things were just not done right here."

Bob introduces me to Dan Wolford from the Coastside Fishing Club, the third plaintiff in the lawsuit, who tells me, "There's no science behind the MLPA. There's been no overfishing on the West Coast for a decade, maybe two. Overfished stocks are recovering using traditional fisheries management. The fish populations here in California are truly healthy."

That's a concise if inaccurate statement, given that the February 2010 *Proceedings of the National Academy of Sciences* had included several studies among dozens of peer-reviewed science reports showing well-managed MPAs benefit both ecosystems and fisheries. There'd also been an emergency closure of federal waters off California due to overfishing within the past decade, and landings of all fish are down from thirty years earlier when fish populations were larger and healthier. The good news is when you set aside parts of the ocean where you're not allowed to kill fish, they tend to grow back.

David Gurney, a curly blond-haired urchin diver from Fort Bragg and one of three conspiracy-minded guys down from Mendocino County, goes up to the public mike and says, "You have to notice that these [no-take] areas mirror the areas of interest to the oil and gas industry." He's come to believe that marine protected areas are being promoted by big oil—working through rich environmental foundations—in order to drill off California, the theory being that if fishermen are excluded from certain waters they'll no longer have the motivation to oppose oil drilling as most other Californians do. Indian tribes are also unhappy with what they see as a lack of consultation on the site designations, although Governor Jerry Brown's secretary for natural resources, John Laird, has gone a long way to assuage them, including an agreement giving them access for some traditional harvesting of fish and kelp.

. . .

I again visit Paul Dayton at Scripps that summer of 2011. The meandering campus overlooks a surfing beach, research pier, and the one-thousand-foot-deep Scripps submarine canyon. Its tree-shaded buildings run chock-a-block up a rising bluff to a NOAA government fisheries lab. Unfortunately, because it's part of the financially imploding University of California system, Scripps's library, which contains the most extensive collection of marine science research publications on the planet, including more than 225,000 books, is about to shut down. The books will be dispersed to other libraries and some rare materials digitalized with help from Google. Fifteen pelicans fly overhead in a V formation, unconcerned with human folly.

Paul turns from his office computer on the third floor of Ritter Hall as I enter. His hair has gone white. His face is more weathered looking than it was a decade ago, though still handsome when he smiles. He's wearing wire-frame glasses and a hearing aid, sporting a T-shirt of a whale, tan shorts, and running shoes. He now has Meniere's disease, he tells me, so he can no longer dive. As a young man in 1954 he built his own dive equipment, including homemade air tanks, and did his first dives in Baja's Sea of Cortez, where he saw groupers "large enough to swallow me whole." He then spent much of his career diving in the six square miles of San Diego's Point Loma Kelp forest, now the most studied kelp forest in the world.

He's unhappy with environmental groups that claim California's kelp forests are in trouble. "Right now the kelp and understory algae are fine—probably they've never been healthier—it's the fish that are in trouble," he explains. "But go into any [fishing] tackle store and ask them if we need marine protected areas and you get this drumbeat of hating government and demonizing scientists. Bob Fletcher and his ilk, we know where they fish, we know where sports fishermen fish, and when they say they're being deprived they're not. These areas [being set aside] are not where the [paid passenger] day boats go. It's where a few lobster and urchin guys go. This attack on the public managing our own resources—all this outrage based on misinformation, Fox News, and what have you, I think it's tearing the country apart.

"I've talked to sport fishermen eight times and couldn't finish because they shouted me down. I had a sport [speargun] diver promise if I set up a reserve he'd go in and shoot all my fish. But I want my grandkids to be able to have fish, too," he explains, looking glum. "There's a whole suite of rockfish and abalones that won't come back without reserves. White and black abalones aren't coming back at all." (He thinks they're too close to extinction to recover.) "Reds and greens are. Some urchin divers are even planting them but won't say where so the sports guys don't target them. The lobster fishery is still sustainable because they have what we call local ecological knowledge of how to fish. They take the small ones and not the great big lobsters [that are better breeders]."

"There's been lots of science on reserves that's been put out, hundreds of [research] papers on this, and when they're big enough to work fishermen love them," he claims, referring to the spill over effect, when larger and more numerous fish swim beyond the watery boundaries of their protected zones and can then be legally taken. One example is in the waters just outside the Cape Canaveral Kennedy Space Center, which has been off-limits to fishing since 1962 for national security reasons, and where there are more world-record catches of red drum, sea trout, and other sport fish than anywhere else in Florida.

I mention I've seen other evidence just down the road at the La Jolla Cove Underwater Park Ecological Reserve, which Scripps helped establish in 1971. Past the yellow buoys that mark the edge of the 514-acre no-take reserve, the sea surface is thick with marker floats for lobster traps, that have been placed there to capture the "spill over," of spiny lobsters migrating out of the reserve.

Dayton says he doesn't see La Jolla Cove as much of a model for marine protection because, "It's too small to work and huge amounts of poaching goes on there." He cites a two-hundred-pound black sea bass that was speared there in 2005 (the poacher was arrested, "but only got his wrist slapped,") and a 150-pounder speared to death in 2007. Back at the beginning of World War II, the cove's Bottom Scratchers Club—of trident spear fishermen—regularly chased and sometimes caught two-hundred- to six-hundred-pound six- and seven-foot black sea bass when not collecting the abundant abalone and lobster also found there at the time.

A 2008 study in the journal *Science* concluded that 40 percent of the world's oceans are now heavily impacted by human activities, including overfishing, while only 4 percent remain in a pristine state.

Paul Dayton believes that big protected zones such as the Galapagos Islands reserve off Ecuador, and the 140,000-square-mile Papahanaumokuakea Marine National Monument in Northwest Hawaii, (home to 70 percent of U.S. corals), and even the twenty-two square miles recently designated around Point Conception (a biological transition zone in California's coastal ocean), have much better chances for restoring marine wildlife and habitat than older, smaller reserves. Still, even California's "mini-reserves," including La Jolla Cove, the Landing Cove on Anacapa, (one of the Channel Islands), and Point Lobos south of Monterey are like small three-dimensional mirrors into the living past and so remain hugely popular with recreational divers willing to take only pictures and leave only bubbles.

In many places around the world fishermen have played a major role in establishing and promoting big marine reserves. Nearly 20 percent of the Channel Islands, 318 square miles of water, came under protection in 2003 at the end of a public process similar but separate from the state's MLPA battles. That effort was launched by a Santa Barbara recreational fisherman named Jim Donlon.

Sean Hastings, resource coordinator for the Channel Islands National Marine Sanctuary, recalls meeting his "ocean hero" back in 1997. Donlon was already in his eighties when he and an old fishing buddy came by to visit Sean and the sanctuary manager, telling Sean, "Son, I've fished these waters since before you were born and I've done damage to the rockfish and I want to change that," and suggesting the establishment of a no-take reserve. "He had a vision that he and his buddies had fished out the big cod but that with this we could bring them back," Sean recalls. "Unfortunately he passed away, but it's been fifteen years now and we do see them coming back. I think we're making progress for him. We need to do more but we're getting there."

Dirk Rosen is the founder of an outfit called MARE, Marine Applied Research and Exploration, that does ocean science contracting out of Point Richmond, California. He was hired to use MARE's ROV robot submarine to survey the Channel Islands' marine protected areas for seven years beginning with their initial fishing closures. He tells me that in 2009, the last year of his surveys that are run off a commercial fishing boat, the ROV cameras were recording a greater abundance and variety of fish, including threatened canary rockfish, and significantly larger fish than when they began. He shows me the tapes. A large black sea bass swims past the ROV's camera and wanders off into the kelp. "There were a lot of BOFFs this time—Big Old Fat Females," he explains. "It's not a good pick-up line in a bar, but it's what you're looking for because they're more fecund and they help rebuild stocks and their presence lets you know these reserves are going to recover from past fishing impacts."

Back at Scripps I ask Dayton if he feels like his work has helped change public awareness.

"I think our work contributed very little to the MLPA process. I'd say my impact has been close to zero," he claims. "If I could, I think I'd have rather done more science and spent less time speaking out."

It's kind of a down note to end our interview on, and later he'll e-mail me to say as much and to point to a key 2006 paper on marine reserve design he helped author that clearly helped advance the cause of ocean conservation. Leaving Ritter Hall (named after Scripps's founding director) I walk down hallways typical of marine stations everywhere with labs full of fridges and glassware and waterproof pelican cases for taking equipment to the field, bulletin boards full of notices on rentals, post-graduate jobs, old Gary Larson cartoons, and science posters. Then I pass an office with a half-open door and spot a pair of surfboards ready for the next swell and I perk up because I'm heading back to the beach. The next morning I go body-boarding in Ocean Beach with my friend Charlie's eleven-year-old son, Nick, and start thinking about my next dive trip.

Avalon, a small hilly harbor town on a 26-mile-long desert island, is just over an hour's ferry ride from the port of Long Beach. Pods of dolphins accompany us on the passage over. The town has a Mediterranean charm with its raft of moored sailboats, small cafés, inns, and steep meandering streets. It reminds me of a mini-Monaco with William Wrigley's green-and-white mansion on Mount Ada (named for his wife) in lieu of the prince's palace. Its population is close to four thousand, most of whom get around by golf cart, with another two hundred residents twelve miles down island in the peninsula town of Two Harbors. We put up at a dive motel at the end of Maiden Lane with a view to the cove and big drum-shaped island casino that, unlike those of Monaco, has never been used for gambling but rather for Southern California's larger industry of entertainment, including a still spectacular movie theater and an old-style dance pavilion that has hosted Cecil B. DeMille, Errol Flynn, and Benny Goodman, the King of Swing, among others (check out the revealing mermaid mural). Looking down I can also see orange garibaldi fish in the gin-clear waters of the harbor.

After a few fish tacos on the pier we negotiate with a local dive operator for some rental gear and head over to the small marine reserve park by the casino, where we put on our wet suits, hoods, booties, gloves, BCDs, regulators, air tanks, and for me twenty-two pounds of weight, half of it to compensate for all that neoprene. My dive buddy Scott Fielder and I then carefully walk down some seaweed-slick concrete stairs into the kelp forest. As soon as we drop down into the bracing 53-degree water we're surrounded by big striped red-and-black California sheephead and more abundant garibaldis, like goldfish on steroids, also shoals of blacksmith and kelp perch and lots of bottom cover, including pink strawberry anemones like tiny living flowers and a decorator crab, covered in red seaweed and green algae, camouflaging itself among the red-plated mollusks, white anemones, and purple ring top snails. The kelp forest is infused with late afternoon cathedral light and some downed pilings and rollers from an old dredging machine that's providing firm placement for the kelp's holdfasts, including a massive thickly tangled collection of brown strands fifteen feet across and rising fifty feet straight up to the ocean's surface. It's like seeing your first redwood, only underwater. Half an hour later, as it's getting dark, we look up and see the illuminated Christmas tree atop the casino through the crystalline water column, unusual for California. That evening we'll go to dinner in the all but abandoned town, its palm trees wrapped in holiday winter lights.

The next day we head out on a forty-six-foot dive boat with four others. It's a warm blue-sky day. Our first dive is at Long Point. We swim along a rock wall of kelp with lots of spiny urchins and I spot four lobsters in caves and a big purple sea hare (marine snail) and then another and there are lots of kelpfish and pencil-thin yellow senoritas and more blacksmiths, a kind of damselfish that, unlike its multihued coral reef cousins, comes only in basic cold-water blue and black.

Motoring to our next site, we spot a pod of big Risso's dolphins, twelve feet long, who are migrating through the area, feeding on squid.

As we anchor at Hen Rock (which looks nothing like a hen—"guano rock" would be a better name), we're greeted by a couple of sea lions dozing on the surface, each with one flipper in the air like a sail or a high five. We dive through more kelp, then along some open sandy bottom when a six-hundred-pound sea lion streaks past us on the hunt like some sleek, flexible torpedo. Sometimes they'll check you out and want to play with the slow, awkward bubble breathers but not this one. He's working. So I examine some turban snails and limpets and an old algae-encrusted dinner-plate-sized abalone shell that reminds me of what's been lost. I get distracted and don't watch where I'm going and then have to untangle my tank and BCD from the clutches of several rubber-hose-like kelp strands. Giant kelp and bull kelp are the dominant marine plant species along the California coast and can grow a foot a day, which sounds awesome till they're yanking on your regulator hose.

After clearing my gear, I check out some rocky crops covered in tangled white mats of vascular meshlike holdfasts that secure the brown kelp's stems, serrated leaves, and bubble floats. While I'm playing botanist with this mass of algal spaghetti, Scott spots an abandoned hoop net used for catching lobsters and frees a four-foot leopard shark trapped inside.

While leopard sharks thrive along the California coast, up to 73 million other sharks are slaughtered each year for their fins used in shark fin soup, a tasteless but expensive vanity item popular in China. California passed a law banning the sale and possession of shark fins in late 2011. This was more than a symbolic gesture given that California had the largest market for shark fin soup outside of Asia. Polling showed that over 70 percent of Californians of Chinese descent supported the ban. Many worry that due to their continued global slaughter sharks may be going the way of the American buffalo. Buffalo, I'm glad to report, are doing okay on Catalina.

We spot one of the shaggy celebrities on a cliff top the next day, along with a few bald eagles, while working our way down the coast from the Avalon pier to the Wrigley Institute for Environmental Studies (marine lab) near Two Harbors. We're aboard an open nineteen-foot boat driven by Trevor Oudin, the lab's sun-reddened, clean-shaven twenty-nine-year-old boat handler. It's turned cold and foggy overnight, though with his black watch cap and jacket Trevor doesn't seem to notice. He was raised in Two Harbors and went to its one-room schoolhouse before being bused cross-island to the high school in Avalon. He left for a few years to go to college at USC but is back now. "I can still get my fix of city life. It's just a boat ride to L.A. and we can get Korean food or Thai or whatever but without all that big-city hustle," he explains. He's engaged to the lab's young manager, Lauren Czarnecki. We pass a harbor seal on a rock waiting for the sun that's not coming out today and a frenzy of seabirds feeding on squid. "Everyone's feeding now." Trevor smiles. It's been a good year for squid. "Here with my fiancée we all eat well," he tells us. "People, my generation of friends, we'll do dinner parties and we all cook. I'll serve venison I hunted or fish I caught. Good, healthy food."

Trevor also used to hunt goats and pigs, but the Catalina Island Conservancy, which owns 88 percent of the island, has eliminated them as invasive species that threaten the native Catalina foxes' habitat. The goats gathered on the highest crags at night to bed down and were relatively easy to eliminate, but the pigs (introduced several times, most recently in the 1930s to eliminate the island's native rattlesnakes at a Boy Scout Camp) were wily, and it required professional hunters using helicopters, camouflage, and night-vision goggles to finally kill them off. There are still some two thousand introduced deer on the island whose elimination is more controversial with local hunters and admirers. The buffalo that once numbered as many as six hundred are descendents from an original fourteen who arrived by barge as extras for the 1925 silent film about Indian life, *Vanishing Americans,* based on a Zane Grey novel. Grey also spent summers fishing in Avalon, whose Tuna Club is the birthplace of modern big-game sportfishing. Catalina was the backdrop for numerous other movies, including *Ben-Hur, Treasure Island,* and parts of the original *Mutiny on the Bounty.* It was already a shooting locale for L.A.'s emerging film industry in 1919 when chewing gum magnate William Wrigley Jr. bought the island from the sons of Phineas Banning, founder of the Port of San Pedro. The island conservancy that the Wrigley family later established, despite its ruthless approach to invasive species control, has decided that a herd of 150 bison is a cultural legacy that is also ecologically compatible with the island's native flora and fauna. For a time they'd been shipping the younger animals to an Indian reservation in South Dakota, but since 2009 they've instead put the herd on birth control.

The Wrigley lab dock area at Fisherman's Cove has been part of a small marine reserve since 1988, where fishermen and divers aren't allowed to remove the wildlife. Under the new MLPA guidelines, the half-a-square-mile protected area will be expanded to three square miles.

"It's been here over twenty years as a reserve so there are big kelp bass and sheephead under our dock," Trevor tells us as we tie off at the pier and I can look down and see some big fish right there. "We've got sand sharks, bat rays, moray eels, Garabaldis, lobster. . . ." He points to where fifty to seventy leopard sharks filled in a narrow arm of the cove the previous summer till a big bull sea lion found them and started trapping them against the shore, pulling them out one by one and tearing them apart. "After that the sharks moved to the other side of the dock"—he points—"near that open pebble beach, so they can't get trapped in a narrow inlet again."

While touring the facilities we meet Trevor's fiancée, Lauren, short and animated with dark blond hair and light brown eyes. She's excited they were able to catch one hundred pounds of market squid off the pier the night before. "It's a big spawning event and everyone's looking happy and full," she says. "The bottom of the cove is just covered in squid nests (egg capsules). They spawn and die just like salmon and other animals higher up the food web. U.C. will save seven hundred dollars just on what we caught last night [since they won't have to buy live feed for their research animals]."

We're at the outdoor display tanks full of study animals including a swell shark and a horn shark and lots of urchins and red- and blue-banded goby that are bright and fluorescent enough to pass for tropical fish but are native to Catalina's waters. Lauren waves a squid over a rock pile in one of the larger tanks and we watch an already stuffed moray eel slowly come out to take this one final squid though he's more playing with his food than eating it at this point. He (or she) bites it, spits it, tentatively chews on its tentacles, and finally downs it. Dozens of other squid hang at the upper corner of the tank. If I were to anthropomorphize, I'd say they look nervous.

Along with her lab responsibilities Lauren is also director of the marine reserve and has been working on the MLPA process for Southern California. That process was strongly debated at public hearings in San Diego, Dana Point, and elsewhere until a compromise was finally reached establishing reserves smaller than what scientists and conservationists had called for but large enough to still protect key habitat and wildlife. "I know Catalina residents who are fishing for subsistence and as a biologist I can see both sides," Lauren claims, "but it was an eye-opening experience for me to come out of school and these groups would sit back and not say anything during these meetings and then sue and its kind of sad because good things could have been done a long time ago and it's unfortunate it's gotten to this point but that's how it goes, I guess."

After our lab tour we have lunch in Two Harbors and take a ride back across the big island to the ferry with naturalist Ellen Kelley. We cross over dirt and gravel roads through desert sage past two thousand-foot-high interior mountains and pig fences left over from the eradication campaign. "It was a war here in the 1990s," Ellen says without irony. We pass through fields of prickly pear cactus and chaparral that took over after the pigs and goats overgrazed the island. We pass stands of coyote brush and bush poppy, toyon, yellow-flowering coreopsis, and native lemonade berry, mountain mahogany, and Saint Catherine's lace with its silvery dusty leaves. All the island's native plants are adapted for drought conditions and to survive periodic brushfires, as are most Southern California native species, though some also burn like kindling. Eleven percent of the island caught fire in 2008 and they evacuated the town of Avalon and barged in fire trucks from L.A. and Ventura. It was aircraft dropping fire retardant that finally saved the town.

Six months later I return to Catalina aboard my friend Jon Christensen's thirty-foot sailboat. It's mid-July and Two Harbors now looks like a maritime tailgate party with more than 250 boats moored at its anchorages and overflowing into Fourth of July Cove and Cherry Cove. Remembering the lab tour, I talk Jon and Charlie Landon into taking our eight-foot rubber inflatable into the cove in front of the lab, where we go snorkeling. The kelp is thick and swarming with big calico and kelp bass, large orange Garabaldis, and lots of shoaling small fry. We spot five-foot bat rays flying through the water column. Closer to the beach we find rocky nooks and caves full of lobster and more big bat rays lying next to each other on the sandy bottom. We make our way to the pier and underneath find a large school of white sea bass about twenty pounds each.

Along the cliffs on the far side of the pier the water is crystal clear, like the Caribbean, only with kelp and the sun bright overhead. Resting on the surface amid the giant brown algae, I can look up at a steep slope covered in prickly pear cactus and Catalina live-forever, a succulent native only to this island. Below the surface I can free dive through open channels in the seaweed to play with small opaleyes, apple green fish with yellow spots, big caramel-spotted calico bass, and hunky orange Garabaldis and suspicious antennae-waving lobsters in crevices and it feels good to be in a wilderness again. I suspect ten or fifteen years from now Californians who today vehemently oppose marine protected areas will shrug and reluctantly acknowledge that something useful and important really did happen when our state park system moved underwater.

One of my favorite things about Catalina is that as wild as it mostly is, it's by far the most developed of the eight Channel Islands, two of which are navy owned. These are San Clemente, a live-fire range that also includes a mock Afghan village that SEALs periodically invade, and San Nicolas, a smaller island used for weapons and systems testing above and below the surface. Five of the islands incorporate national parklands and marine sanctuary waters: Santa Barbara, Anacapa, Santa Cruz, Santa Rosa, and San Miguel. San Miguel, the most western of the islands, is living proof that the Marine Mammal Protection Act works with more than one hundred thousand seals, elephant seals, and sea lions hauling out on its breeding beaches every year. Anacapa has the largest brown pelican rookery in the United States. Some twelve to fifteen thousand birds roost there today, up from a few hundred in 1972 when DDT, which weakened their eggshells, was banned.

While the Farallon Islands off San Francisco are known for the dozens of white sharks that congregate there every fall, few are aware that the Channel Islands provide a similar draw for blue whales. More of the largest animals ever to live on earth can be seen in and around these waters than anywhere else on the planet. Some two hundred blue whales gather here in the California Current each summer and stay on through the rainy season feasting on tiny shrimplike krill. The islands also attract humpbacks, fin whales, twenty thousand migratory gray whales, some white sharks, and some orcas who have been known to kill white sharks. One such attack was even videotaped off the Farallons back in 1997. The day after the attack there wasn't a white shark in sight. Apparently they can also detect their own blood in the water.

Given the Channel Islands' biological diversity and rugged backcountry landscapes, it's no surprise there's an "All Eight Club," made up of those who've touched all of the islands (members get a bill cap). Sean Hastings, the sanctuary resource protection coordinator I mentioned earlier, is a seven islander and anxious to visit Santa Barbara, the smallest island at 644 acres, so he can claim his cap.

"It's amazing there are eighteen million people less than hundred miles from the islands yet it feels like old California—what the coast was like one hundred and fifty years ago when Henry Dana sailed it," he tells me at the sanctuary office behind the maritime museum in Santa Barbara harbor. Sean is a laid-back lanky native Californian with gray eyes and brown hair graying on the edges. He looks like an aging grad student in his short-sleeved white cotton shirt, black jeans, and tennis shoes without socks. I notice a poster on his cluttered office wall reading, "3459 Species live on the California Coast—Only one is destroying them." It's from his time running the Adopt-a-Beach program at the California Coastal Commission.

He shows me a map with different colors representing concentrations of blue and humpback whales that feed on the north (landward side) of Santa Barbara County's islands and fin whales that feed to the south. "Growing up in San Diego and living in San Francisco the ocean was always to the west. It's hard to get used to the ocean being to your south," he admits, noting how the coast takes an eastward bend between Point Conception and San Pedro.

Sean grew up in Del Mar, a beach town in North County San Diego and attended Torrey Pines High School, which, like a number of other California schools, has its own surf team. He did his undergraduate study at U.C. Santa Cruz under famed marine biologist Ken Norris. At the time there were no ocean policy programs in California (U.C. Santa Barbara now has one) so after a few years working for the coastal commission in San Francisco, where he also spent part of his time getting beaten up by big gnarly waves in the Ocean Beach section of the city, he went on to the University of Washington for a master's in coastal zone management. That got him hired by the sanctuary. "I was living as a coastal Californian and then found a job to match, so now I can go into my kid's first-grade class and talk about whales." He smiles, showing even, white teeth.

I ask about a photo on the wall of someone standing tall on a surfboard inside an aquamarine overhead tube. I ask if it's him. "No, that's actually my buddy. We took a Zodiac [inflatable raft] north past Gaviota to this place by the Hollister Ranch. It breaks there on this shallow rock shelf with seaweed and you really have to cut out [back through the wave] before it breaks, which it does hard but not that often, only on certain days of the year when the tide, the wind, the waves all come together, you know. . . ." He smiles more softly this time, no doubt reflecting on another regular visitor to the waters off California, one that could arguably be called a marine mammal and certainly an indicator species for the health of the ocean, the California surfer.

CATCH A WAVE

*From out of the sea he has leaped upon the back of the sea,
and he is riding the sea that roars and bellows and
cannot shake him from its back.*

—JACK LONDON ON SURFING

I learned to bodysurf by doing it, including near drowning, where I'd drop over the falls and get pushed under by the force of a wave so that I was in a dark, churning cauldron with my limbs and head being twisted in different directions from my body and seeing nothing but bubbles and a few times floating black dots from hypoxia, a lack of oxygen. I'd surface just in time for a quick breath that was half salt foam before the next big wave in the set would hammer me back down again. Still, though I eventually drown proofed myself in waves six to eight feet high and got to enjoy some great adrenaline rushes, I never made the pilgrimage north to the Wedge in Newport Beach, where the swells bouncing off the seawall into the next set can create peaks thirty feet high and deadly steep. The Wedge is to body-surfing what Mavericks is to board surfing, which is to say completely terrifying.

Mostly I spent my beach years in the waves off lifeguard tower 3 in Ocean Beach, San Diego, although I've gotten pounded at Pounders on Oahu, almost drowned in fifteen-foot surf at Sunset Beach (also on Oahu) and took a longboard to the throat after an otherwise perfect day at Stinson Beach by the redwoods in Northern California. I figure the risk/benefit calculus more than pays off just waiting in the lineup on a glassy day for those kick-in moments of well-timed transcendence when I catch a wave and am shooting across its face, having the best kinetic rush of speed and immersive flow I can experience in the ocean, at least until the next one. But enough about my feeble attempts to imitate a dolphin; let's talk about how Jack London introduced surfing to California.

As even the youngest grommet knows, surfing, or he'e nalu (wave sliding), was the Hawaiian "sport of kings," although Hawaiians of all classes participated beginning shortly after their arrival on voyaging canoes from Polynesia around A.D. 1200. Still, the olo, the first true longboard, was reserved for the ruling alii class. About seven hundred years later, on July 20, 1885, three visiting Hawaiian princes, Jonah Kuhio Kalaniana'ole, David Kawananakoa, and Edward Keli'Iahonui rode fifteen-foot, hundred-pound redwood boards that they had ordered from a local sawmill off the main beach in Santa Cruz, impressing the locals with the first recorded incident of surfing for fun in California. Fifty years earlier, Richard Henry Dana Jr. had described his first small boat landing in Santa Barbara where, following the example of some Sandwich Islanders (Hawaiians) he and his crew surfed their launch ashore, taking advantage of "a great comber," pulling their oars strongly until "the sea got hold of us and was carrying us in with the speed of a racehorse, we threw our oars as far from the boat as we could and took hold of the gunwales . . . we were shot up upon the beach, and seizing the boat ran her up high and dry."

By 1896 the local boys of Santa Cruz were in the surf trying to "wave slide" like the Hawaiians. Seventy years later Bruce Brown's *The Endless Summer* hit movie theaters nationwide and a million new surfers headed west to crowd up the waves. Today Santa Cruz and Huntington Beach south of L.A. have competing surf museums (as does Oceanside in San Diego County) and claims to the title "Surf City, U.S.A."

"He is Mercury—a brown Mercury. His heels are winged, and in them is the swiftness of the sea," Jack London reported on seeing his first surfer back in 1907. He was standing on the beach at Waikiki, having spent some of the royalties from his bestselling novel *The Call of the Wild* to build a sailboat, the *Snark,* that he and his wife, Charmian, took to Hawaii. After traveling farther around the Pacific he'd write *The Cruise of the Snark* in 1911 and include a chapter on surfing.

London was a natural waterman. Growing up in San Francisco, the son of an absent father and unstable mother (she later remarried a man named London whose name he took), Jack was largely self-reared and self-educated, working twelve- to eighteen-hour days in a cannery by the age of thirteen. Desperate for a way out, he borrowed money from his black foster mom, an ex-slave named Virginia Prentiss who'd helped raise him, and bought a small sloop, becoming an oyster pirate and skilled sailor on the bay. After the boat was damaged he hired on with the California Fish Patrol (later writing *Tales of the Fish Patrol*). At age seventeen he signed aboard a sealing schooner bound for Japan. On his return during the economic Panic of '93 (caused by a railroad speculation bubble), he joined worker protests and bummed around as a hobo for a time, including jail time, before making his way back to the bay. There he made himself at home in Heinold's, a sailors' bar on the Oakland waterfront whose owner lent him money to attend Berkeley and study writing. Around the same time he became an avowed socialist and was arrested for public speaking in front of Oakland City Hall. A year later, at twenty-one, he dropped out of college to join the Klondike Gold Rush to Alaska, where he went hungry and developed scurvy.

On his return in 1898 he began working full-time as a magazine writer and book author, using his own experiences as the basis for his stories. In 1903 he published *The Call of the Wild*. It became a national bestseller. Later books would include *White Fang, The Iron Heel, The Sea-Wolf,* and *Martin Eden*.

By the time his childhood home burned down during the 1906 earthquake, London had married, had two children, divorced, and married his second wife and "soul mate," Charmian Kittredge. They would stay together till his death in 1916 at the age of forty from a combination of dysentery, alcohol, failing kidneys, and a possible overdose of morphine, which he was using as a painkiller.

By the time Jack and Charmian arrived in Hawaii in 1907, he was already a world-famous celebrity admired for the same muscular brand of outdoor adventuring and rugged individualism that defined then-President Teddy Roosevelt. So it was no surprise that his first reaction on seeing the local "Kanakas" surfing was to join them, taking half a day to learn how to stand up on Waikiki's gentle rolling waves. Immediately he wrote a long essay, "A Royal Sport," displaying the kind of unbridled enthusiasm for surfing he usually reserved for brave dogs. Run in the October 1907 edition of the widely circulated *Women's Home Companion,* it brought surfing into the national conversation from whence, dude, it's never quite departed.

George Freeth, credited with showing Californians how to surf was the son of an English father and part-Hawaiian mother, an expert swimmer, platform diver, and one of Hawaii's top surfers at a time when, due to the destruction of Hawaiian culture by foreign colonialism and disease, there were not a lot of watermen left. On seeing him practicing his easy style of stand-up surfing, London described Freeth as "a young god bronzed with sunburn." A few months later, with letters of introduction from London and others, plus the widespread publicity London's article had provided, Freeth booked passage to San Francisco planning to introduce surfing to the mainland. He soon made his way south to Los Angeles, a booming city of 275,000.

Beginning in the 1870s, railroad companies like Collis P. Huntington's

Southern Pacific opened up the seashore and the southland to vast numbers of holidaymakers and urban day-trippers. Fabulous resorts soon followed, including the many-gabled Victorian beachfront Hotel Del Coronado in San Diego, which opened in 1888 as the largest resort in the world. Similar wooden palaces included the enormous Hotel Redondo, built in 1890 by Collis's nephew Henry Huntington, who also owned L.A.'s Red Car trolley line, which ran to Redondo and other beaches. Additional wonders included Monterey's Hotel Del Monte, built by railroad magnate Charles Crocker, which featured California's first golf course, and San Francisco's Victorian Cliff House, built in 1896, which survived the great earthquake of 1906 only to burn down a year later.

For those who couldn't afford that level of luxury, holiday cabins, tent cities, bathhouses, amusement piers like Santa Monica's, and swimming plunges such as San Francisco's Sutro Baths and Santa Cruz's heated saltwater Natatorium drew hundreds of thousands more people to the shore.

Having learned about Freeth from London's writings, Henry Huntington hired him to do Redondo Beach exhibition surfing including his famous headstand, which he also demonstrated in the surf fronting the competing resort area of Venice Beach. In 1908 Freeth rescued seven Japanese fishermen, leaping off the Venice pier to pull them out of the surf one by one after their boat capsized during a winter storm. For his valor he received the U.S. Life Saving Corps Gold Medal.

Two years earlier Long Beach had been the first California city to hire a lifeguard, or "tag man," as they were known at the time, the idea being to run into the water and "tag" or grab a drowning person by their hair or bathing suit, then haul them back to shore.

Freeth moved to San Diego, where he helped organize lifeguard programs following the drowning of thirteen men on a single day in 1918 when they were caught in a riptide at the new Wonderland Amusement Park in Ocean Beach. Eleven of them were servicemen bound for the war in Europe. Freeth also taught improved surf rescue techniques to the lifeguards in Long Beach and Los Angeles, and he happily taught anyone who asked how to surf and how to make a surfboard. Many of his young acolytes would go on to form the first cadre of dedicated California surfers and surf clubs that sprung up in the 1930s. Unfortunately he wouldn't live to see that. George Freeth died during the great influenza epidemic of 1919. He was thirty-five years old.

A few years before his death Freeth had been visited by his friend Duke Kahanamoku, a younger waterman from Hawaii who would become known as the father of modern surfing for his promotion of the sport. Kahanamoku had already won gold and silver medals swimming for the United States at the 1912 Olympics in Stockholm, breaking the hundred-meter freestyle world record. Twenty-one at the time, he would win more gold and silver at three future Olympics, coming in second to Johnny Weissmuller in 1920 and later claiming it took "Tarzan" to beat him. A superb athlete, the handsome native Hawaiian's love of surfing combined with his fame as a swimmer gave the sport a huge boost.

On his return home from his first Olympics he gave surfing exhibitions in Atlantic City, New Jersey, and to more than a thousand people in Long Beach, California. Later he would introduce stand-up surfing to Australia and New Zealand and meet with Jack London during London's last extended trip to Hawaii a year before his death. Duke, who would also become a major figure in the introduction of beach volleyball, moved to Los Angeles in 1924, where he became a supporting actor in Hollywood and in 1925 rescued eight fishermen at Newport Beach after their vessel overturned in heavy surf. This was "the most superhuman surfboard rescue act the world has ever seen," Newport Beach's police chief claimed, and Duke was soon designing large surfboards specially adapted for lifesaving work. By then surfing and lifesaving were merging along California's beaches as ocean drowning became a risk for growing numbers of day-trippers and holidaymakers, not just the traditional victims such as fishermen, ships' crews, and their passengers.

On the East Coast, with its extensive barrier islands, coastal shallows, and long history of horrific shipwrecks within sight of the land, the need for a shore-based maritime lifesaving service had been recognized early on. Beginning in 1848, the federal government helped fund lifesaving stations in New Jersey, including boathouses, surf boats, beach apparatus, line-throwing Lyle guns, and breaches buoys for getting "surfmen" and their rescue lines out to foundering ships and then rowing or roping the survivors back to shore alive.

The West Coast's newer maritime frontier, with its steeper continental shelf, coastal fog banks, winter storms, and hundreds of miles of inaccessible coves and rocky bluffs far from any town, meant that ships in trouble off California often had to rely on their own masters' skills and blind luck to assure their survival.

In 1877 the U.S. Lifesaving Service became an agency of the Department of the Treasury, overseeing 189 lifesaving stations, but only twenty of them on the West Coast. At Point Reyes north of San Francisco, the surf was so dangerous that the station lost three of its four surfmen in just four years of lifeboat drills. It was also badly damaged during the 1906 earthquake. The six stations in the San Francisco Bay Area also suffered extensive damage. Still, the Bay Area Lifesavers helped fight the fire that followed the earthquake, rescued people trapped under collapsed buildings, and served more than thirty thousand meals to those who came to their half-wrecked stations for refuge. One hundred miles north of the ravaged city of San Francisco, the Arena Cove station was also damaged and the Point Arena lighthouse destroyed. Statewide, only the far northern Humboldt Bay Surf Station escaped the effects of the earthquake.

By the turn of the twentieth century, the lifesaving service had rescued more than one hundred and fifty thousand people, but not many of them in California. Typical of a good California rescue was the shipwreck of the *Hanalei,* a steam schooner that had been converted from the Hawaiian sugar trade to the California timber trade. During a winter storm in 1914, en route from Eureka to San Francisco with passengers, railroad ties, and wooden shingles, it ran aground on Duxbury Reef just off Bolinas. Over the next eighteen hours lifesavers in motor lifeboats, one of which capsized, and others on the beach who'd humped their equipment over Mount

Tamalpais after hauling it by truck from Sausalito, made repeated forays into the massive waves, including forming a human chain through the freezing surf and deadly debris when line guns failed to reach the ship, managing to rescue thirty-nine people but losing twenty-three others after the battered vessel disintegrated.

It was with the emergence of recreational beach going in the early twentieth century when few people knew how to swim and when Newport Beach alone lost eighteen swimmers to the sea in a single weekend, that local municipalities began stationing lifeguards on the sand. Many early lifeguards were policemen sent down to watch the beaches, piers, and boardwalks. They might have been physically fit, but few had water skills. For areas like San Diego, Long Beach, Santa Monica, and Santa Cruz, it was essential to local tourism-dependent businesses that their holiday visitors not be afraid of the water. Beachgoers needed to know there was someone there to help them if they got into trouble. This, of course, was at a time when some of the most skilled watermen were surfers like George Freeth and Duke Kahanamoku, who helped develop the paddleboards, hand buoys, and other tools and techniques that would later become the standards of rescue swimming.

In 1915 the federal Lifesaving Service joined the Revenue Cutter Service to become the modern Coast Guard. The lighthouse service would later be added on, with California's lighthouses eventually being automated or handed over to nonprofit historic trusts. Lifesaving stations became Coast Guard surf stations, including Morro Bay, Golden Gate (San Francisco Bay), Bodega Bay, Noyo River (Fort Bragg), and Humboldt Bay. It's at these stations that today's top Coast Guard surfmen and women, qualified to do tows in thirty-foot seas and fifty-knot winds or rush into eight-foot shore break and pull people out of harm's way, get to do their work in the most challenging conditions imaginable.

I spent a fair amount of time with the "Coasties," as they call themselves, at surf station Golden Gate, located at Fort Baker in Marin close to the famous bridge while working on a book about them called *Rescue Warriors*. This is the busiest surf station on the West Coast with some six hundred cases a year. They have a map in their hallway marked with different colored stickpins. Crossing the Golden Gate it's thick with black pins—suicide jumpers. Along Crissy Field inside the bay is a larger clump of pink pins—wind and kite surfers who got in trouble and had to be rescued before the tide dragged them out to sea. Scattered offshore are green pins for disabled vessels and blue ones for "taking on water/capsized."

I was there during the winter of 2007–08, when California was battered by a series of boxcar lows, big soaking Pacific storms that kept the station hopping with SAR (Search and Rescue) cases including on December 4, "Black Tuesday," when well-known California surfer Peter Davi died at Ghost Trees, a famous big break off Pebble Beach, and two crab fishermen were lost when their boat was smashed in thirty-five-foot waves at Pillar Point by Half Moon Bay, close to Mavericks. By the time one of the surfboats got on scene all they found were chunks of wood and a floating survival suit.

A month later Northern California was hit by an even bigger storm and two surf crews were called out in thirty- to forty-foot seas on a SAR report of a surfer in trouble off Pacifica. I was listening to the station radio when a Coast Guard H-65 Dolphin helicopter arrived on scene to report, "He's paddle surfing. He's doing fine. We're gonna make another pass, but he's in there with a purpose for surfing."

The boats were recalled to station where their soaking wet crews seemed agitated, despite having gotten a major hit of adrenaline. "It's okay when someone's actually in trouble, but it bugs me when we get into it like that and it turns out to be nothing," explained one of the boat drivers, whose forty-seven-footer had been dumped on by several breaking waves.

Chief Kevin Morgan, their CO tells them to rest up. Given the degrading conditions, they probably won't be going out again, but if larger cutters or helos aren't available they might have to. "Luckily none of the fishermen, none of the commercial guys, are going out in this."

"Surfers are the only real idiots who'll go out in this kind of shit," Greg,
the boat driver complains.

"And us," Kevin points out.

"Yeah, and us."

The earliest California lifeguards also tended to be pioneering surfers. It
was two Santa Monica lifeguards, Tom Blake and Sam Reid, who in 1927
trespassed onto privately owned Malibu ranchland and became the first
surfers to ride its "perfect wave" (smooth, long, and consistent). Blake went
on to design lighter hollow boards that were quickly adapted by both lifeguards and Depression-era surfers. His most significant design contribution, however, was the stabilizing fin he introduced in 1935. Screwed onto
the bottom of one of his hollow boards, it prevented the board from slip-
sliding all over the waves. Fins would stabilize surfboards even as the
boards became lighter and more hydrodynamic with new shapes and built
of new materials. Ankle leashes introduced in the 1970s would further expand the popularity of surfing as falling off the board no longer meant a
long swim chasing it back to the beach.

The Depression of the 1930s saw increased use of California's beaches
across the board, largely because they were public and didn't cost anything.
Gene "Tarzan" Smith, one of the hardcore surfers of the time, lived in a
sandstone cave near Newport Beach and cooked seafood he caught on a
driftwood fire. Because of the glamour attached to surfing by Duke Kahanamoku and his new friends in Hollywood, Smith never faced the police
harassment or vigilante violence encountered by unemployed hobos riding
the rails or migrants looking for work in the Central Valley as depicted in
John Steinbeck's *The Grapes of Wrath*.

The Depression saw the first mass-produced surfboards put out by a kit
house (early pre-fab) building company. Their subsidiary was called Swastika Surf-Board and the swastika, seen as a good luck sign not yet associated with Hitler's nazis, was emblazoned on each new board. By the time

World War II broke out, the company had changed its product's name to Waikiki Surf-Boards.

Dedicated surf clubs also emerged in the 1930s, and new isolated surf spots were ridden for the first time including the point break at Rincon on the Santa Barbara/Ventura county line with its long rides and waves that could grow huge, and San Onofre, whose break would later be named Trestles because of nearby railroad overpasses. Even when other spots were flat there were always well-shaped waves at Trestles. With surf clubs also came competitions, and one of the earliest was held at San Onofre. Santa Monica lifeguard Pete Peterson was an early and regular San Onofre contest winner. Weekend camping at San Onofre with fish, mussel, and abalone stews and guitar and ukulele jams helped define what would become the laid-back California surfer lifestyle, according to surf historian Matt Warshaw, author of the definitive book, *The History of Surfing*. This idyllic interlude would end on December 7, 1941, with the Japanese attack on Pearl Harbor, America's entry into WWII, and the marines' takeover of San Onofre for their new Camp Pendleton base.

World War II saw the California coastline built up with artillery fortifications, training camps, shipyards, piers, and other works of war. It also saw Californians of Japanese descent deported from the coast to internment camps in the interior. Many Depression-era surfers went off to the war. At the same time the war brought millions of new defense workers into the state along with soldiers, sailors, and marines on their way to the Pacific. Many would later settle in California after they were discharged from the military. Some two million people moved to California during the war and another two million in the postwar boom of the late 1940s and 1950s.

Southern California took the brunt of this demographic tsunami with nut, avocado, and citrus orchards being plowed under to make way for massive new suburban developments connected by a system of federally funded freeways. Orange County stopped being about orange trees just as Oakland had stopped being about oak trees a century earlier. Auto traffic replaced the Red Line and other light-rail trolleys around L.A. and air pollutants brought out the colors in Pacific sunsets. *Sunset* magazine, founded to promote California for the Southern Pacific railroad in 1898, now promoted the "California lifestyle" of single-story ranch houses and royal palms, barbecuing, avocado and tangerine salads, beach going, and surfing. After the courts forced the Rindge family to sell off much of their coast-hugging Malibu ranch, the area quickly became a bedroom community for Hollywood moguls and a leading surf scene where the future Marilyn Monroe learned to ride tandem (two on a board) with a surfer she was dating.

Southern California's postwar aerospace industry that would supercharge the economy during the Cold War also brought new engineering skills to surfboard design. Boards got shorter and lighter. Noses more pointed and rails (edges) more tapered and rounded. Twin fins emerged and wood and balsa boards sealed with shellac gave way to two new industrial war products, polystyrene foam (Styrofoam) for board cores or "blanks," and fiberglass for sealing them. Soon Clark Foam in Laguna Niguel was producing nine out of ten foam blanks for shapers worldwide. When founder Gordon "Grubby" Clark shut its doors in 2005, production shifted to China.

Despite the mass-production focus of the 1950s and '60s, surfboards continued to be customized by individual shapers to fit the needs of particular waves, riders, and conditions. Among these postwar artisans were Laguna Beach's Hobie Alter, who went on to design the Hobie Cat sailboat; ex–Coast Guardsman Bing Copeland, and San Diego soul surfer Skip Frye, who turned out distinctive egg-shaped surfboards. Other changes during the Cold War included new understanding of ocean waves, wave trains, currents, gyres, upwelling, and weather developed during World War II by marine scientists at Scripps Institution of Oceanography in San Diego. This meteorological and oceanographic information now became part of an emerging arsenal of surfer knowledge used to find the best waves on surf safaris and dawn patrols up and down the coast, reading wave forms from the front seats of "Woodie" station wagons and VW vans with hot coffee and donuts (later Pop-Tarts), visual data collection that today can be carried out with the click of a mouse linked to an array of online surf cams.

Out of California's expanding surf culture whole other sports would emerge and take on their own identities including windsurfing, kiteboarding, bodyboarding (using the Boogie board developed by surfer/mathematician Tom Morey) and more recently stand-up paddling, along with crossover sports such as ocean kayaking, skateboarding, and snowboarding that also gained traction thanks to California's unique geography, which encompasses every kind of terrestrial habitat except the tropics. At Pomona College in Southern California they have an annual ski-beach day where students go up to Mountain High resort to snowboard in the morning and down to Newport Beach to surf or bodyboard later in the day.

Lighter, shorter surfboards developed in the 1950s and '60s also meant it was possible to take off higher on the wave just below the curl and do more radical turns and cutbacks that became known as the Malibu style. Riders shifted from a squared-off gunfighter stance to more of a karate stance, positioned sideways to the wave and leading with one foot. The left-handed tend to lead with the right foot, and are known as "goofy-footed."

Lighter boards also brought more girls onto the Malibu scene twenty years after California's first accomplished female surfer—and Esther Williams stunt double—Mary Ann Hawkins rode the waves at Palos Verdes for *Life* magazine and shortly before Joyce Hoffman made a big splash in the 1960s.

Still it would take another generation until four-time world women's champion Lisa Andersen of Huntington Beach opened up the surf scene to younger women with her aggressive wave-shredding competition style of the 1990s. The fact that she also created a half-billion-dollar female-oriented product line for the Huntington Beach–based Quiksilver corporation did not go unnoticed among executives of the Surf Industry Manufacturers Association (SIMA) and the $6.2 billion surfwear and board sports industry they represent. Until the 1990s women made up around 3 percent of the surfing population. Today it's more like 20 percent.

I was recently sitting on a bodyboard waiting for a set in San Diego listening to a couple of twenty-something surfer guys nearby discussing another surfer who'd just caught a last ride in.

"That chick on the longboard was something," one said.

"Yeah, she was serious good."

"And she's out here every day on her own even like on a cold gray day like now."

"Yeah, some chicks won't come out unless they're with two or three girlfriends on a weekend sunny day, but she's hardcore."

"Hardcore," his buddy agreed.

That kind of respect is earned but also was fought for by generations of surfer girls who wanted to claim their waves.

"We're gonna ride those boys right out of style, we're gonna shoot the curl for one clear mile," sang The Honeys in 1963.

One of the real-life Malibu "honeys" of the postwar era was a five-foot-tall ninety-five-pound teenager named Kathy Kohner, who Terry "Tubesteak" Tracy, the original surfer/slacker nicknamed Gidget, a contraction of *girl* and *midget*. Kathy's dad, screenwriter Frederick Kohner, inspired by her enthusiasm, wrote *Gidget*, a fictional version of her adolescent beach adventures that came out as a book in 1957 and a movie two years later. At the time there were probably no more than five thousand surfers in California, but the movie starring Cliff Robertson, James Darren, and Sandra Dee as Gidget was a huge nationwide hit, particularly with teenage girls and the beginning of surfing as a pop-culture phenomenon, not unlike the early Beatles, only with more clothing and sports gear to buy. Beach party dance-and-romance movies starring singer Frankie Avalon and ex–Disney Mouseketeer Annette Funicello followed and were also hugely popular despite a noticeable absence of actual surfing. In California, surf documentaries were working the opposite end of the celluloid experience, all surf and no story. They made the rounds of local beach town movie theaters where surfers got to see the best waves and riders as documented by early one-man shooter/editors with 16mm cameras including Bud Browne in the 1940s and '50s and San Clemente lifeguard Bruce Brown (no relation) who produced *The Endless Summer* in 1966, a mellow round-the-world surf safari set to music with a narrative and visual flow that seamlessly wove the surf culture into the emerging counterculture. From then on the lines between surf films and Hollywood films would begin to blur like fresh water in salt from *Five Summer Stories* to *Big Wednesday* to more contemporary films such as *Step into Liquid, Blue Crush, Riding Giants,* and the sweetly respectful *Surf's Up,* the best animated surfing penguin movie ever made.

Elvis Presley, whose adoption of African American R&B "race music" mainstreamed rock and roll for white youth (if not their parents), also pushed the link between film, surfing, and music in his 1961 movie *Blue Hawaii.*

In the early 1960s fast-riffing instrumental surf bands like Dick Dale and his Del-Tones, the Ventures, and the Surfaris with their visceral feel for hormonal young men and fast-moving water were drawing huge crowds to waterfront venues such as the Rendezvous in Huntington Beach, but it was the Beach Boys with their pop vocal harmonies that soon topped the charts. Again, much was borrowed from black music, but little credited. Brian Wilson took the melody of Chuck Berry's "Sweet Little Sixteen," and changed the lyrics to produce their first major hit, 1963's "Surfin' U.S.A," with its list of favorite California surf spots. After Berry sued, an agreement was reached and the song was cocredited to Wilson and Berry.

In California, as opposed to Hawaii, surfing remained an almost exclusively white pastime as a kind of freeway apartheid separated low-income African American and Hispanic communities from the evolving mostly white middle-class surf scene along the coast. Even today surfing as a sport remains pretty monochromatic.

However, in the late 1950s and early '60s when the white Anglo-Saxon protestant WASP was the cultural norm, there was a feeling that California represented the nation's best and brightest future with its heady mix of military defense industries that employed many of the nation's top engineers, an emerging public university system to feed the industry's needs, year-round sunshine (in the southland), and a pioneering, largely rootless, but highly mobile middle-class band of suntanned adolescents cruising the coast in pursuit of the endless ride of youth, Ponce de Leon's fountain of immortality as a perfectly formed tubular wave.

Surfer magazine and other dedicated surf journals featuring stunning surf photography began appearing in the 1960s. Fifty years later, *Surfer* is still around along with other magazines and Web sites including *The Surfer's Journal,* a literary coffee table bimonthly that appeals to older professionals who never left the waves.

Today California's lifeguard services are also highly professional. In L.A., San Diego, and elsewhere they are integrated into municipal fire departments and include hundreds of skilled full-time staff along with thousands of seasonal employees acting as critical first responders along the shore.

Back in the 1960s, experienced L.A. lifeguard Greg Noll began surfing big waves at Palos Verdes before moving to Hawaii and pioneering giant North Shore waves including the never-before-ridden Banzai Pipeline. California's winter surf was considered respectable but not really comparable to Hawaii's giant waves.

Few people knew that a local from Half Moon Bay named Jeff Clark had, beginning in high school, been taking occasional opportunities to ride solo on one of the world's biggest, gnarliest waves at Mavericks outside Pillar Point. It was only after *Surfer* magazine ran a photo of the wave in 1990 (and a cover story two years later) that others joined Clark, and Mavericks's mythic size and power caught the surfing world's attention. With Mark Foo's death in 1994, it became both infamous and also commercial with an annual contest (waves permitting) despite its obvious hazards, including bone-chilling water, fog, rips, rocks, and at least two surfers thrown off boards hit by white sharks (one rider doubled up on the shark's snout). The break itself is named in honor of a surfer's German shepherd who tried to take on the wave back in the 1960s. (Jack London would have been proud of that dog.)

To the south there is Ghost Trees off Pebble Beach, where Peter Davi died in storm surf and another surfer was lost at sea and his shark-bitten board later recovered. Even farther south there's the wave known as Killers at Todos Santos, a desert island off the Pacific coast of Baja.

Another giant California wave not discovered until the 1990s can be found 115 miles off San Diego at the Cortes Bank, a chain of seamounts a mile deep, some of which rise to within a few feet of the surface. Long recognized as a hazard to navigation (which didn't stop the captain of the nuclear-powered aircraft carrier U.S.S. *Enterprise* from running up onto it, putting a forty-foot gash into his hull back in 1985) the bank can, given the right conditions, generate hundred-foot waves. In 2008 San Clemente–based surfer Mike Parsons was photographed riding a seventy-seven-foot wave at Cortes Bank, till recently the largest wave ever ridden. It takes an expedition complete with boats and Jet Skis to get to the bank, and that's part of its attraction. When you reach the wave it may be deadly, but at least it's not crowded.

Dr. Mark Renneker is a big, strapping, long-faced rumpled guy who trends toward jeans, cotton Ts and a perpetual three-day growth of beard (he's never actually shaved down to the skin). He is also one of the pioneers at Mavericks. He's in the movie *Riding Giants* and is also the subject of a 1992 two-part opus by William Finnegan in *The New Yorker* magazine that may have shocked its sophisticated readership with the realization that not all surfers are clones of Jeff Spicoli from *Fast Times at Ridgemont High*.

Renneker grew up in West L.A. and joined the junior lifeguard program in Santa Monica at age eleven, when he was taken surfing by the lifeguards and found his passion. Along with Mavericks, "Doc" Renneker has surfed Hawaii, Fiji, Alaska, the Arctic, and Antarctica but is most content with the wave trains he can see from his new home in the Ocean Beach neighborhood of San Francisco a block from the rent-controlled apartment on the Great Highway he had occupied for the previous thirty years. He likes to show a picture he took from a U.C.S.F. classroom window two miles inland when he arrived there as a medical student in 1975. It's of a big wave breaking beyond the urban heart of the Sunset District and oddly compressed by the zoom lens so that it looks as if a tsunami is about to swallow the city.

"I have a love affair with the ocean and this neighborhood," he explains before going on to describe how Ocean Beach (site of a recent Rip Curl Pro contest) can get forty- to fifty-foot winter waves breaking half a mile off-shore plus generate five-foot or better waves 90 percent of the rest of the year.

The first time I visited the Coast Guard's Golden Gate Station they'd just broken the windshield on the flying bridge of one of their forty-seven-foot rescue boats training in the surf zone off Ocean Beach. Even paddling through its thundering whitewater shore break to get outside requires what Doc calls "a kind of Zen approach, not just powering out but figuring how to flow through the water, to use its strength." Still when he'd reach the outside waves he'd sometimes see even bigger waves breaking on the Potato Patch (Four Fathom Shoals), miles offshore. He had a number of failures trying to paddle out to them with friends or getting a boat to drop them off. "Finally I realized there was this current off Cliff House that I could ride out on my own at a certain time." He rode it three miles offshore where he had to triangulate his position using landmarks including the Golden Gate Bridge directly in front of him, which meant his takeoff point was in the middle of a major shipping lane. On the day he paddled out he caught the big wave he was looking for that deposited him back in front of Ocean Beach. "It was a three-minute ride," he says, still astounded by what must have seemed the interminable rush of a lifetime. "My legs started shaking because you don't ever have that long a ride. Most people just don't appreciate what spectacular surf we have here."

Then Ocean Beach was eclipsed in his life by Mavericks, a much more powerful wave. "It's a true freak wave the way it comes out of deep water," he says. "I felt like a turncoat to Ocean Beach."

He was at Mavericks the day Foo died in the water. They'd met earlier at Doc's house and had driven down together. Nobody saw Foo surface after he wiped out that day on a fifteen- to twenty-foot wave, but everyone assumed he was okay. "The wave wasn't exceptionally large for Mavericks," Doc recalls, even if people measure them by the Hawaiian standard, which means from behind the shoulder (the back of the wave) so that the faces are about twice the height they call them. It wasn't till later that afternoon that Foo's body was spotted floating near the harbor breakwater. "I examined him and we still don't know what happened. It appeared to be a drowning—his body wasn't damaged. We think the leash caught on the bottom," Doc explains.

"The next year a wave pushed me down to the reef, twenty-one feet down, and I hit it three times and then I was washed down the back of the reef twenty feet further down to the hard bottom. I was being held there and started to panic. I had a twenty-foot leash and my (nine-foot) board was standing vertical [above it] what we call 'tombstone' and guys on the surface could just see the top of it. I was scrambling for the surface and a third of the way up I realized if I got there and was knocked down again I wouldn't survive and realized I had to slow down and I'd been down sixty to ninety seconds but I stopped and let my wet suit's buoyancy take me up, and I made it."

In 2011 Hawaiian pro surfer Sion Milosky died at Mavericks. "We call it 'just off the boat syndrome,'" Doc claims. "They sat in the wrong place because they didn't know this wave like we do. Now you have all these new people showing up and taking off on waves we wouldn't. We don't take off unless we have about a 90 percent certainty we're going to make the wave, but these guys see all the [surf magazine] cameras on shore and take off on anything and it's what I call 'Kodak Courage.' They take off to get the picture taken and a lot of them wipe out and get hurt."

During the El Niño winter of 1997–'98, Doc and his friends had their own kind of contest. "We had notch wars, just hilarious and brutal competitions where every day you surfed and if you caught a wave you got a notch, seeing how many you could get that year and [his friend] John Raymond and I tied. We rode eighty-six days out of maybe one hundred days we were down there. We just became fixtures down there."

When not in the water, Doc works as a family practitioner specializing in complex and life-threatening diseases. He is also a founder of the Surfer's Medical Association, which now has hundreds of Surf Doc members who hold clinics in medically underserved communities (villages) impacted by surf tourism in Fiji and elsewhere, as well as doing sports medicine for surfers.

"You talk about surfer's ear (also known as swimmer's ear or exostosis) bony growths in the outer ear canal, and 95 percent of physicians have no idea that it's a pure function of hours in cold water with exposure to cold, wet, and wind in particular," Doc explains. "As wet suits got better, people spent more time in the water and in colder water, and there's a clear relationship to which ear is exposed to the prevailing winds. Looking west in California it's 90 percent in the right ear. In the Southern Hemisphere, where the wind is from the south, 90 percent of exostosis is in the left ear. And now that more surfers surf later in life, surfer's ear is close to 100 percent [detectable in older surfers]." As he describes the symptoms, water getting stuck in the ear canal, more frequent ear pain, a plugged sensation, I realize what's been bugging me for the last decade.

One of his other concerns is the increase in pollution-related illnesses. A study by the Los Angeles environmental group Heal the Bay found that one in twenty-five people swimming or surfing near storm-water outflows get sick from things like stomach flu and upper respiratory infections. Their risk of getting sick is 57 percent greater if they're within five hundred feet of a storm drain.

Doc shows some pictures of surfers with swollen faces at the beach where he lives. "Red tides (toxic algal blooms) are getting worse in Ocean Beach. I don't know why. All I know is it's a small slice of coastal California and we want to keep it a clean environment," he says.

Being in the water as much as they are, it is not surprising surfers started their own environmental group. The Surfrider Foundation, with more than fifty thousand members organized into surf club–like chapters, was founded in Malibu in 1984 and has been involved in countless clean-water campaigns ever since. During a 1990 Huntington Beach oil spill, some of its members carried signs reading "No way dude, we don't want your crude!" In 2008 the Department of Commerce and California Coastal Commission ruled against an extension of a private toll road just above Trestles by Camp Pendleton that Surfrider and others worried would ruin the watershed and pollute the San Onofre lagoon and state beach there. With its headquarters based in San Clemente just north of Pendleton, Surfrider's staff finish up many of their workdays catching waves at Trestles.

For ten years I lived in "O.B.," Ocean Beach, San Diego that, like San Clemente, Cayucos, Santa Cruz, San Francisco's Ocean Beach, and Stinson Beach in Marin has retained its identity as a surfer town.

In 1970, radicalized surfers fought the police on the north end of O.B. to stop the Army Corps of Engineers from building a seawall for a marina and hotel complex that would have destroyed the surf just as earlier seawalls and marinas killed surf breaks at Dana Point, Corona del Mar, and Long Beach. O.B.'s surfers won their battle: Ocean Beach still faces into wind-driven Pacific swells. Its main palm-lined street, Newport Avenue, ends at the beach by the longest municipal pier on the West Coast, reaching almost a third of a mile offshore before terminating in a T. It was built in 1966, and surfers regularly "shoot" its cement pilings, riding waves between its barnacle-encrusted pillars. After surfers beat back the threat of development, water quality became the next issue.

Donna Frye is slim with straight blond hair, aquiline features, and a raspy ex-smoker laugh. She left the San Diego City Council in 2010 because of term-limit restrictions. Years earlier Donna and her famed surfer/shaper husband, Skip, ran Harry's Surf Shop in Pacific Beach, just up the coast from O.B. On the low bluff outside Harry's I'd observed sunbathers and surfers scattered across the beach sand beyond a bilingual sign reading "CAUTION: Storm drain water may pose an increased risk of illness. Avoid contact near outlet." This warning and others like it up and down the California coast are a direct result of Donna's work.

"Around 1994 I got very active because I was dealing with a lot of sick surfers, Skip being one of them," she recalls. "It didn't make sense. These healthy, athletic people were getting sick from pollution."

"I was running for state assembly in 1996 and heard Donna was an environmental activist and owned a surf shop, so I went to meet with her," recalls former state assemblyman Howard Wayne. "She took me behind the store and pointed to these storm drains pouring into the surf and told me her husband and friends and customers were bathing in this toxic soup." He agreed to do something if elected; Donna campaigned for him, and after he won he invited her to Sacramento and asked her to take a crack at creating a bill. With support from surfer/lawyer friends, she crafted a bill that set statewide standards for water quality, required weekly testing of recreational beaches, and ordered warning signs and hotlines be made available to inform the public if their coastal waters were polluted. It passed into law in 1997.

A few years later Surfrider helped pass the federal Beaches Environmental Assessment and Coastal Health (BEACH) Act, a national version of California's law that requires coastal states to test their waters for pollutants and inform the public of the results. Frye was then elected to the city council in 2001 and lost a write-in mayoral race in 2004 when the city registrar refused to count more than five thousand of her votes because people who wrote in her name failed to fill in an oval bubble for the optical-scan voting machines.

I ask Donna how she and Skip first got together. She tells me she walked into Pancho Villa's bar in Pacific Beach back in 1980 and won a bet with him on an L.A. Rams game. I ask if she knew who he was. She looks at me like I'm a complete hodad. "Of course," she says, and breaks into her husky laugh.

Along with Skip Frye and his generation of "soul surfers," California has been home to countless other famous surfers, including Mickey Dora, Greg Noll, Tom Curren, and Lisa Andersen. Oddly, today's biggest brand name and multiple world champion Kelly Slater comes out of Florida, though he has a second home in California (and a third in Hawaii). Slater, who won his eleventh World Surfing Championship in San Francisco's Ocean Beach, is the Tiger Woods of surfing but without the zipper issues, just as Hawaiian big-wave surfer Laird Hamilton is the Barry Bonds without the steroids (his rage is organic).

While they can often amaze with their wave-riding skills, professional surfers and semipros (paid to surf but not full-time) are not the real story of surfing or ocean sports in California. More significant are the hundreds of thousands of dedicated wave sliders who despite jobs, family, and school-work, still find time to get into the water at least once a day because it's healthy, sustainable, and addicting. Millions more ride boards, paddle, swim, dive, or sail as often as they can.

When I think of a typical surfer I think of my friend Charlie Landon, now the senior cameraman for the CBS affiliate in San Diego. He lives with his wife, Sheila, two boys, Nick and Joe, and their little girl, Alise, in a glass-walled alley house on O.B.'s main beach just above the volleyball nets and a surf break called Avalanche. Charlie is five foot eight with curly gray hair and, at age fifty-seven, still wiry from forty-five years of surfing and cross training that's included skateboarding, mountain biking, plus three decades spent carrying twenty-five pounds of camera gear through fires, coastal floods, and race riots. He's goofy-footed and when he surfs has a kind of simian grace that occasionally gets him into the green room, inside a curling tubular wave.

His dad, Joe, was a screenwriter whose credits included *Von Ryan's Express*. They lived in Pacific Palisades but every summer rented a Malibu house in Los Flores. "I wasn't allowed a surfboard till I was twelve and had taken endurance swimming lessons. It was an eight-foot Bing," Charlie recalls. "My friends and I were already accomplished rafters. We'd take the biggest drops with no hands and push each other to knock the other off the wave. During the winter I surfed State Beach at Santa Monica canyon."

After high school, Charlie hitched around Canada and worked construction in Northern California before returning to school as a communications major at San Diego State.

"I went there to continue my lifestyle with the ocean—surfing, living close to the ocean in Mission Beach. One of my instructors said, 'If you think you can be a surfer and get a job in broadcasting you've got another thing coming,' but in passing he also mentioned they [the school] had a sister station in Guam, and right then I knew I was going to do an internship there." There he got to surf Guam's Turtle Cove and the famous left break at Boat Harbor.

After graduating, Charlie got a job shooting and editing news for a Tijuana TV station before getting hired by CBS Channel 8 and moving to Ocean Beach.

"I'd have to say my connection to the ocean was primary to my staying in San Diego," he admits. "By then I'd become a specialist in breaking news and SWAT-type stories. Around 1987 I met Sheila, my wife, on the beach. Where I lived I surfed a wave that no one else surfed because it was too rocky and low quality and I wanted to be alone. I wasn't interested in competing for waves. I want to commune with nature, so I surfed this unpopular wave that became known as Charlie's Reef. It was on this pocket beach below Santa Cruz Street and there was this girl lying on the beach and she was very attractive and I was shy but wanting to meet her. I was body-womping the shore waves and one threw me up to her feet, so I mustered the courage to ask her name and start a conversation. I was thirty-two and she was twenty-two and we've been together ever since. She was very impressed with me," he adds. "I was one of the few people pursuing her who actually had a job."

"He had this shorty wet suit half pulled down real low so I could see this patch of fur on his lower back and I thought that was sexy." Sheila confirms the story. "He was in good shape and had a job and surfing's kind of a cool thing, don't you think?"

They now live on the beach with their kids, plus Charlie has a place in Hawaii on the Big Island where he also gets to surf. "It's hard not to feel better after being in the ocean," he explains. "It's the dance we do. There are very few parts of nature where you can dance and interact with it the way you do with the sea."

Also it's generational. While his oldest, eleven-year-old Nick, is a dedicated fisherman searching the tackle shops for the perfect lure when not on the pier or fishing off a boat, and his middle son Joe, age nine, likes the water but also just playing in the sand and running around, Alise at three is dedicated both to dressing up as a ballerina and gypsy and also to getting into her spring wet suit whenever allowed and having her dad drag her on a bodyboard through the wet sand and water by the surf's edge, holding on to the pull leash with one hand while throwing surfer poses with her free arm, moving her feet like her dad on his boards and smiling like a blond pixie. There are posters of surfers Bethany Hamilton (a shark attack survivor) and Alana Blanchard in her bedroom. "She's our hope to be the next surf champ," Charlie confesses with a slight grin and obvious delight.

California's ocean is about more than finding your stoke, of course. As with Charlie, it's also about hard work. One surfer I recently encountered is the security chief for one of the major port terminals in L.A. A member of Surfrider, he doesn't agree with their plan, now under official study, to remove part of the neighboring port's seawall in order to restore the waves at Long Beach. Still, finding that right balance of recreation, conservation, trade, and industry while also restoring and protecting the seas everyone depends on is what life along California's golden shore is all about.

PORTS OF CALL

*It is not the going out of port, but the coming in
that determines the success of a voyage.*

—Henry Ward Beecher

climb onto the bow of the yellow-and-green pilot boat three miles past
the breakwater. It's 4:30 A.M. and still dark except for the frothing white
bow wake from the 60,000-ton, 958-foot container ship we're about to
board south of the sea buoy. The *Sea-Land Intrepid* has slowed to 7 knots
and dropped its Jacob's ladder over the side. Captain Rob Lukowski, a
twenty-seven-year veteran harbor pilot, casually reaches out to grab it. Step-
ping over the frothing watery gap, he climbs up the rope and wood-slatted
ladder. The pilot boat backs off and then comes in close again. I reach and
grab on to the ropes and climb up, planting both feet on each orange rung

until I can step across open air onto the partially extended metal embarka-
tion ladder about twenty-five feet off the water. Once we've climbed onto
the deck, we're escorted inside to a narrow elevator and are soon on the
ship's wide bridge, one hundred and twenty feet above the water. The captain is not thrilled when I introduce myself as a writer. No one informed
him I'd be coming aboard.

The crew offers Rob black coffee as he instructs them to move "slow
ahead" and "ease in mid-ship . . . mid-ship steady 298" and then "dead slow"
as we approach the breakwater, where two tugs are waiting for us in the
dark.

For more than an hour I watch as Rob, craggy, shaven headed under his
fleece cap, with winter gray eyes and wearing a thick pilot's parka, carefully
guides the vessel into the Port of Long Beach.

Long Beach and the adjacent and even larger port of Los Angeles are the
two biggest in the United States and together the fifth largest port complex
in the world. Its sixteen square miles of mammoth ships and piers is also
home to: mountains of shipping containers or "cans"; top stackers and
stacking cranes; dozens of thirty-story-high gantry cranes, many shipped
whole from China; thousands of diesel trucks and trailers; miles of trains
and locomotives belonging to Burlington Northern and Southern Pacific;
dry and liquid bulk silos; scrap metal yards; Mercedes car lots; Carnival
and Princess line cruise ships and terminals; boatyards; rail yards; fence
lines; pipelines; Exxon, BP, and Shell refineries and tank farms, as well as
still-active oil wells that have been producing for eighty years; fishing boats,
tugboats, patrol boats, and Coast Guard cutters; recreational marinas; a
World War II Victory ship; a self-propelled platform that can launch large
commercial rockets into space; customs storehouses and radiation detectors
alongside secured truck gates near bridges and quays; the Terminal Island
Federal Prison; overhead power lines; a sewage plant; and seemingly endless commercial shipping terminals: CUT (California United Terminals),
Matson, Evergreen, Mitsubishi, COSCO (China Ocean Shipping), Hanjin,
and APL (American Presidents Line, now owned by Singaporeans). These
two largely indistinguishable ports move thousands of tons of goods a day,

both essential and frivolous, thanks to the skill and labor of more than thirty thousand longshoremen, mariners, and port workers behind an eight-and-a-half-mile-long breakwater. The one million California jobs tied to these ports are a tribute both to global trade and mass consumption. The ports handle around 40 percent of the nation's imports. Odds are fifty-fifty that anything you buy that says "Made in China" came across these docks.

Of course for most of its history San Pedro Bay was little more than a shallow fishing port and wetland with a wide, rocky, seaweed-covered beach and small offshore island once called Rattlesnake in honor of the serpents that washed down the Los Angeles River and found refuge there.

Phineas Banning was a square-jawed stagecoach operator who arrived in California at the age of twenty-one by clipper ship and Panama mule at the tail end of the gold rush in 1851. Twenty years later, a successful business-man and shipper, he got Congress to vote to fund a rock jetty from Rattle-snake Island (now Terminal Island) to Dead Man's Island in San Pedro Bay. Unfortunately he died in 1885 at the age of fifty-five before his vision for a new breakwater port at San Pedro could be realized.

In the 1890s there was a seven-year fight over where Los Angeles's main port would be located. On the one side was Collis P. Huntington, one of California's "Big Four" robber barons, who controlled the South-ern Pacific Railroad and had built a long wharf in Santa Monica at the rail terminus, the perfect site, he decided, for Southern California's main deepwater port. His opponents in this epic, if largely forgotten battle, included the chamber of commerce, businessman Harrison Gray Otis of the *Los Angeles Times* and U.S. Senator M. Stephen White who wanted a "free port" in San Pedro—free, that is, of Southern Pacific's monopolistic powers, later portrayed in Frank Norris's muckraking 1901 novel *The Octopus.*

In 1896 Congress approved funds for a breakwater at Huntington's Santa Monica wharf, but his opponents added an amendment to the bill establishing a review commission, and in 1898, after the commission's report was released, Congress, by a one-vote margin, decided to build the federal breakwater at San Pedro instead.

San Pedro would expand to become California's major port with an early focus on timber and tuna, while Santa Monica Bay would develop as Los Angeles's recreational beachfront, including the 1905 opening of "the Coney Island of the Pacific," Venice Beach, with residential canal homes and imported gondolas, an amusement pier, music pavilion, and other scenic attractions. In 1906 Los Angeles expanded south along a narrow strip of land it called "the shoestring addition" to annex the port area as a source of municipal revenue.

Writing about Santa Monica Bay or San Pedro Bay could be interpreted as a serious abuse of language. Neither is a bay in the true geographical sense. Santa Monica is a gentle crescent curve in the California coast and San Pedro more an eastward bend than large body of water partially enclosed by land. Long Beach, just to the other side of the Los Angeles River, used to have great ocean-exposed surf, proclaiming itself the "Waikiki of California," until 1949 when they finished the federal breakwater and killed the break.

The port complex, being a largely human artifact, is also built on landfill including most of Terminal Island, Pier F, Pier G, Pier J and Pier 400, the largest commercial shipping terminal in the United States, completed in 2002. These man-made constructs are all within a ship's turning radius of the San Andreas Fault. Port security folks I talked to confess that their biggest worry is not terrorists, oil spills, or tsunamis but the next inevitable earthquake that could see much of the port's landfill liquefy and turn to quicksand with rail tracks and eight-lane truck roads becoming twisted steel and muddy rubble as giant cranes slip their tracks and tumble across the piers into the port channels and basins that are the veins and arteries of American commerce. Given the "just in time," intermodal (ship, truck, train) transport delivery systems now in place, a port shutdown in Southern

California could slow the national economy within twenty-four hours and cripple it in seventy-two.

Rob and the fourteen other watch captains from Jacobsen Pilot Service will guide eighteen ships in and out of the Port of Long Beach the day I join up with him. The L.A. pilots will do a little more, moving more than twenty ships.

"Hard left," Rob instructs on the darkened bridge of the *Sea-Land Intrepid*. "Hard left." The bridge helmsman repeats the order.

"Right twenty."

"Right twenty."

The *Sea-Land* is ending an eleven-day run from Yokohama, Japan, lightly loaded with fifteen hundred TEUs or twenty-foot equivalent unit shipping containers (it can handle four thousand).

We turn into a narrower channel—"Zero, zero five"—and pass an oil tanker on our port side. "Right twenty." We pass a scrap metal yard with its rusting mounds of one of America's major exports. Rob heads out onto the open bridge wing, as does the captain. Both carry their radios with them. I follow into the cold predawn darkness. By now the silvery radiance of moonlight sparkling on the water has been replaced by the harsher yellow reflections of high-intensity lamps mounted on the port's cranes and docks. Dock tractors and trucks with rotating blue and green roof lights flash warning as they drive around the still dark piers. We make our way under the Gerald Desmond Bridge into the inner harbor and turning basin. There'll be a press conference later today to announce the planned billion-dollar replacement of this 155-foot-high bridge with something bigger (and seismically safer) that larger ships can fit under. A billion dollars for a bridge seems like a lot of money till you remember these ports move about $1 billion of goods every day. It looks like we're about to T-bone another oil tanker when Rob orders a full stop and slowly begins to turn us into a second narrower channel with help from the tugs at our bow and stern. We pull past another oil tanker from Abu Dhabi. Now we've begun reversing power and are backing alongside the pier at the Long Beach Container Terminal. A full moon is shining through the arms of its big gantry cranes. One of the tugs drifts behind the ship, slipping away from the narrowing space between our starboard hull and the long pier. I notice there's only one guy on the dock below us standing next to a white van. He shouts up to Rob, then uses the van's open hatch to haul two thick mooring lines for the ship. Normally there'd be a docking crew of half a dozen, but it seems like the stevedore and his driver are doing okay on their own. A few other cars arrive, including security folks. The ship pushes up against thick metal dock plates and more lines are tied off.

Down on the pier, waiting for a lift back to the pilots' office, Rob tells me he's probably "taken the con" (controls) of ten to twelve thousand ships in his career. He grew up in the Fell's Point section of Baltimore with tugs a block away. His uncle was a tugboat captain, his dad served in the Coast Guard during World War II, his brother was in the navy and another uncle was a longshoreman. "So the whole family was on the waterfront. The tugboats were my playground when I was seven and eight. So later I got my mariner's license and worked tugs for ten years, but it got hard finding jobs by the early '80s. I went to the union hall and they said there was work in Wilmington. I thought that meant Delaware but they said no, [Wilmington], California [just north of the port], so I came out here and have been working here ever since."

Geraldine Knatz is a slim, neat as a pin, self-assured woman who favors tortoiseshell glasses, a flip hairdo, and a staccato speaking style reminiscent of her New Jersey origins. She also spent more than twenty years working in the Port of Long Beach. Then in 2006 she moved over to become the first woman executive director of the Port of Los Angeles, also the first marine biologist to ever run a major American port.

Right after taking the job, she arranged the first joint meeting of the L.A. and Long Beach port commissions since 1924. Although largely indistinguishable to outside visitors, the two San Pedro Bay ports remain fierce competitors. When I asked Cosmo Perrone, director of security for the Port of Long Beach, about the risk of industrial disasters like the 1976 conflagration in which a Union Oil tanker blew up, killing nine people, injuring fifty-six, and damaging more than 250 ships, he replied, "Oh, that was the other port."

Knatz's unique joint meeting was to promote efforts to green up the ports with a particular focus on improving air quality under what's called the Clean Air Action Plan or CAAP. Since then, while continuing to work as chief of the Port of L.A., she's become a global leader in the movement for greener ports, being named president of the International Association of Ports and Harbors (a two-year position) at their conference in Busan, South Korea, in May 2011.

Within her first five years on the job, air pollution at the Port of Los Angeles was cut by more than half, including a close to 90 percent reduction in diesel fumes from trucks and 80 percent reduction in ship emissions after 2009 when the state required ships to burn low-sulfur diesel fuel within twenty-five miles of the coast. Of course, as the region's largest air polluter the port had a lot of dirty air to begin with.

In 2001, the Natural Resources Defense Council, working with a San Pedro homeowner's association and other community activists, sued to halt planned port expansion until the massive amounts of nitrogen oxides, which cause smog, and small particulate matter (diesel smoke and soot) being emitted in and around the port complex from ships, tugs, trucks, and trains was dealt with. One study attributed 120 premature deaths a year to living close to the ports. While cancer rates were dropping in the L.A. area as a whole, in the San Pedro, Wilmington, and Long Beach neighborhoods closest to the docks they had increased 15 percent between 1998 and 2005. The lawsuit and community protests blocked the expansion of a new China Ocean Shipping terminal and a subsequent settlement led to most of the ships docking at that terminal now hooking into shoreside electrical power (what they call "cold ironing") instead of burning diesel or bunker fuel, the sludgelike dregs of the petroleum process, as their source for in-port power. In 2011 California's other major port, Oakland, also began the transition to dockside power.

In 2006 incoming mayors Antonio Villaraigosa of Los Angeles and Bob Foster of Long Beach agreed there needed to be a more comprehensive plan to clean up the ports if they hoped to continue expanding them.

"From the perspective of the mayor and the new board [of harbor commissioners], they were looking for a change agent to get us out of the situation we were in. L.A. hadn't approved a new port development in five years." Knatz recalled a critical moment in her job interview. "I told them, 'We need to eliminate this health-risk issue and get rid of old trucks.'"

A major source of port pollution was the sixteen thousand trucks hauling containers in and around the docks, a number that's easy to believe if you drive down the 710 freeway near the port or on the least scenic stretch of Pacific Coast Highway where it crosses Santa Fe Avenue in Long Beach and where six hundred trucks an hour have been counted moving shipping containers through that intersection.

The only candidate for executive director who addressed the health issue, Knatz was surprised but resigned when she received a pro forma rejection letter. Her husband insisted it had to be a mistake and that she call the headhunting company running the job search. Reluctantly she did so and was informed that yes in fact they'd sent her the wrong letter. After a few more interviews she was hired.

Shortly after taking charge, she established the joint ports Clean Trucks Program that's seen five thousand older diesel spewing trucks replaced with cleaner greener ones. The port helped pay for the new trucks, putting close to $100 million into the program, even during the recession-driven slowdown of late 2008 and 2009. The program has slashed truck-related pollution despite suits and threats by the American Trucking Association and others opposed to the cleanup. Knatz is now focusing on electric trucks and port vehicles, cleaner locomotives for the rail yards, more million-dollar dockside electric plug ins for the ships, hybrid tugboats, and other innovations including a possible mag-lev (magnetic levitation) carrier for moving cargo off the docks.

"All we see now are these new trucks. You no longer see smoke-belching half-broken-down trucks," harbor pilot Rob Lukowski tells me. "When I started here there was no kelp [in the bay] and the water quality was terrible and the air was terrible and now the air is much better. Ships all have better standards and the crews are better trained."

"We want our customers to expand their business but only by signing on to our cleaner action plan," Knatz says. "The thing is that Los Angeles and Long Beach [the San Pedro port complex] is so huge the companies need to do business with us. [The Port of] Oakland couldn't say, 'Customers, here's our plan.' Their customers would bolt. But it's harder for them to do that here [since the two ports are the gateway for over 40 percent of the nation's container trade, while Oakland accounts for only 7 to 8 percent]. You want them to grow but in a certain way," she explains. "We traded off their ability to expand [their port terminals] to sign on to our cleaner action plan. For them it was terrible—our setting standards—but if one of our standards fell down through litigation [lawsuits] we'd fall back on another measure. And the thing is, as soon as we adopted our plan, within eighteen months our board approved sixteen EIRs [Environmental Impact Reports required for a development to move forward], so we also delivered for them [the shipping industry]. I did not take this job to maintain the status quo," she adds with a quick grin.

Nor did she take the usual course through the maritime trades or big business to get where she is. As a graduate student in marine biology at the University of Southern California in the 1970s, Knatz spent time at USC's Wrigley marine lab on Catalina Island and also worked on a project evaluating the effects of discharges of effluents (scales, tails, and guts) from the big fish canneries that operated in the harbor. "They called it 'bio-enhancement' and claimed it was a good thing for the water. I'd go around the harbor with concrete weights and hang things off piers with wooden plates and collect data. We'd collect water samples and be happy if there was any [dissolved] oxygen in the water. At the time, instead of paying to have their bottoms scraped, people would bring their boats up the main channel to clean their hulls."

In other words, barnacles, seaweed, and other living things that cling to the bottom of vessels and create drag would simply fall off after a short exposure to Los Angeles's oxygen-starved and polluted harbor water.

"It was a Disneyland of toxic waste," recalls Kenneth Coale, director of the Moss Landing Marine Lab in Monterey Bay who also did underwater research in L.A. harbor in the 1980s. "It was black-water diving and we'd wear full face masks with radios because there are big ships going through these channels and basins and we'd move around [with full wet suit protection] but our hands were exposed 'cause we had to move by feel and had to place these sensors, these benthic flux chambers, on the bottom.

"At the *Queen Mary* [historic ship and tourist attraction in Long Beach] where the L.A. River lets out, a quarter inch of rainfall is like pulling the flush lever on a toilet. The surface would get thick with plastic containers and condoms, and they have barriers to contain that, but the nutrients [runoff from freeways, lawn fertilizer, dog droppings, etc.] would also run out and turn the water a bright [algal] green, but three feet down it was almost black. When taking core samples in Fish Harbor about a foot down in the bottom sediment you'd hit this hard layer of fish scales from the processing plant days."

In the 1950s and '60s, Fish Harbor, just off the port's main channel, had the largest cannery row in California with some eighteen plants including Van Camp ("Chicken of the Sea") and StarKist, employing close to twenty thousand production-line workers and fishermen. In the 1970s and '80s, with rising labor and fuel costs and declining fish stocks, much of the state's fishing industry, including the entire San Diego—based Tuna Fleet, relocated to the Western Pacific. Today some eighty fishing boats and one small processor remain in the harbor, bringing in squid, mackerel, sardine, bonita, tuna, and deepwater hagfish or slime eels (for the Vietnamese and Korean markets). The harbor water, instead of *copious* fish guts and green algae is now cleaner, clearer, and full of seagulls, pelicans and hungry barking sea lions annoying the fishermen.

"When the [cannery] discharges were reduced the harbor made a phenomenal turnaround," Knatz explains. "I was a scuba diver and we'd go transplant kelp from Catalina to the harbor breakwater, and we'd go re-move the urchins [that eat kelp] and today you can find kelp growing in the main channel," she says with pride.

Around that time she saw a job listing to do entry-level water-quality work for the port of Long Beach, becoming one of the first environmental hires at an American port. Later she moved over to planning and manage-ment and rose to the number two position in the port before taking her present job in L.A.

Among her myriad new responsibilities she has to address another water-quality issue, invasive species. These are critters ranging from viruses to full-sized fish found in the ballast tanks of ships that use tons of intake water for stability at sea but then often discharge it into harbors elsewhere in the world where these ride-along critters can become a major nuisance. Aquatic nuisance species (ANS) including Asian carp, Zebra mussels, and European green crabs have had devastating effects on local ecosystems and cost the United States some $9 billion a year. San Francisco Bay is con-sidered the most invaded of all California and U.S. waterways with close to three hundred alien species, many of them considered harmful, including the overbite clam and New Zealand carnivorous sea slug. One of the sim-pler if not completely effective ways to deal with ANS in ballast water is to have ships exchange their water at sea rather than in port.

"I think we've done well on the ballast-water issue," Geraldine Knatz tells me. "We're doing education where every harbor pilot would slap a flyer into each captain's hand and if you look at compliance it is now over 90 percent. We educate the captains that you can't exchange water in the harbor."

The Coast Guard is also overseeing development of various control methods, including biodegradable chemicals and ultraviolet light to kill off invasive species in ballast water. In March 2012 the Coast Guard issued new rules that require all oceangoing cargo ships to begin using onboard treatment systems to get rid of invasive organisms before they're allowed to flush their ballast tanks in U.S. waters. The rule limits the number of organisms permitted in certain volumes of water. California has, not sur-prisingly, passed the toughest law in the nation, one requiring no detectable discharge of invasive species from ballast water by 2020. The shipping industry, like every industry faced with an environmental deadline, claims the technology doesn't exist to meet such an onerous standard and that the regulation will cost the state jobs and money.

Still, the invasive species most hated by the shipping industry, at least from a historical perspective, would have to be Harry Bridges, an Australian import who went on to lead the ILWU, the International Longshore and Warehouse Union.

During one of the many hearings in which the U.S. government tried to deport him back to Australia, one of his lawyers suggested, "There are eight bridges in San Francisco, and the one you don't want to cross is Harry."

The gold rush established San Francisco as the West Coast's major port, a position it maintained till the 1920s when San Pedro passed it by. Across the bay, Oakland's port development was stymied by a battle with Collis P. Huntington and the Southern Pacific Railroad, similar to what was taking place almost four hundred miles south in L.A. In 1893 Oakland's mayor, George Pardee, personally kicked down a fence the Southern Pacific had erected to enforce its ownership claim over the city's waterfront. It would take another thirteen years of lawsuits, protests, and conflict before the California Supreme Court ended the dispute, ruling in the city's favor.

Even as the politically powerful railroads began to link the nation and provide new means of moving people, beef, and grain, California continued to ship its central valley grains around Cape Horn to Europe by sail. In 1881 no fewer than 559 ships assembled in San Francisco Bay to load grain bound for northern Europe. The *Balclutha,* a steel-hulled, square-rigged, three-masted cargo ship built in 1886, was typical of this trade, rounding Cape Horn seventeen times in thirteen years. The *Balclutha* carried everything from grain to coal, timber, and salmon, sailing across the globe from California to Europe and Australia to Alaska. It's now docked at the Maritime National Historical Park near San Francisco's Fisherman's Wharf.

Pacific and Asian commerce was also a major source of maritime activity. The iron-hulled, four-masted *Falls of Clyde* traveled between Hilo, Hawaii, and San Francisco carrying trade goods, sugar, and passengers from 1899 to 1907 when it was converted to a tanker hauling kerosene from Santa Barbara to Hawaii and returning with molasses for cattle feed. Today you can find the *Falls* rusting out on the Honolulu waterfront.

San Francisco's docks were also jammed with timber ships from Eureka and other points north, and local ferries and fishing boats that worked both the bountiful offshore waters as well as the bay itself.

Unfortunately for the seamen and stevedores on the docks, little improvement had come into their lives since the anarchic days of the gold rush and the Shanghaied sailor, but at least the mariners could count on steady if dangerous work. To work as a longshoreman you had to survive the "shape up," where crowds of desperate men gathered around a foreman who would pick a work crew for each ship to be loaded or offloaded. Often the only way to ensure a shot at the job was through bribery or physical force.

Things improved a bit during the boom years of the 1920s. Then the Great Depression hit the waterfront hard. By 1933 an able-bodied seaman was earning $53 a month, down from $85 in 1920. A longshoreman who could find work earned around $40 a month, about a third less than before the crash.

As discontent grew, the International Longshoremen's Association of the American Federation of Labor began a union drive on the docks. Among its more effective organizers was a short, hawk-faced Australian and fiery orator named Harry Bridges.

On May 9, 1934, Bridges led the San Francisco longshoremen out on strike demanding higher wages, shorter work hours, and a union hiring hall in place of the shape-up.

By July 3, with the strike continuing into its second month, the mayor sent the police down to the Embarcadero waterfront to "open up the port." This led to widespread rioting, with tear gas and bricks flying. After a Fourth of July truce, the battle resumed on "Bloody Thursday," July fifth, when the police opened fire with tear gas, pistols, and shotguns, killing two workers and wounding hundreds. California's governor then ordered in thousands of National Guard troops to secure the port, and Bridges thought the fight was lost, but after forty thousand mourners attended the funeral for the two dead workers, Howard Sperry and Nicholas Bordoise, the bay's trade unions organized a general strike in solidarity with the longshoremen. Close to 130,000 strikers shut down San Francisco and Oakland. Sympathy strikes shut down ports around the country. Under pressure from President Franklin Roosevelt, the shipowners agreed to recognize the longshoremen's union and meet its demands. Later that year, facing the threat of another strike, they recognized the Seaman's Union and its demands for eight-hour at-sea watches, an eight-hour day in port, and better pay.

With labor peace restored, San Francisco managed to keep its port business going strong until after World War II, when a different kind of revolution broke out. In 1956 Malcolm McLean, a North Carolina trucker turned entrepreneur, introduced "the box," a reinforced truck trailer with its wheels removed. He put fifty-eight of them on the *Ideal-X,* a ship he modified and sailed from New York to Houston. That voyage marked the beginning of containerization in shipping.

Bridges, still leading the ILWU, recognized this would mean fewer men working the docks (women had not yet joined the union in significant numbers). Rather than fight the new technology, he negotiated contracts that allowed older union members to retire with their benefits intact while guaranteeing the remaining jobs stayed in union hands. It was a hard sell to the membership.

"My dad said that first container was a longshoreman's coffin and each one after a nail in that coffin," recalls former ILWU president Dave Arian, who began working the San Pedro docks at the age of seventeen and is now an L.A. port commissioner. Over time Arian has come to disagree with his dad. "Today you look at the cranes. There are twenty workers per crane. I've seen a Maersk ship being worked with eight cranes. You get fifty cranes working in the port with everything else going on—that's a couple of thousand jobs involved." Today the Union's two San Pedro locals have close to ten thousand members, and the ILWU remains a powerful force providing secure jobs for its members up and down the West Coast and in Hawaii.

Unlike the union, the city of San Francisco failed to make the transition to containerization. With its waterfront fully utilized and increasing demand for downtown commercial office space, the port authority found itself trapped in a different kind of box with no space to expand its facilities. Today its piers are largely gentrified, including some cruise ship terminals, cafés, and an America's Cup regatta "village." Only Pier 92 south of the ballpark still functions as a classic marine terminal. That's where Darling International processes tallow from animal fat using restaurant grease and butcher scrap instead of Mexican cattle. With its on-site rendering plant able to produce shiploads of tallow, it dwarfs the barrel loads Richard Henry Dana's *Pilgrim* might have taken aboard, but in the spirit of turning a sow's ear into something other than soap, in 2010 Darling opened a new facility to convert its animal fat into biodiesel fuel.

Across the bay, the Port of Oakland, with a deepwater channel first dredged in 1874, had better options to deal with containerization, including extensive estuarine mudflats to fill in and a competitive drive that led to its becoming the first West Coast port to invest in terminals designed specifically to accommodate container ships. On September 27, 1962, Malcolm McLean, now chair of the newly formed Sea-Land corporation thanked six hundred Oakland dignitaries for helping mark "a new milestone" in world trade as the S.S. *Elizabethport,* the world's largest freighter (and first container ship to dock on the West Coast) began offloading its boxes. A converted war surplus T-2 tanker, the *Elizabethport* was just over five hundred feet long and carried 476 containers. By the late 1960s the Port of Oakland had become the second largest container port in the world. Today it's the fifth largest in the United States. Still, it continues to plan for the future. In 2009 the port granted a fifty-year lease for a 175-acre outer harbor terminal to Ports America (owned by AIG), which plans to invest $2.5 billion upgrading it to handle fully automated (robotic) yard cranes and trucks, something the local ILWU isn't too happy about.

"In the next five years as the technology increases our membership will decrease," warns Richard Mead, the big, gray-haired president of ILWU Local 10, which includes 1,300 members, a majority of them African Americans, working in the port of Oakland. "We've got to organize the truckers and the unorganized people beyond the [terminal] fence line if we're going to keep the power in our numbers," he tells a crowd of more than two hundred men and women outside Local 10's San Francisco union hall a few blocks up from Fisherman's Wharf. He goes on to recall some of the union's past and more recent glories, including tearing down swastika flags from German merchant ships that docked in San Francisco in the 1930s, making Martin Luther King Jr. an honorary member in the early 1960s after he spoke at the hall, and shutting down the Port of Oakland for twenty-four hours on April 4, 2011, in solidarity with the public workers of Wisconsin whose collective bargaining rights were under attack. Just over six months later, on November 2, 2011, close to twenty thousand anticorporate "Occupy Oakland" demonstrators marched on the port and shut it down again. A week earlier the police had used tear gas, flash-bang grenades, and "nonlethal" weapons on the demonstrators, seriously injuring Scott Olsen, a twenty-four-year-old marine veteran of Iraq who was struck in the head by a projectile (he recovered). While the ILWU local did not officially join the protestors' call for a 1934-style general strike, they respected their picket lines that shut down the port's night shift for eight hours. A month later a smaller Occupy demonstration shut the port again.

Today's crowd is here to commemorate a different event, the seventy-seventh anniversary of Bloody Thursday, an annual union holiday marked by speeches, picnics, and a boat ride on the bay less than two miles from where the 1934 street battles played out along the Embarcadero. Lest anyone forget, there's a chalk outline of the two bodies of Sperry and Bordoise on the sidewalk surrounded by flowers and yellow letters reading "Shot in the back by the police."

In San Pedro today's Bloody Thursday picnic will draw some four thousand people, a function of the size difference between California's two (excuse me, three) major ports. It will also commemorate two workers, Dickie Parker and John Knudsen, shot and killed by the shipping industry's private guards on the L.A. waterfront in May 1934.

The ILWU, like the Coast Guard, surfers, coastal tribes, and other maritime people, has its own internal culture and traditions it holds sacred. Taps for the dead "union brothers" is played. The local color guard parades the Stars and Stripes and union flag, and when the drillmaster calls, "Present Arms," they hold their fists across their chests. Next, ten-year-old Aaliyah Washington-Purry, a daughter of the union, sings the National Anthem. Paul "from 'da Hall" Williams sings "Amazing Grace." Supervisor David Chu gets up at the mike and says he's honored to represent this neighborhood and city that "was built on the backs of labor and honors those who toil by the sea."

"Good morning, brothers and sisters," eighty-eight-year-old Cleophas Williams greets the crowd as a trolley passes by. "I came to the union when I was twenty and that first day I was taught how to make a sling load and was offloading coffee," he says proudly. "And they gave me a union book and it needed a stamp that your dues were paid and I needed a stamp that I was registered to vote and one that I had in fact voted. Back in Arkansas my father couldn't vote because of Jim Crow and the poll tax." The aged African American pensioner pauses. "So I want to recognize the union and Sadie [his wife] who raised children with me and now we have great-grandchildren. I met Harry Bridges one time and he told me when we didn't have any that we were going to have vacations and have pensions and we did. Working together we did great things with our unity."

After a few more speakers, San Francisco Mayor Ed Lee arrives and talks about the strength of labor and people coming together, and just before lunch is served he presents Rich Mead and the union with an official proclamation declaring July 5 "Bloody Thursday Memorial Day in San Francisco." I wonder what former mayor Angelo Rossi, who sent the cops down to clear the docks back in 1934, would have thought about that.

• • •

Maersk's Pier 400 in Los Angeles harbor is the largest shipping terminal in the world owned by a single company. It's a big L-shaped landfilled island with a notch taken out of the heel of the L so that a new generation of "Super Post-Panamax ships" can turn around inside the harbor and head back out the breakwater at Angels Gate. Post-Panamax was the original designation given ships too large to fit through the Panama Canal before its 2014 expansion. Today there are 1,300-foot long-container ships bigger than any aircraft carrier, cruise ship, or supertanker in the world. In 2014 Maersk will launch a new fleet of still larger ships that will be able to carry 18,000 containers each plus enough fuel to create their own major oil spills. In 2007 the Chinese-owned 901-foot *Cosco Busan* hit the San Francisco Bay Bridge on a foggy November morning, spilling fifty-three thousand gallons of toxic bunker fuel, killing thousands of seabirds, fouling the bay and coastal beaches for months, and wiping out the herring fishery for several years.

The day I visit Maersk's 484-acre APM Terminal at Pier 400 it's about to sublease ninety-one acres to CUT, California United Terminals, that is owned not by Californians but by Hyundai of Korea. CUT wants to fill in another 130 acres and call it Pier 500. There are also plans for a new crude oil terminal at Berth 408 that would require drilling a pipeline through the artificial island.

We're standing in the MRC, or Management Resource Center, on the top floor of Maersk's three-story administration building. It's surrounded by sixteen giant cranes, including two delivered from China a week earlier, plus several big ships, acres of asphalt, and a whole Lego city of shipping containers in yellow, red, green, blue, gray, and white stacked four and five stories high. The MRC reminds me of a big-city railroad control center, and with good cause. To access Pier 400 you have to drive out a long peninsula built to carry several rail lines that expand to twelve sets of tracks along with an eight-lane road—seven lanes for trucks and one marked "Thru traffic—cars only," which is how we got out here.

The MRC has an array of workstations facing half a dozen large video screens. There's also a big model ship to one side. The three key MRC operators manage the rails, vessels, and yard (pavement where containers are temporarily stored). Operator Tim Caldon is casually dressed in slacks and a sports shirt with lightly gelled hair, a light fuzz of a beard, and a yellow vest indicating he's the vessel guy. "We spot where the vessels will berth," he explains, pulling up some charts and video of a ship on his computer screen.

"We plan thirty-six hours out what's being discharged and what's loading out. This week we have a TP [Trans-Pacific ship] that may have nine thousand TEU [twenty-foot equivalent unit] capacity but is only carrying eleven hundred containers. We've got one that's only offloading one hundred and taking on four hundred and eighty, including empties. That's unusual. We have one coming in with four thousand on and maybe three thousand will be for local distribution by truck [to California] and the others will go out on rail. This week has been slow because of Thanksgiving," he adds apologetically. It's a few days before the holiday and all the Walmarts, Targets, Staples, and other retailers across the United States have already stocked up off of the docks.

Although he's not the rail guy, Tim explains that the first train of the week "always goes to Chicago, but they also go to Dallas, Houston, Memphis, Kansas City. They go all over the place. We have BNS, the Burlington Northern and Santa Fe, and also the Union Pacific railroad."

He takes the joystick on his console and shows how he can bring up video images from any of 130 surveillance cameras on the island. He zooms one camera in to show me the tracking numbers on a stack of containers in the yard, then zooms in on a white security truck and its driver, who's yawning.

He shifts to another camera showing a crane offloading a ship. "Watch the spreader on the crane," he instructs. We watch the spreader (flat, rectangular metal plate that locks onto the top of a container) as it drops toward the ground and hovers over some twenty-ton deck lids. These lids are removed to gain access to containers stored inside the hold after clearing the cans (containers) stacked six high and sometimes eighteen wide on top of the deck. The cans are eight tons empty or, when filled with something heavy, such as imported water from Fiji or couches from China, can weigh twenty-five tons each.

Jeremy Ford is a dark-haired ex–New Yorker in his thirties, the terminal's director of vessel operations. He's been with the company for ten years. "We deal with both the maritime side and the stevedore piece," he explains. "We handle eighty-six hundred TEU vessels. Some are nine thousand to ninety-two hundred TEU and twelve hundred and five feet long like the Grete Maersk that's in port now." I'd spotted the ship earlier, its wide, flat, blue hull reminding me of a paddleboard, though one only Godzilla could sweep along. Motoring around the channels with the Coast Guard Auxiliary I spot similarly sized monster ships owned by Yang Ming, Hyundai, and COSCO.

"Maersk now has [1,305-foot] Emma-class vessels that can handle fourteen to fifteen thousand TEUs, though they haven't come here yet," Jeremy tells me. "But we can handle them. That's why the facility cut off the end of the island, to keep the turning radius for the Emma class. We presently get a million plus containers a year [at Pier 400]," he adds.

That's out of some eight million that pass through the port of L.A. and fourteen million through the combined San Pedro ports—half a trillion pounds of consumer goods, give or take.

"China is the number one source. Everything else is a distant second or third for us," Jeremy says. He thinks about one-third of their cargo stays in California, a third is bound for the East Coast and a third ends up "in the heartland."

While China is the number one importer into California, America's top three exports are scrap metal, waste paper, and air, as in empty containers headed back overseas. Oakland's major export in terms of dollar value is almonds. That pretty much says everything you need to know about our trade deficit.

In addition to consumer goods, the port also imports some twelve billion gallons of fuel a year while boarding a million passengers onto cruise ships and the Catalina ferry.

. . .

"Coming in with a van in two minutes," Jessie Cuevas lets his people know so they don't mistake us for intruders. Cuevas, Damien Ludwick, and I drive around the terminal yard in a big white Ford van. Ludwick is a tall, friendly Coast Guard lieutenant raised in L.A. who's been escorting me around the port. Cuevas is a former Coastie and the terminal's security officer, shorter with spiky dark hair and thin frame glasses. He grew up in Orange County.

Port security has become its own industry since 9/11 with between $15 and $36 million a year flowing to the San Pedro ports, their major new source of federal funding. The Coast Guard's L.A. Maritime Safety and Security Team, one of thirteen armed MSST units formed under the Maritime Transportation Security Act of 2002, patrol the port's waters on twenty-five-foot orange Defender boats along with port and harbor police while Coast Guard Vessel Traffic System (VTS) centers track incoming ships by radar and compare their Automated Information System (AIS) tracker signals against cargo manifests, previously recorded histories, and other data, looking for anything out of the ordinary. Customs and Border Protection (CBP) takes responsibility for container security, tracking, and inspecting cans from before they're loaded in foreign ports to when they leave the port complex aboard GPS-tagged trucks and railroad cars. Civilian volunteer waterfront watchers also keep an eye out for anything suspicious. Meanwhile, port gates, perimeter fences, and in particular dockworker IDs continue to be standardized and upgraded.

In 2010 there was a "port protector" security exercise with the navy, Coast Guard, CBP, port agencies, and customers (shipping and terminal companies) based on a "Mumbai-style attack," in which "terrorists" in Zodiac rubber boats hit the port at several locations at once. A year later there was an exercise combining a terrorist attack with a major oil spill in the harbor. I figure Coast Guard Captain Roger Laferriere must have had something to do with that one.

As captain of the port he's the federal official responsible for vessel safety, security, and navigation, also waterways and bridges. He shows me around his command center at the Coast Guard Station on Terminal Island next to the federal prison, highlighting some areas of concern on satellite maps, including several recreational marinas to the north and west of the port where small boats operate freely and could become platforms for terror attacks.

I don't feel as concerned as the last time I saw Roger, a highly effective organizer with a large forehead and strong brow that gives him an air of skepticism even when he's being friendly. He was running the Louisiana's Incident Command Center at a BP facility near Houma during the massive BP oil blowout and spill of 2010. He'd been on detached duty from his L.A. command for several months at the time that the Coast Guard was forced to surge its top personnel and assets to the region, stretching its resources, including the captain of "America's Port," to their absolute limits. Now he was back where he belonged and things seemed safe enough provided no earthquake faultlines slipped.

Back at Pier 400 we drive across open fields of asphalt and down wide lanes of stacked containers five stories high. Forty-foot containers seem to make up most of today's stacks. Designated "scrollers" in small trucks drive around finding containers by their numbers and then inputting them into handheld devices so the MRC can keep track of them. They might be stored for up to a week in the yard. A rubber-wheeled stacking crane about eighty feet high is building a new stack of cans, and I know my neighbor's six-year-old boy would love to help out. On the next aisle there's a big blue top handler that looks like a front loader you might take on a Mars mission. It's got white stripes on huge thick tires and a ladder up to its raised cab. We watch its giant flat hydraulic clamps pull containers off a pile, then load them onto a line of waiting utility tractors, skinny white cab trucks with open-frame "bomb-cart" chassis that are not street legal and so can only operate in the yards. Somewhere beyond lane 936 we pass hundreds of Maersk truck chassis, some stacked four thick, that will be linked up to private-contractor tractor trucks after they enter the terminal. The main entry gate is twenty-four lanes wide.

We check out the truck inspection garage and the rail yard with its carloads of double-stacked containers where I take some pictures of trains waiting for their locomotives to hook up. Next we drive by the *Grete Maersk,* where half a dozen overhead cranes are working to offload containers—pulling them up on cables, sliding them along their big arms, lowering them onto waiting yard trucks, and detaching the spreaders. "The hope is each crane can do thirty moves an hour," Jessie explains. I ask about talking to one of the crane operators and he gets nervous. "If I haven't gotten permission from the ILWU it isn't possible. Even taking their picture could cause a work stoppage," he warns. Later I tell my friend Peter Olney, chief organizer for the ILWU, that the companies seem on edge about what the union will and won't allow. "They should be," he smiles coolly.

In 2002 the shipping companies staged a lockout at the port in an attempt to win job-reduction concessions, but containerization, computerization, and globalization had replaced most warehouse inventories with "just in time" delivery systems. As a result the lockout caused a backup of goods clogging the yards. Within weeks the industry had to back down under pressure from the Bush administration as the West Coast lockout began to threaten the entire U.S. economy.

We approach the twenty-lane exit gates where transaction tickets are checked to make sure the right trucks are hauling the right containers. Radiation-monitor truck portals, like matched yellow Santa Claus poles, stand near a darkened glass guard post.

Back in Jessie's office I ask him and Damien if they ever thought about the port while growing up in Southern California.

"Not at all. I was clueless," admits Damien.

"I had no awareness of what goes on here," Jessie agrees. "It just becomes this wow factor once you get here."

The Marine Exchange Vessel Traffic Center overlooking the port from a hillside in San Pedro has another kind of wow factor with its panoramic wraparound view of the sun-dappled Pacific stretching across the curve of the earth, the working harbor, and the Southern California coastline spread below us from Point Fermin east to Seal Beach and beyond (remember, the coast faces south here). Established in 1923 it's the only non-Coast Guard Vessel Traffic System in the United States, though the Coast Guard partnered up with it in 1994 so that they now share the same air-traffic-control-like functions as other VTS centers in San Francisco, Seattle, New York, and elsewhere. Though housed in a modest two-story cinderblock building 306 feet above sea level (310 at low tide) it has the usual state-of-the-art digital radar screens with live AIS feeds of ships that can appear as circles, squares, or triangles depending on their designations. The AIS provides the name of the vessel, ID number and call sign, what type of vessel it is, its tonnage, crew size, flag country, location, course, and speed. This helps the operators monitoring San Pedro traffic. Unlike New York's constricted natural harbor channels, San Pedro can afford to designate three-mile-wide-shipping lanes with 1.5-mile separation zones and oversee the new unofficial lane that's emerged since the California Air Resources Board ruling that ships have to burn cleaner low-sulfur fuel within twenty-five miles of shore. As a result many ships now approach the port from outside the Channel Islands to avoid traveling within twenty-five miles of the coast until the last possible moment.

On the morning I visit, the mixed crew of civilians and Coasties are monitoring an outgoing oil barge headed to the Chevron refinery in El Segundo and several incoming ships approaching the pilot station seven miles offshore. Video feeds show a couple of escort tugs waiting by the breakwater and a container ship moving up channel. I'm trying to take good notes but distracted by the awesome view.

This is where the navy's Great White Fleet once sailed into port and where coastal defenses were established at Fort MacArthur during World War II (also where Japanese fishermen and their families on Terminal Island were arrested and sent east to be interned). I can see an early-morning Catalina ferry heading out along with sailboats from Marina del Rey. People will soon be escaping on three-day Carnival cruises to Avalon on Catalina and Ensenada in Mexico before returning to Los Angeles. Tonight the spotlights of squid boats and the navigation lights of cargo ships will pierce the ocean's darkness. I go over to the window and spot an oil tanker on the horizon. "I grew up sailing here with my dad and never realized how much goes on here in terms of maritime trade," someone says.

The previous evening I'd attended a joint meeting of the Los Angeles and Long Beach harbor commissions at the Banning's Landing Community Center down in the Wilmington port area. Along with Geraldine Knatz and Dave Arian, there were a hundred other people willing to spend four hours listening to a discussion of the port's cleanup efforts, including dozens who gave public testimony in which they spoke passionately about the role of the port in their communities, their workplaces, and their lives. Now, staring out across the bright morning sea, I can't help wondering if, before he died, stagecoach operator Phineas Banning fully appreciated what he'd started here. Port towns San Pedro, Wilmington, and Long Beach have become as vital to our national security and way of life as San Diego is as a navy town.

NAVY TOWNS

*Every Navy town I've lived in was great, but I think
San Diego embraces the Navy more than any other place."*

—Captain Jim Landers, USS *Makin Island*

The history of the U.S. Navy is not so deeply tied to California as California's history is tied to the navy's. Commodore John D. Sloat commanded the navy's ten-ship Pacific Squadron, including the sloops *Levant* and *Cyane* and the frigate *Savannah,* which acted as his flagship. On the morning of July 7, 1846, these three ships lay anchored in Monterey Bay. The Mexican-American War was less than three months old and Sloat was under orders to seize California once it started. The problem was he didn't know if the war of annexation that President James Polk was keen to have had, in fact, commenced. He might have been thinking about

Commodore Thomas ap Catesby Jones who, four years earlier, had raised the Stars and Stripes over Monterey only to be informed there were no active hostilities under way between the United States and Mexico. Despite his uncertainty, Sloat ordered Capt. William Mervine from the *Cyane,* one of the ships Catesby Jones had earlier commanded, to go ashore with 140 sailors and 85 marines and again raise the flag of the United States over the customs house, which was done without opposition on the part of the Mexicans. Sloat felt he had no choice but to act before the arrival of the heavily armed British man-of-war HMS *Collingwood,* which had been spotted in local waters. He feared the British might take advantage of the situation the United States had created in order to seize California in payment for debts owed England by Mexico.

Two days later, on July 9, seventy bluejacket sailors and marines from the U.S. sloop *Portsmouth* seized San Francisco. On July 11 American settlers who'd declared their own "Bear Republic" replaced their homemade grizzly flag with an American flag at Sutter's Fort by what is now Sacramento. On July 23 Sloat, old and ailing, handed his command over to Commodore Robert F. Stockton, captain of the frigate *Congress,* before sailing home to the United States. On July 29, sailors and marines from the *Cyane* seized San Diego's presidio before disembarking Army captain John Charles Fremont's "California Battalion," a mixed band of volunteers, mercenaries, and mountain men. In early August navy sailors and marines under Stockton took control of Santa Barbara and San Pedro. Just over a week later, a contingent of 360 men under Stockton and Fremont took control of Los Angeles. On August 12 a U.S. Navy sloop arrived in Monterey with official confirmation that the United States was, in fact, at war with Mexico. Two days later, Mexican forces in California surrendered.

This might have completed a relatively peaceful transfer of power as many Mexican Californios, were dissatisfied with rule from Mexico City and sympathetic to the enterprising spirit of the United States. In San Diego, for example, arriving troops found their flag already flying, the banner having been sewn together from white muslin sheets and red and blue flannel by three daughters of Juan Bandini, a leading citizen of the pro-American town.

Unfortunately, Stockton put marine captain Archibald Gillespie in charge of Los Angeles. Gillespie imposed a heavy-handed martial law that, by late September, had sparked a rebellion. He and his men were surrounded and forced to surrender before being let go. Scores would die in subsequent battles across Southern California, and many others would be injured, including the Army of the West's general Steven Kearny, who'd just arrived, and Captain Gillespie, who had returned to the fight, both wounded by horse-mounted lancers at the Battle of San Pasqual, where twenty-three American troops were killed. Eventually some six hundred sailors and marines under Stockton, cavalry troops under Gillespie, and Fremont's irregulars marched north out of San Diego and, with superior numbers and firepower, were able to defeat the rebels in early 1847. A few months later, an army regiment of more than six hundred additional troops arrived by ship and relieved the sailors of their garrison duties. Commodore Stockton appointed Fremont governor before departing for the east, but General Kearny thought he ought to be governor. Fremont would not yield the governorship. Kearny had Fremont arrested for disobeying an order and escorted back to Washington, D.C., where he was convicted of mutiny in a court martial. Pardoned by President Polk and allowed to return to California, Fremont briefly became one of the state's first senators and, in 1856, the first Republican candidate for president. During the campaign an incident in which he'd ordered Kit Carson to murder three unarmed Mexican civilians was recalled to his disadvantage and James Buchanan went on to become the fifteenth president of the United States.

During the gold rush that followed California's annexation, navy sailors joined merchant seamen in deserting their ships to pan for gold. The army didn't have much better luck keeping their troops from deserting, though those they did keep command over were ordered to kill a lot of Indians while also protecting some other Indians who'd survived massacres by local miners' militias that had not been authorized by the military.

In 1854 David G. Farragut, the navy's first admiral (until then the term was "flag officer"), was assigned to establish a naval yard at Vallejo. He stayed on for four years, completing construction of the first West Coast navy shipyard on Mare Island, twenty-five miles northeast of San Francisco. During the Civil War he would gain fame for damning Confederate torpedoes (floating mines) and ordering "full-steam ahead," at the Battle of Mobile Bay.

California was admitted to the union as a free state in 1850, but its sympathies during the war divided between Northern and Southern California with a number of pro-union volunteer brigades from the Bay Area, along with federal troops from western forts occupying proslavery towns such as Los Angeles and San Diego through much of the conflict.

At the outbreak of the Civil War the navy's Pacific Squadron was stripped down to six wooden sloops of war including the old *Cyane* while army fortifications like the citadel at Alcatraz (later to become a federal prison) were built up to protect California's harbors from privateers, be they foreign or Confederate.

Meanwhile, naval engagements in the east were changing the nature of warfare with the introduction of new tactics and technologies, including steel hulls, steam engines, and gun turrets as demonstrated by the inconclusive March 9, 1862 battle of the two ironclads CSS *Virginia* and USS *Monitor* off Hampton Roads, Virginia. Unfortunately it would take the navy's leadership another thirty years to realize the potential of these new warfighting techniques. In 1890 Captain Alfred Thayer Mahan, one of the first faculty at Newport, Rhode Island's new Naval War College wrote *The Influence of Sea Power upon History* that argued the navy's tradition of commerce raiding and brown-water coastal defense was unworthy of a global power able and willing to confront foreign fleets on the high seas. His work electrified both naval strategists and an upcoming politician and future president named Theodore Roosevelt. It also promoted the cause of a two-ocean Navy for the United States.

The need for completion of the Panama Canal, started by the French, to link America's seas, Pacific coaling stations to fire the engines of newly built U.S. cruisers, dreadnaughts, and battleships, and expansion of West Coast military ports all came into focus with the Spanish-American War. After the Spanish were accused of blowing up the USS *Maine* in Havana harbor, killing 253 sailors (a century later U.S. Navy investigators would determine it was an accidental explosion in the ship's coal bunker that sank the ship), the United States declared war on Spain and occupied its colonies in Cuba, Puerto Rico, and the Philippines, where the locals, already in rebellion against Spain, were soon fighting a jungle-based guerilla war with U.S. troops, eighty thousand of who shipped out through the Presidio army base in San Francisco.

With the United States now in possession of Hawaii, the Philippines, and Guam and emerging competitors including Japan, Germany, and Britain loose on the western sea, California's strategic importance for the United States as a Pacific power became more apparent.

A survey of San Diego harbor in 1900 by the navy ship *Ranger* found it to be an attractive site for a major port if the shallow bay entry could be dredged. This was exactly what the San Diego Chamber of Commerce hoped the navy could be persuaded to do for them. A steam explosion aboard the visiting gunboat *Bennington* in 1905 rattled the city, killing sixty-five sailors and reminding locals of the risks associated with welcoming the navy. Still, the city's leading men of wealth were convinced this was the town's future. They included John Spreckels, a sugar baron who, on the night of the 1906 San Francisco earthquake, had loaded his family onto his yacht *Lurline* and sailed south, never to return. Instead he became the dominant power broker in San Diego, buying up the Hotel Del Coronado, the streetcars, newspapers, and coal wharfs, using vigilantes to bust the city's unions and having the police arrest thousands who tried to protest. "Out there in San Diego where the western breakers beat, they're jailing men and women for speaking on the street," wrote one union bard. While boasting that San Diego was the finest possible military port (given enough federally funded dredging), Spreckels wined and dined navy admirals aboard his 226-foot steam yacht, *Venetia*, which he later leased to the navy during World War I.

California had formed its own naval militia in 1891, an adjunct of its National Guard that reflected the state's unique interest in the Pacific. It eventually grew to some one thousand officers and men, trained on more than a dozen navy ships and was mobilized for the 1906 earthquake, the Spanish-American War (guarding the coast against a possible Spanish invasion), and World War I, after which it began to fade. Today it provides a small number of lawyers and strategists who advise the state on military matters.

From 1907 to 1909, President Teddy Roosevelt sent sixteen new battleships and escort vessels from the Atlantic fleet on a round-the-world tour to show off America's new sea power. The Great White Fleet, was scheduled to make California port calls in San Pedro and San Francisco, bypassing San Diego, but a chamber delegation chartered a vessel that made for Baja, intercepted the fleet, and convinced the commanding admiral to make a courtesy stop in San Diego. He agreed to send the destroyers into the shallow bay but would keep the deep-draft battleships at anchor off the Silver Strand. The four-day party that San Diego threw for the fleet on its arrival drifted from the city's grand ballrooms and finest homes to its bars and bawdy houses and would be fondly remembered by the visiting sailors, including many who would go on to become leaders of the service.

In 1903 the navy built and operated its first submarine torpedo boats, *Grampus* and *Pike,* in San Francisco, commissioning them at Mare Island. The first submarine base with tendering (supply) ships was established in the port of San Pedro in 1913. World War I proved the value of submarines in warfare (one example of their lethality being the German U-boat sinking of the armored cruiser USS *San Diego* off New York). Mare Island was assigned to build and repair submarines for the navy, which it would continue to do for the next eighty years.

In 1910 aviation pioneer Glenn Curtiss established San Diego's North Island as a center for teaching army and navy personnel to fly, winning it the designation "birthplace of naval aviation." This is where he staged the first seaplane flight in 1911. That same year one of his demonstration pilots, Eugene Ely, made the first landing and takeoff from a warship using the fantail of the battleship USS *Pennsylvania* in San Francisco Bay after it had been covered with 130 feet of wooden planking. Six years later, North Island, still mostly empty sand flats little changed since Richard Henry Dana Jr. had labored in its hide-drying barns, became Naval Air Station San Diego.

In 1914 the United States opened up the Panama Canal, claiming sovereignty over a ten-mile-wide strip across the isthmus that would be home to generations of "Zonians" (U.S. residents of the canal zone) before being returned to Panama in 1999. Today San Diego's Balboa Park and San Francisco's Palace of Fine Arts are both artifacts of competing Pan-American fairs that celebrated the canal's opening from which these cities hoped to gain increased trade and naval traffic.

In 1919, President Woodrow Wilson transferred two hundred warships by way of the canal to the newly established U.S. Pacific Fleet. With San Diego still not dredged deep enough, San Pedro, California, and Pearl Harbor, Hawaii, became the navy's major battleship anchorages.

For many newly arriving navy captains, the coast of California north of Point Conception, with its rugged cliffs, winter storms, coastal fog, and jagged sea stacks, would prove a new and unfamiliar challenge.

California's greatest single shipwreck disaster occurred during the gold rush era in 1854 when the sidewheel steamship *Yankee Blade* loaded with close to one thousand people and more than a ton of gold hit the rocks and sank off Point Honda. Four hundred fifteen lives were lost along with its treasure, which was recovered a short time later. This was just north of where the California coast forms an elbow marked by the Point Arguello headland and Point Conception to its southeast. If you round Point Conception and sail east you come into the waters of the Southern California bight where the coast faces southward, the beaches are wide, and the waters more gentle than not. However, if you mistake Point Arguello for Point Conception, you'll find yourself turning too soon, sailing into miles of steep cliffs and dangerous sea stacks.

On September 8, 1923 a flotilla of fourteen destroyers sailing from San Francisco to their home base in San Diego followed their lead ship under the command of Capt. Edward Watson through heavy coastal fog. Unable to see Point Conception's lighthouse beam or to decipher garbled radio messages, Watson went with his gut, ordering a change of course when he thought he was rounding Conception and led the warships, traveling in tight formation at twenty knots, onto the rocks of Point Honda. The seven lead destroyers were lost, along with twenty-three sailors. It was the worst peacetime shipwreck disaster in U.S. naval history. During subsequent navy salvage operations the *Yankee Blade*'s ship bell from 1854 was recovered.

In 1924 San Diego became homeport to the *Langley,* the Navy's first aircraft carrier. The *Langley* had a wooden deck but no bridge or super-structure above the deck level, giving it an odd appearance that led to the moniker "The Covered Wagon." Still, San Diego's fleet including the *Langley* and a few dozen destroyers remained smaller than San Pedro's. By the 1930s there were fourteen battleships, two aircraft carriers, and thirty other ships based in San Pedro. The weather was good, the depth better than San Diego's, and they could use the nearby Channel Islands for artillery practice. In 1934 the navy purchased San Clemente Island, which eventually became its only ship-to-shore live-fire range off California.

Even during the Depression of the 1930s with its dock strikes, labor disputes, and dust-bowl migrants, the navy continued its West Coast buildup. Hanger One at Moffett Field in Silicon Valley, a 198-foot high, eight-acre freestanding structure with two hundred-ton rolling metal doors, is one of the more interesting artifacts of the era. It was built in 1933 to house the navy dirigible USS *Macon.* The *Macon* was one of the largest aircraft in history, a 785-foot rigid-frame helium filled airship that acted as a flying aircraft carrier with five Curtiss Sparrowhawk biplanes stored in an internal hanger. They could be launched and recovered from a skyhook suspended below the airship. In 1935 the *Macon* was lost to a violent gust of wind that drove it into the sea just south of Monterey by Point Sur, killing two crewmen. Eighty-one others escaped by raft. Fifty-six years later, the wreck was discovered in 1,450 feet of water by an ROV robot submarine from the Monterey Bay Aquarium Research Institute (MBARI). The outlines of the biplanes could be seen in the debris field as the images were broadcast live to Big Sur, where David Packard, founder of MBARI, was holding a barbeque for his friends to show them how one strange craft could find another.

In 1939 San Francisco held a world's fair on Treasure Island, a newly filled-in artificial island adjacent to the natural island of Yerba Buena, which was spanned by the three-year-old San Francisco–Oakland Bay Bridge. The new island also had a view of the Golden Gate Bridge, completed two years earlier, the largest suspension bridge in the world at the time. The theme of the fair that ran into 1940 was Pageant of the Pacific, and President Franklin Roosevelt inaugurated it with a call for "the unity of the Pacific nations," a nice thought that wasn't to be.

In 1940 San Pedro's battleships forward deployed to Pearl Harbor as a deterrent to possible Japanese aggression. That didn't work, either. After the December 7, 1941, Japanese air attack on Pearl Harbor, what was left of the fleet never returned to San Pedro.

The "Day of Infamy" surprise attack that killed 2,400 Americans and brought the United States into World War II transformed the world, the navy, and California. It had been coordinated with military offensives against Malaysia, Hong Kong, Guam, Wake, Midway, and the Philippines, and many in California thought the West Coast was next to be invaded.

Militarily, the Japanese attack in Hawaii was a great but not unqualified success. The battleship fleet was shattered, but the aircraft carriers were at sea or, in the case of the *Saratoga,* in port in San Diego, where it was outfitted and under way within twenty-four hours, arriving at Pearl Harbor a week later. The carrier battle groups would soon be hammering the Japanese starting with B-25 bombers that were loaded onto the carrier *Hornet* in Alameda, California, and launched on a raid over Tokyo in April 1942. More important than military considerations, however, the Japanese ruling circle misjudged the American people's response to the Pearl Harbor attack. Rather than undermine the U.S. will to fight, December 7 unified a divided nation in its commitment to total war against Japan and its fascist partners, Germany and Italy. In California coastal fortifications were quickly built up or reinforced. Many of these concrete artillery and observation bunkers, particularly in the Bay Area between Devil's Slide and the Marin Headlands, can today be seen hanging precariously close to exposed cliffs as erosion threatens to do to them what the Japanese were never able to.

Still, a Japanese submarine that surfaced off Santa Barbara in February 1942, firing on several oil tanks ashore and then sinking two cargo ships, followed by a massive antiaircraft barrage over L.A. three days later in response to rumors of an air attack, put California seriously on edge. Soon submarine nets were stretched across the state's harbors, including a seven-mile net across San Francisco's Golden Gate, below which a minefield was planted. Fear of invasion also fed darker more atavistic attitudes among those Californians who'd once championed the Chinese Exclusion Act and had long opposed any Asian immigration. When you visit the immigration station on Angel Island State Park in San Francisco Bay where 550,000 people were processed between 1910 and 1940, you'll find the detention barracks were segregated between Europeans and "Asiatics," mostly Chinese and Japanese who had a much harder time gaining entry and citizenship. In 1942, California attorney general Earl Warren argued for the removal of all Japanese, including U.S. citizens, from the coastal region. Lt. Gen. John L. DeWitt, head of the Western Defense Command, agreed, telling a congressional committee, "A Jap's a Jap." In the summer of 1942, 110,000 Japanese, Americans and immigrant Japanese, including California farmers, shopkeepers, and fishermen, were forcibly relocated from the coast and sent to military internment camps such as Manzanar and Tule Lake in Eastern California. Forty-six years later, in 1988, President Ronald Reagan signed legislation apologizing for this human rights abuse, stating that the government action was based on "race prejudice, war hysteria, and a failure of political leadership." Earlier in the 1970s I'd written an article for the *San Diego Reader* interviewing a number of young men who'd been interned. They were older men by the time I met them at their VFW post in National City. They'd all volunteered for the army out of the internment camps and joined the 442nd Regiment that fought in Italy, becoming the most decorated unit of the war, a tough way to prove their patriotism.

Other examples of prejudice during World War II included the L.A. Zoot Suit riots of 1943, in which young white servicemen targeted slightly younger (not yet drafted) Mexican American males. There was also the court martial of fifty African American servicemen who refused to load ammo ships until safety measures were put in place following a massive munitions explosion on July 17, 1944, in Port Chicago north of San Francisco that killed 320 people and injured 390, two-thirds of them black ammunition loaders. The striking sailors were convicted of mutiny by a jury of seven white officers. There were no black officers in the navy at the time.

At the same time the war also became a democratic experiment in collaboration and a template for the multicultural state California would later become as working women (glamorized as "Rosie the Riveters"), African American, Hispanic and "Okie" dust-bowl refugees seeking defense jobs filled the cities of Richmond, Oakland, Alameda, Los Angeles, Long Beach, and San Diego to overflowing. They lived where they could in temporary housing, tents, and trailers while producing thousands of warships, tens of thousands of military aircraft, and packing and loading hundreds of millions of rounds of ammunition in defense plants and shipyards that sprouted like eucalyptus across the state.

More than two million men—draftees and volunteers—soldiers, sailors, and marines trained at Camp Pendleton, Camp Roberts, Camp Cooke, Fort Ord, and elsewhere. More than one million were processed through Camp Stoneman in the North Bay before shipping out of Fort Mason in San Francisco. More than 250,000 jeeps and tanks were assembled and shipped from the Bay Area. Fourteen thousand ships and submarines poured out of the Kaiser shipyards in Richmond, Marinwork in Sausalito, Mare Island in Vallejo, and Bethlehem, Moore, and Hunters Point in San Francisco. Even small yacht builders like the Stephens Brothers in Stockton, California, turned out wooden minesweepers and rescue boats.

In terms of training and shore leave, Northern California was known as army country and Southern California as navy and marine territory, although Northern California produced warships for the navy while Southern California turned out warplanes for the Army Air Corps. Still, it was the unified might of Americans on the frontline and the factory line, from Guadalcanal to the Hollywood Canteen, where Hollywood actors served beer and food to enlisted GIs that turned the course of the war and transformed California's golden shore into an industrial and economic powerhouse.

By the time Nazi Germany and then Japan were forced to surrender in 1945 and the world war quickly transitioned into the Cold War with the Soviet Union, California had become the production center of what President Dwight Eisenhower would call "the military-industrial complex." This was the combination of war factories, politics, and military might that supercharged California's emerging aerospace industry, helped launch its computer industry with navy contracts to Hewlett-Packard and other companies based around Stanford University, and made San Diego one of the world's major navy ports while simultaneously promoting undeclared wars, military coups against elected leaders, and waste, fraud, and abuse in government contracting.

At the height of the Cold War, fifteen of the twenty-five largest aerospace firms, including Lockheed, Hughes, Convair, and Northrop were based in Southern California. Marine scientists from Scripps, who'd played a vital role in World War II's development of antisubmarine and amphibious warfare, now helped the navy test a nuclear depth charge off San Diego and develop nuclear missiles that could be launched from submarines lest the navy's most feared Cold War enemy, the U.S. Air Force, gain a death hold on the nation's atomic weaponry. After the Soviet Union developed its own bombs, America's first-strike nuclear plans evolved into a strategy called MAD, for mutually assured destruction.

The missile age also brought new missile ranges to California, including the navy's China Lake test range that's the size of Rhode Island, its missile facility at Point Arguello on the coast, and San Nicolas Island offshore, all part of the Pacific test range. In 1958 the Air Force established Vandenberg (formerly Camp Cooke) along thirty-five miles of pristine California coast as its own ballistic missile test base, later incorporating the Navy's launch site at Point Arguello. Today its six space complexes regularly launch government and commercial satellites into polar orbit. By firing the rockets due south over the Pacific from Southern California's most westerly point they avoid any potential impacts on land from booster rockets or classified payloads, at least not till they reach Antarctica. Also, as an example of something uniquely Californian in its mix of militarism and environmentalism, the state coastal commission got the U.S. Space Command at Vandenberg to agree to restrict its missile launches over the Channel Islands during the four-month pupping season for harbor seals, elephant seals, and sea lions.

During much of the Cold War, troops were deployed to hotter wars, including Korea and Vietnam, from the Oakland Army Base and later by charter jet from Travis Air Force Base in Solano County. During the Vietnam War the Oakland Army Base became both the largest military port complex in the world and a major draft induction center that drew massive antiwar protests that were beaten back by the police. Fifty-five thousand Americans and more than two million Vietnamese would die in what the Vietnamese call "the American War."

In the bitter wake of America's Vietnam experience the military became all volunteer and for cities like Los Angeles and San Francisco less connected to the daily lives and routines of the civilian population. San Diego was different. The city leaders had tied their fate to the navy and it had paid off handsomely. Even before President Ronald Reagan's military buildup of the 1980s, military expenditures in San Diego County topped those of any other county in the nation with the military employing some 20 percent of the workforce and generating thousands of additional jobs at defense-related companies, including SAIC, NASSCO, General Atomics, and Convair, which built cruise missiles.

In 1987 the navy proposed homeporting the recommissioned battleship *Missouri* at its Hunters Point Shipyard in San Francisco. This idea got enthusiastic support from then-Mayor (soon senator) Diane Feinstein but less so from the next mayor Art Agnos, who wanted guarantees of jobs for the mostly African American residents of Hunters Point and equal treatment in the hiring of gay people. Antiwar critics of the Reagan administration's wars in Central America and battleship bombardment of Beirut also opposed bringing "the Mighty Mo" to the city. The fight ended with the ship being mothballed after President Reagan's budget office cut funding for it.

At the time of the controversy producer Steve Talbot and I did a documentary for KQED, the local PBS station, titled *Navy Town*. In it we visited and highlighted the many navy facilities around the bay that contributed to the local economy and national defense, including Naval Air Station Moffett Field, Naval Air Station Alameda, Naval Supply Center Oakland, Hunters Point Naval Shipyard, Naval Station Treasure Island, Naval Weapons Station Concord, and the Mare Island Naval Shipyard.

Despite the thousands of jobs the navy provided to Oakland, local Democratic congressman (and later Oakland mayor) Ron Dellums was a harsh critic of the waste, fraud, and abuse he saw in many Department of Defense (DOD) contracts and programs, including the MX Missile and B-2 bomber. As the first African American chair of the House Armed Services Committee from 1993 to 1995, this hard-charging former marine and self-styled socialist also got under the skin of a lot of Pentagon brass who had to testify before him.

In 1989 the Berlin Wall came down as democratic uprisings in Eastern Europe signaled the beginning of the end of the Soviet Union, which collapsed two years later. During the subsequent U.S. base closures of the 1990s, which also saw navy consolidation in San Diego and Norfolk, Virginia, a number of U.S. towns experienced some losses of military installations, but only the San Francisco Bay Area saw all its major navy facilities shut down. If the intent was to punish Ron Dellums and San Francisco for their perceived lack of enthusiasm for the Department of Defense, it failed to take into account the region's economic dynamism linked to Silicon Valley (the dot.com bubble was just about to inflate) and voracious real-estate market always on the lookout for new waterfront property.

Still, a generation later, all seems forgiven, at least during the Blue Angels flybys at the annual Navy Fleet Week festivities on the bay that draw large and enthusiastic crowds both on and off the water.

Meanwhile, faced with post–Cold War, post-9/11 threats including rogue states, stateless terrorism, pirates, criminal cartels, and climate change, the U.S. Navy continues to haul greater ship tonnage through the world's oceans than the next thirteen largest navies combined.

San Diego is today homeport to several nuclear aircraft carriers, including the *Ronald Reagan* (whose F-18 Hornets fly out of a naval air station near Fresno when not deployed) and USS *Carl Vinson,* home to the inaugural NCAA basketball Carrier Classic staged on its flight deck with President Obama in attendance on Veterans Day 2011 (six months after the body of Osama bin Laden was dumped into the sea off the same deck), also the private USS *Midway* aircraft carrier museum on the downtown waterfront. Naval Base Coronado includes the North Island Naval Air Station with more than 235 aircraft, a nuclear weapons depot, an amphibious base and Navy SEAL school, plus SEAL Team 2. Point Loma has a nuclear submarine base and marine mammal program with eighty dolphins and twenty-six sea lions employed by the Space and Naval Warfare Systems Center. There's the Imperial Beach helicopter training station, Balboa naval hospital, and a host of other sites, most important, Naval Base San Diego at 32nd Street. The base is homeport to the Pacific Fleet, fifty-seven ships of the line, including a dozen amphibious assault and landing ships, Aegis guided missile destroyers, cruisers, frigates and the littoral combat ship *Freedom,* a new-generation warship designed to fight in the near-shore environment.

Still, even as most people in L.A. and Long Beach don't think or know much about their commercial ports, most San Diegans live their lives without really delving into what it is exactly that the navy does. Unless you're sailing out of the harbor you might not realize that every day navy and marine corps' volunteer warriors are training offshore in a 120,000-square-mile Southern California Range Complex, preparing to go in harm's way for the next cause, be it wise or reckless, that our nation's elected civilian leadership directs them to champion.

Rotors whir and AC steam runs like a small waterfall between the cockpit and the cabin as water droplets condense on the metal airframe above me. We're rolling down the runway, blades thrumping, past dozens of other H-60 helicopters (like Army Blackhawks only navy gray). We come to a stop then lift straight up like a fast, wobbly elevator over the North Island Naval Air Station, roaring out over San Diego harbor, over three Los

Angeles–class nuclear attack submarines at their piers and a fourth in dry dock, past the Point Loma lighthouse and kelp beds, and on out to sea. It's a cloudy day. Riffles and wind drifts give shape to the water five hundred feet below, blue and copper colored where shafts of sunlight have broken through the low cloud layer.

Behind me facing to the rear is Adm. Gerry Hueber, the head of Expeditionary Strike Group 3, an eleven-ship amphibious fleet that can deliver combat-ready marines, their vehicles, tanks, artillery, and air support anywhere in the world. The tall, slender white-haired officer is heading out for a briefing aboard the USS *Makin Island,* an amphibious warfare ship twenty-five miles off the coast now training with the *New Orleans,* a smaller transport dock ship last in the news when it collided with the nuclear sub *Hartford* in the Strait of Hormuz back in 2009. They and a third San Diego–based ship, the *Pearl Harbor,* will go on a six- to eight-month Western Pacific deployment this fall that will take them to the Persian Gulf unless called to duty elsewhere. It's August and they're working on the first of three training evolutions, what they call the "crawl, walk, run" phases of their preparation. It's early in the cycle for the Blue/Green Team, which includes 1,060 sailors and 1,690 marines who will be deployed aboard the *Makin Island.* Back on the tarmac, Admiral Hueber told me how yesterday they'd practiced retaking a ship hijacked by pirates, using both helicopters and a boarding team on a rigid-hull inflatable. An oceangoing tug simulated the target ship.

Half an hour after takeoff we approach the *Makin Island,* which looks like a small aircraft carrier, dropping onto its flight deck lined with helicopters and Harrier Jump Jets where we're hurried under the loud rotor wash and inside the superstructure and relieved of our floatation vests and cranial helmets. The admiral is taken off for his briefing on tonight's mission while I'm shown the stateroom I'll share with a ship's surgeon and briefed by a chief petty officer from public affairs.

At 844 feet and more than 41,000 tons, the *Makin Island* is one of the biggest ships in the navy other than aircraft carriers, which are about a third longer and carry twice the weight and crew. While both have flight decks and hanger decks for jets and helicopters, the amphibs also have warehouselike spaces to store weaponry and supplies behind their well deck and aft ramps that drop open to the sea. Hydraulic valves can then sink the ship eight feet for bringing on and launching landing craft or to sea level for receiving eighty-eight-foot hovercraft called LCACs, Landing Craft Air Cushion." These roaring monsters function along the same lines as the Harriers on the flight deck, redirecting their jet engines' thrust downward to give them vertical lift. Their drivers are even called pilots, as underneath the landing craft's rubber skirts they actually fly four to six feet above the water. While aircraft carriers are designed to deliver airborne bombs, missiles, and rockets, assault ships carry an even deadlier payload, U.S. Marines.

The *Makin*'s main cargo is the Eleventh Marine Expeditionary Unit, or MEU, led by Col. Mike Hudson, a tall, intense fellow with brush-cut brown hair, jug ears, a creased brow, and two tours in Iraq. "We continually train because as long as the flag flies people won't like us, and I'm not into the home game, I'm into the away game, which is why we're forward deployed," he succinctly states expeditionary ideology. "We're engaged and ready now, but I also like to sell our soft side because people think we just break things."

He takes offense at my suggestion that marines, "the first to fight," might not make the best humanitarian relief workers, one of the *Makin Island*'s other roles. "The Coast Guard's too small. We've got the capacity, the size and we're good at projecting soft power," he insists forcefully.

Aside from being one of the Navy's bigger and newer ships, commissioned in 2009 at a cost of $2.5 billion, the *Makin Island* is also the navy's greenest. This mostly has to do with its hybrid propulsion system of gas turbine engines linked to diesel electric motors that has gotten it labeled the "Prius of the Navy."

At between 12 and 25 knots it can run on its gas turbine jet engines but gas turbines don't perform well at low speeds, so for slower cruising the ship can switch to diesel-fueled electric motors that also power its lights, galley, water makers, radar masts, combat information center, and other essentials. In the ECC, the engine central control room Senior Chief Jeff Brotherton explains the advantages of the two 35,000-horsepower gas turbines and twin diesel electric motors over the navy's more common steam boilers that have been in use since 1950. "One is you can get under way in three hours," he says instead of the half day it takes to build up a head of steam. Also, the hybrid engine room rarely gets above 85 degrees—"a lot more comfortable for my guys," he explains, compared with the 120 to 140 degrees typical of a steam-fired engine room.

Most impressive, sailing from their shipyard in Pascagoula, Mississippi, fourteen thousand miles around the horn and on to San Diego they used just 33 percent of the fuel that other ships of their class would have used, making the same speed while saving the navy more than $2 million. They're expected to produce $250 million in fuel savings and a huge reduction in carbon dioxide emissions during the projected forty-year lifespan of the ship.

"We're based in California and so it makes sense this ship start weaning the navy off fossil fuels given that California is the most environmentally sensitive state," says Capt. Cedric Pringle, the ship's executive officer, who is scheduled to take over as commanding officer during the deployment. His attitude reflects Secretary of the Navy Ray Mabus's ambitious commitment to cut navy and Marine Corps use of fossil fuels in half by 2020.

There's another way the *Makin Island* functions as a hybrid. It can be used both for war fighting and as the largest humanitarian aid ship in the navy. Similar ships have been sent to help in the Southeast Asian tsunami, mass flooding in Pakistan, earthquake in Haiti, earthquake and subsequent tsunami and nuclear accidents in Japan, as well as other disasters. I remember the assault ship *Iwo Jima* tied up in New Orleans next to the Carnival Cruise ship *Ecstasy,* both being used for emergency housing and support in the wake of 2005's Hurricane Katrina. Along with its ability to move relief supplies by air and sea and generate two hundred thousand gallons of potable water a day from its desalinization plant, the *Makin* also has the biggest hospital unit in the navy outside of a hospital ship.

The ship's speakers announce a mass casualty drill. We head up a couple of ladders and through various bulkheads to the hanger deck, where the marines are launching a tactical communications balloon to eighty thousand feet, then walk halfway up a steep nonskid boarding ramp that leads to the flight deck. We're passed by a group of marines in full battle rattle with guns ready and hundred-pound packs on their backs, all wearing digitalized desert-tan camouflage. A second group of marines brings stretchers down the ramp to a door that opens into a hospital bay where they've set up a triage unit to sort out the casualties. Several marines are made up to match their medical status with painted wounds and splints.

"We had a gunshot to the chest that was through and through, a bowel evisceration with the guts hanging out, a burn victim with 40 percent burns to the body, and an arm amputation, also two dead," Chief Medical Officer Lt. Cdr. Adolfo Granadoes, a short, solid internist and one of six doctors on board, tells me as he tours me around his unit. He has a full X-ray suite, four operating rooms, and is particularly proud of his fifteen-bed Intensive Care Unit. He shows me the forty-two-bed primary ward, then takes me into a marine berthing area where there are 252 more beds that they could use for casualties by asking the marines to move out and putting navy medical corpsmen on watch. I notice that the navy areas of the ship have blue floors with white splotches. The marine areas are bloodred with white splotches.

I head up to the ship's air control tower, known as PRI Air, behind the ship's crowded bridge. From time spent on an aircraft carrier, I know this is where a lot of the action takes place. In between the tower and the bridge is an open walkway known as Vulture's Row, where the brass can watch air ops and witness any mistakes (common in training) or accidents (rare in practice) on the 2.5-acre flight deck.

"We've already gotten sixteen helos airborne today and four Harriers," Cdr. Mike Dowling tells me. He's gray haired and sun reddened, with blue eyes behind shades and a sharp nose on a well-proportioned face. He wears a radio headset with a control switch that almost never leaves his hand and a yellow Jersey reading "Air Boss" across his back. Lt. Cdr. Dan Boutros his number two or mini boss, is a little younger with darker skin, a shaved head, and a green flight suit, his rough look only slightly undermined by big brown doe eyes and lashes. These two will work twelve- to fourteen-hour shifts here, their meals brought to them, their leather chairs rarely used as they stand or pace among a small crowd of operators including a marine watchdog who represents the aircraft on deck and a landing signals officer who grades landings for pilot qualifications.

The air boss checks the NAVAIR weather monitor above him and clears "bullet," the H-60 search and rescue helicopter, to launch. It rises and banks off the deck to fly protective circles nearby during the long hours that air operations are under way.

Though the pace is less frenetic than on a carrier, PRI (Primary Flight Control) Air comes with its own challenges.

"Debark (disembarkation control next door) needs certain speeds and courses to launch boats (landing craft), but I also have to get into the winds for the helos and jets and doing it all at once takes a lot of synchronization," Mike explains.

Down on the flight, deck dozens of crew members in helmets, Mickey Mouse ear protectors, goggles, and multicolored jerseys are preparing for the next wave of launches in what looks like choreographed chaos. Four CH-46 Sea Knight helicopters (smaller versions of Chinooks) are lined up, their double blades turning. They will soon be replaced by V-22 tilt-rotor Ospreys, marine aircraft going operational after thirty years of program glitches, crashes, and cost overruns. Behind the 46s, several Harrier Jets are chained down on the starboard side near one of the aircraft elevators. Guys in purple jerseys unhook a fuel hose from one of the helicopters and retreat to the outer edge of the flight deck. Blue shirts remove blocks from in front of the helo's tires.

"The blue shirts are the chocks and chains," Mike explains.

"The tie-down guys?"

"Right. It's a blue-collar job, mostly eighteen- nineteen- twenty-year-old sailors and they want to work up to be red shirts, the crash and salvage and weapons guys, and then yellow shirts who move the aircraft around the deck. They're my eyes and ears on the deck. The white shirts are [responsible for] combat cargo and safety. The green jerseys are my mechanics, and the brown ones are mechanics attached to the aircraft, not to me. The purple shirts are the grapes, the fuelers."

White shirts are now directing lines of marines in battle gear across the flight deck, where they head up the rear ramps of the grasshopperlike 46s.

"Dragon 4 deck run approved" the air boss tells one of the helicopter pilots. "Let's try and launch them together," he tells Dan.

The 46s begin to lift off, noses down. The door gunner in the open window of the first one to fly past us makes rowing motions in the air, likes he's moving a big canoe, before the aircraft peels out to sea. The others follow.

The deck is empty for a time. Then a Chinook makes a nervous-seeming landing, hesitating before hitting the deck hard.

"Marine pilots have lots of flight time and combat experience but not a lot of ship-time experience," Dan explains. "It's just because of the reality of recent years with their doing a lot of flying in the deserts of Iraq and Afghanistan."

Later I watch three giant CH 53 Super Stallions, two Hueys whose airframes go back to Vietnam, and a Cobra gunship take off, the yellow shirts standing in front of them giving hand signals before waving them off the deck. The 53s are huge beasts, their tail rotors the size of a small helicopter's main rotor. The line of aircraft heads off toward a blinding white patch of sunlit sea below low, dark clouds.

The blue shirts are now moving the Harrier jets into position. Designed to support marine ground troops, they're best known for their short take-offs and bansheelike vertical landings. The air boss radios the CO and gets the ship to come around into the wind.

"The bridge will kick it up to twenty-five knots," Dan, the mini boss lets him know. Unlike a carrier, there's no steam catapult on this ship to launch the Harriers off the deck—just 750 feet of no-stick surface with a yellow centerline.

"Flying a Harrier is rewarding because its not fly-by-wire—it will let you do something that will tear the wing off and kill you. So it's challenging," Harrier pilot Capt. John Dirk, a slight, balding ginger-haired marine (call sign Ike) tells me straight-faced. He and his wingman are here in the air control tower to assist the marine watchdog representing the pilots on deck before taking off in their own jets to support the marines who left earlier on the helicopters. They will leapfrog past them to a target outside Yuma, Arizona.

The blue shirts push a Harrier out of its "slash," its deck position, and onto the rear center flight line, turning it to where its tail is almost over the rear edge while its pilot, looking out his egg-shaped canopy at a yellow shirt, makes radical adjustments with the plane's small front wheel.

"It's real tight at the end of ship. This is where my yellow shirts make their money," the Air boss says as the small, hump-shouldered jet moves a good ways forward down the centerline.

"He needs a push back, sir," the watchdog reports.

Eighteen guys in multicolored jerseys move to its wings and push it back a few yards.

"Not ideal," the air boss says.

"Just put the tail over the end," one marine suggests.

"This is very much an art," Mike explains.

A crew in silver firefighting suits, bosun mates Marcus Castillo, Mario Fulgenzi, and James Keough drive their white crash truck onto the deck. The cart carries 750 gallons of water and sixty of firefighting foam in case anything catches fire.

"Dragon Fifty, winds are thirty knots down the deck. You're cleared to launch on launch officer's command," Mike radios.

The Harrier takes off, leaving a brown, smoky contrail behind.

A second Harrier is pushed out and turns almost 180 degrees at the far corner of the deck, behind which the ship's luminous blue-white wake marks its pathway through the sea. After some radio glitches it's launched with another roar, leaving another haze of brown smoke behind.

The 108 helicopter-borne marines who'd taken off earlier will soon land and capture a "terrorist camp" in the desert two hundred miles from here at the army's Yuma Proving Grounds in Arizona. Eighteen thousand feet overhead, Ike and his wingman will paint targets for them with laser-generated green dots visible only through night vision goggles. They will then drop down to the deck to provide close air support.

"We do raids," Col. Hudson tells his troops the next day during a commemoration for the original 1942 Makin Island raid in which a pair of submarines dropped off two companies of marines who attacked the Japanese on Makin Island and prevented them from reinforcing other Imperial troops fighting on Guadalcanal. It was an early precursor to today's special-operations raids. On the hanger deck there's a big banner that reads "Raiders."

The colonel compares the 1942 operation to the previous night's practice raid. "If they're plotting against this nation in a country in chaos or without a government, all they'll hear is incoming aircraft and then bad things happen to them. . . . Ooh-rah." He concludes his remarks.

"Ooh-rah," the marines respond.

I'm sitting next to twenty-five-year-old Cpl. Nick Kniffen, a combat engineer with a thin mustache who missed last night's practice because he was on watch in the berthing area. Almost everyone in his First Combat Engineers Battalion has deployed to Iraq. He's recently returned from Helmand province in Afghanistan, where he used a metal detector to find IEDs (improvised explosive devices).

"Did you find any?" I ask.

"I found one IED with a detector and two with a truck."

"Was anyone injured?"

"No, we were in MRAPs [mine-resistant ambush-protected vehicles] so we were all safe. The Humvees below [loaded onboard the *Makin Island*] won't take a blast at all." I ask if this is his first WestPac [Western Pacific Deployment].

"This is my first boat deployment. I figure it's better than Afghanistan. A lot better than getting shot at."

Ooh-rah for common sense!

Today's training scenario involves passing through narrow straits and responding to small boat attacks. I climb down a ladder and through a floor hatch into the narrow stern gate machinery room where four young sailors are watching an LCAC hovercraft approaching us like a waterspout surrounded by a big cloud of spray until it roars off the sea and onto the well-deck floor. Through the spray thrown up by its giant fans and jet engines I can just make out a sixty-ton Abrams A-1 tank in its flatbed. The tank, its cannon reversed and "Pucker Factor" painted on its barrel, is soon clanking off the LCAC and up the well-deck ramp to join two other tanks brought aboard earlier.

Soon I'm being toured around the landing craft by one of its crew, fireman Carlos Acosta, who tells me it rides like a roller coaster. The two big aft fans and forward thrusters are powered by four jet turbines, allowing it to bump along at 50 to 55 knots without a load or 30 to 35 knots when carrying a heavy battle tank or other dangerous stuff.

Up on the flight deck I look out at the foggy ocean and spot a second LCAC that's gone DIW, dead in the water. Apparently one of its nearly twelve-foot-long fans blew apart approaching the ship and spun it around. It's now waiting for another LCAC to tow it back to Camp Pendleton. Luckily we're close to shore today, about ten miles off through thick morning fog. The ship's air horn sounds one long and two short blasts to signal other vessels in the area we'll be staying our course.

With morning flights canceled, I spend some time on the flight deck talking with young mechanics, including Marine lance corporals Tiffany Johnson, Keenan Millar, and John Richards, working on a big Super Stallion 53 helicopter based out of Miramar, the navy's old "Top Gun" School in North County that was turned over to the U.S. Marines. The three of them live in the barracks at Camp Pendleton. "We do airframes and avi(onics)," Richards volunteers.

"Mostly busting rust. Keeping corrosion down and then treating the helos to deal with sea conditions," Tiffany adds enthusiastically.

"So do mechanics get to fly?"

"We hardly ever fly," Keenan admits. "If you're a good kid they do a drawing and let you fly in a Huey."

Later back in PRI Air, the weather has cleared and flights have resumed. The *New Orleans,* which looks like a stealthy freighter with a big flight deck, is running one thousand yards ahead of us, convoy fashion, as if we were transiting a narrows like the Strait of Hormuz, keeping an eye out for enemy boats or incompetent submarine drivers. Suddenly a go-fast orange boat is shooting across the sea toward the lead ship's bow, throwing a rooster tail of water behind it. Within thirty seconds an H-60 helo is hovering above the intruder, guns ready. Shortly, two more speedboats with white hulls and orange decks appear off our port. Glassing them with binoculars, I see "Navy" written across the side of the nearer one. More training. Two days later the *New Orleans* will respond to a distress call from a fishing boat and seize 1,800 pounds of marijuana, turning the drugs over to the U.S. Coast Guard and the three drenched fishermen they pull from the sea over to the Mexican navy, proof that training can turn operational at any time, even in the waters off California.

I talk with search and rescue pilot Lt. Cdr. Will Eastham, who tells me his work is essential, monotonous, and sometimes surprising. "We'll see tons of dolphins and whales while flying. I don't know what kind of whales we're seeing, but we saw some the other day. We also saw something weird. We made three or four passes trying to figure out what it was—it looked like a turtle on its side and . . ." Like every aviator, he uses his hands to describe what he saw and I tell him it sounds like a Mola mola, an ocean sunfish, a not-uncommon sight in the waters off California. They can weigh more than a ton and look like a giant halibut swimming on its side with a guppy mouth and big vertical tail fins where the back half of its body should be. A few hours later the air boss points out another big sunfish sliding past the ship, and then a large pod of dolphins off our starboard side. I count eighty to one hundred white-sided dolphins, many leaping clear of the water, including a juvenile who seems particularly impressed with himself. Mike tells me he once wanted to be an oceanographer and studied for it in college before becoming a navy helicopter pilot and now air boss.

I'm reminded how things tend to blend once you cross over the beach, how war fighters and harbor pilots might also be surfers and divers, and marine scientists get to work for the navy and ex-navy, and Coast Guard officers can end up running ocean conservation groups like two of my friends have. Salt water tends to erode professional stovepipes.

"The Cold War was the focus of my first ten years in the service, and the Middle East the last ten," says the *Makin Island*'s outgoing C.O. Capt. Jim Landers, a dark-haired twenty-four-year veteran in a leather aviator's jacket (he used to fly P-3 Orions). He tells me he's a big fan of *New York Times* columnist and author Tom Friedman. "I agree with him that we have to become a world leader in alternative energy. In February we were doing operations between here and the Channel Island and we did ten hours a day of Harrier qualifications and one day our ship burned eighty-eight hundred gallons of fuel and we pumped twenty-two thousand gallons into the jets. Normally jets burn less than half the fuel of the ship, but we burned less than half of what the jets did. I mean we aren't using alternative energy here, but we could be the transition ship to the clean-energy ships of the future."

As for aviation, in 2012 the navy aircraft carrier tested its "Green Hornet," an adaptation of its F-18 Super Hornet jet fighter that can operate on a fifty-fifty blend of jet fuel and camelina biofuel.

Getting off of fossil fuel is certainly one of the great national security challenges of today, with the Department of Defense remaining the major U.S. consumer of Middle Eastern petroleum and the navy and marines committed to being 50 percent fossil fuel free within a decade. Interestingly, within one hundred miles of where the *Makin Island* is now training to head out to the oil-rich Persian Gulf, California once launched the world's offshore oil and gas industry and later experienced an oil disaster that would forever transform how Californians, if not the nation, relate to their coast and ocean.

SAVE OUR SHORES

The coast is never saved;
the coast is always being saved.

—PETER DOUGLAS

Five months after I moved back to California in 2007, the Chinese-owned container ship *Cosco Busan* hit the San Francisco–Oakland Bay Bridge, spilling more than fifty-three thousand gallons of bunker fuel into the bay. Within hours, dead and oil-covered seabirds, including scoters, grebes, gulls, and cormorants, started washing and flapping onto the marina rocks and beach by my house. The toxic fuel oil left rainbow sheens on the water and boat hulls, as well as greasy green and brown smudges that looked like marbled meat gone bad. Tar balls and asphaltlike chips and shards fouled local beaches and salt marshes. After covering the disaster in my home waters for a week, I flew off to the kingdom of Bahrain and from there caught a Navy Seahawk helicopter to the Northern Persian Gulf between Iraq and Iran, where I spent the next week aboard U.S. Coast Guard cutters guarding Iraqi oil terminals. I rode with armed boarding parties climbing onto local fishing dhows and supertankers headed to the platforms. Later I watched natural gas being flared off oil-production platforms as we made our way down the length of the gulf, one of the most lifeless seas I've ever been on. When I returned home they were still cleaning up the spilled oil. Three years later I was in the Gulf of Mexico reporting on the BP Deepwater Horizon oil blowout that was four thousand times the size of the *Cosco Buson* spill. There I flew over more than one hundred dolphins and a humpback whale trapped and dying in oil slicks that stretched from horizon to horizon. Years later oil, tar, and dead dolphins are still washing onto the beaches and wetlands of the gulf. Recently BP lobbied unsuccessfully against oil spill prevention legislation in the California statehouse, giving new meaning to the term *chutzpah*. All of these petroleum-related activities have their origins in coastal California.

The Santa Barbara Channel's more than two thousand natural oil and gas seeps are among the most active in the world. The La Brea tar pit in Los Angeles is another example of oil that naturally bubbles to the earth's surface. The Chumash used oil tar from the channel's seeps to caulk their tomol canoes. Later, local asphalt deposits were mined and shipped north to pave the streets of San Francisco. So it didn't take a petroleum geologist or particularly brilliant mining engineer to guess where the oil was. In 1896, less than forty years after the first rock oil derrick was drilled in Titusville, Pennsylvania, the world's first offshore oil drilling piers were built out from the newly established spiritualist center of Summerland, California. Soon the more secular oilmen were at war with each other, hiring gunmen, stringing barbwire, and dynamiting and sabotaging each other's piers and derricks while racing to suck up as much oil as possible before their wells lost pressure and had to be abandoned. Abandoned wells, sabotage, and poorly controlled gushers soon led to widespread pollution and badly fouled beaches. "The whole face of the townsite is aslime with oil leakages," reported the

San Jose Mercury News in 1901. The resort town of Santa Barbara just up the coast quickly voted to ban oil piers and derricks to protect its beaches.

California's first oil boom had begun a few years earlier in 1890 near Bakersfield in Kern County, site of both the largest uncontrolled gusher in U.S. history (nine million barrels) and the Elk Hill Naval Petroleum Reserve that sparked the Teapot Dome scandal during Warren Harding's presidency. State oil production then exploded with the discovery of three major Southern California fields at Huntington Beach, Santa Fe Springs (east of what's now LAX), and Signal Hill in Long Beach. By 1923, the year of the Teapot Dome scandal, the south coast was a forest of wooden derricks and California was the top oil-producing state in the nation, responsible for a quarter of the world's petroleum production. That year Signal Hill alone produced sixty-eight million barrels of oil. Today, nearly tapped out, it has produced close to 950 million barrels. Estimates of California's existing offshore resources are about ten times that figure.

In San Diego the oil boom intensified a long-held civic debate between "smokestacks and geraniums," those who favored industrialization, including manufacturing and oil refining, versus those who wanted to retain the city's Mediterranean charms with a focus on tourism and real estate. In the end the navy tilted the argument in favor of heavily armed geraniums.

As the oil industry rapidly grew, the state imposed a 5 percent royalty fee that inspired a rush of new lease applications by Standard Oil, Union Oil, and other big companies tired of wildcatting and looking for a regulatory structure that would guarantee their claims under the law. In 1929, as charges of favoritism and corruption and evidence of marine pollution mounted, California placed a moratorium on any new offshore lease sales. By then Standard Oil had developed slant-drilling technology that allowed it to tap into state-controlled "submerged lands" from its onshore rigs in Huntington Beach.

By the 1930s Louisiana was going through its own oil boom in its southern swamps, lakes, and marshes, but with its thin coastal population along the flood-prone delta there was little resistance to the oil companies' blowouts, fires, and pollution. Soon they would begin drilling offshore, later joined by Texas oilmen, so that today the Gulf of Mexico has become a center of global oil and gas production with more than four thousand off-shore platforms.

After World War II and the Truman Proclamation dividing the Gulf's waters between the United States and Mexico, the leasing of oil and gas became the federal government's second largest source of revenue after in-come taxes (and in competition with custom duties). To date, the govern-ment, despite industry-favorable subsidies and tax holidays, has generated more than $125 billion for the treasury from offshore drilling while the oil companies have earned more than $1 trillion.

In 1968 the Department of Interior, anxious to increase government revenues, sold seventy-one OCS (Outer Continental Shelf) drilling tracts in the Santa Barbara Channel for $603 million despite strong objections from local residents whose fears traced back to the Summerland spills at the turn of the century. The government assured the city and county that off-shore drilling technology had become much safer. Then in January 1969, Los Angeles–based Union Oil (now a part of Chevron) got federal waivers permitting it to reduce the length of its primary ocean floor drill-pipe cas-ings off Santa Barbara from the standard five hundred feet to just fifteen feet and secondary casings from 861 to 238 feet. The casings, cemented into the bore hole, were designed to help prevent contamination, cave-ins, and blowouts. Drilling their fourth well, the Union Oil crew hit a snag, and oil and gas exploded up the pipe string. When it was capped it began leaking below the shortened casings. Within days some three million gal-lons came ashore, covering sandy beaches with a viscous black coating of crude oil that gave the waves a sludgy pulse and the air a gas-station odor. For months afterward any hardcore surfers willing to risk going into the water had to finish their sessions with stinging turpentine baths—the only way to remove sticky oil and tar balls from their skin, hair, and eyelids. When President Richard Nixon came to look at the fouled beaches he was greeted by the stony silence and harsh glares of thousands of angry residents.

"Get oil out!" became a local then national rallying cry for the emerging environmental movement. Dying oil-soaked birds in Santa Barbara became one of the iconic images of this new movement, along with the oil- and garbage-soaked Cuyahoga River, which caught fire and burned in Cleveland that summer. The next year, on April 22, 1970, more than twenty million Americans turned out at rallies for the first Earth Day.

The next serious push to expand offshore drilling in California took place in the 1980s under Ronald Reagan's controversial Secretary of Interior James Watt who suggested that since Jesus would be returning soon, now would be a good time to "mine more, drill more, cut more timber," on public lands and in federal waters. He was fired after eight months on the job, largely because he kept alienating people, including the California couple living in the White House when, for example, he refused to allow the Beach Boys to play a free Fourth of July concert on the Washington Mall, claiming they were morally suspect. Watt's successor, Don Hodel, a pious man who would go on to cochair the Christian Coalition, continued Watt's resource-exploitation policies. Watt wanted to open up a billion acres of the Outer Continental Shelf to drilling and undersea mining, including eighty-three million acres of federal waters off the California coast from Santa Monica to Mendocino. At the same time the Environmental Protection Agency was proposing that three large "incinerator ships" be allowed to burn hazardous waste two hundred miles off the coast, assuring critics the plumes left in their wake would contain nothing more harmful than carbon dioxide and hydrochloric acid. When I asked Secretary Hodel about congressional opposition to the drilling plans, he replied that not drilling oil off California "would be putting a sign on America that says we're willing to blindfold ourselves to our God-given resources and place ourselves at the tender mercies of OPEC."

Working on a local PBS documentary called *Troubled Waters* back in 1986, I got a helicopter ride out to a Chevron oil platform off Santa Barbara where I got to see the skilled roughnecks and less-skilled roustabouts in their coveralls, hardhats, and steel-toed boots working the water-slick drill deck like they were doing a choreographed blue-collar ballet, securing the hydraulic tongs and spinning chains around the pipe stem after they manhandled a length of pipe into position below the derrick with its massive yellow top drive and block. The driller responsible for this scene kept one eye on his control console and the other on his crew as they threaded pipe into the open end of the previous section, sealing off the brown fountain of seawater burbling over its lip with a slow, creaky rotation. The platform seemed huge to me at the time (though small compared to BP deepwater platforms I later visited in the gulf) with its helipad that we'd landed on, truck-sized power generator, crew housing, production controls, and shoreline pipe connections, lifeboats, flare stack, and freestanding metal legs rising four hundred feet off the bottom then several stories above the water whose motion you could watch through the open grating of the rig's metal walkways. I came to appreciate the challenges and difficulties faced by offshore operators both in terms of engineering, production, and safety as well as the physical risk, commitment, and skill of these oil patch workers out there producing energy in the channel.

Hodel's five-year leasing plan for California would have seen the number of drilling platforms expanded from 20 to 1,100 if all leases were opened and bid on. While that level of interest was unlikely, even the possibility set off massive protests with thousands of people turning out at public hearings up and down the coast, some dressed up as dolphins and whales. The California Coastal Commission claimed the lease sales threatened sea otters, gray whales, and commercial fishing. Court challenges, rulings, and appeals quickly mounted. Then opponents came up with a new strategy and unique way to shift the balance of influence from the feds to California coastal communities. In their 1985 off-year elections, 82 percent of Santa Cruz voters supported an initiative that would require any zoning changes allowing construction of onshore facilities for offshore oil had to be approved by a vote of the electorate.

"So it wasn't an outright ban [that could be challenged in court], but we did also vote funds to educate other cities and counties about our plan and some thirty cities and counties adopted this ordinance," recalls former city councilman and now California Secretary for Natural Resources John

Laird. "And the Western Petroleum Association took it to court after about the first thirteen cities [adopted the ordinance] and lost, and it's still on the books up and down the coast." He grins. "It was this practical activism and we had a press conference by the pier with these two stuffed ducks and poured Valvoline oil over them and called it Duck ala Hodel."

After his 1988 election, President George H. W. Bush, who'd run promising to be an "environmental president," set aside Hodel's five-year-plan for lease sales off California.

Another impact of the fight was a vast expansion of the National Marine Sanctuary system, including the largest sanctuary established off central California in 1992. The National Marine Sanctuary program was created as a rider to an ocean dumping act in 1972 on the hundredth anniversary of the creation of Yellowstone, America's first national park. Rather than being fully protected like national parks, however, sanctuaries were established to be more like multiuse national forests in that they were supposed to protect "conservation, recreational, ecological, historical, research, educational or aesthetic qualities." Also, Congress provided no money for the program during its first seven years. The first significant sanctuary designations were under President Jimmy Carter, including the 1,658-square-mile Channel Islands Sanctuary off Santa Barbara established in 1980, but what struck a responsive chord with many antidrilling activists around the nation was that there could be no oil exploration or drilling inside sanctuary boundaries. This led to large new sanctuaries being established off New England, in the Florida Keys, and off Monterey.

Antidrilling activists like Richard Charter from Sonoma and Dan Haifley from the Santa Cruz group Save Our Shores began to advocate for a large sanctuary to protect the Central Coast and made common cause with local politicians including John Laird then the mayor of Santa Cruz, and Congressman Leon Panetta, the son of immigrants who'd grown up in Monterey among Italian farmers and cannery workers and who would go on to become White House chief of staff under President Bill Clinton and CIA director and secretary of defense under President Barack Obama.

Farmers, fishermen, local governments, the tourism industry, and leading citizens of the area including David Packard of Hewlett-Packard and his daughters Julie and Nancy, who'd encouraged him to help establish a world-class aquarium in an old abandoned cannery, all joined the sanctuary cause. "I'd never seen such a broad coalition form so quickly in my life. It was a real groundswell," Panetta later recalled. So, he added a rider to the Hurricane Andrew Relief Act of 1992 that would create a new sanctuary of uncertain size off the coast of Monterey. Sanctuary proponents drew up maps for a small-, medium-, and large-sized reserve. The biggest would cover more than 350 miles of coastline and extend 53 miles out to sea.

"Leon said, let's compromise on the middle one, but the people just went nuts at all these public hearings and insisted on the biggest deal," Representative Sam Farr recalls. Farr now represents the seventeenth district seat that Panetta vacated when he went to the White House.

"Luckily '92 was an election year," Farr continues, "and we reminded George Bush that in '88 he'd run a TV ad in California showing the Big Sur coastline, saying he was going to be the environmental president, so he went for the biggest boundary."

"If we could have a presidential election every three months we'd have the best coastal protection in the world," Laird told local reporters at the time.

On the weekend of September 19 and 20, 1992, the Monterey Bay National Marine Sanctuary was dedicated with shoreside crowds turning out in Santa Cruz and Monterey (at either end of the bay) and much maritime pomp and circumstance, including tall ships firing loud smoky volleys from their guns, fishing boats, Coast Guard cutters, kayakers, the Monterey Symphony playing "Ode to the common man," and dozens of barking sea lions. I remember standing in the Monterey crowd and the woman next to me turning to her husband as the big sea lions swam around the somewhat nervous-looking kayakers and asking, "How do they get them to do that?" Bush still lost California to Clinton that November.

In 2009 when President Obama, a supporter of expanded offshore oil drilling, sent Secretary of the Interior Ken Salazar to San Francisco to hold hearings on new Outer Continental Shelf energy leasing, the opposition was still unified and vociferous. More than five hundred people, including Senator Barbara Boxer, then–Lieutenant Governor John Garamendi, and four house members testified and rallied for clean energy and against any new oil drilling. People carried signs of a crossed-out derrick reading "Pointless" and wore dolphin, turtle, and polar bear costumes. Surfrider women in bikinis and wet suits walked around covered in oil (chocolate syrup actually). Senator Boxer noted that the coast was a treasure and a huge economic asset "just as is," generating $24 billion a year and 390,000 jobs. Sailors, longshoremen, green-energy entrepreneurs, and fishermen all agreed with her. The only two people advocating for new oil drilling were a guy from the Western States Petroleum Association (people held dollar bills up as he spoke) and the operator of a Motel 8. The secretary decided not to offer any new oil and gas leases off California, Oregon, or Washington.

Today twenty-six oil platforms still operate off the coast of California along with four ten- to twelve-acre artificial islands called THUMS (for Texaco, Humble, Union, Mobil, and Shell) in Long Beach harbor that are disguised to look like resort islands, including drilling rigs camouflaged as high-rise apartments and landscaped walls, waterfalls, and palm trees surrounding the oil-production facilities at the center of the islands. California's oil platforms also have some of the best safety records in the industry thanks to tough regulation. They also have the largest state-mandated oil spill response infrastructure in the nation. When I went to the gulf to cover the BP oil blowout in 2010, I discovered that California had more oil spill response vessels and standby crews than the entire Gulf of Mexico region. Many of them were down there to lend a hand.

Still, the greatest legacy of the Santa Barbara oil spill may not have anything to do with offshore energy production but rather with onshore development, coastal conservation, and public access to the beach.

I stop at the ocean end of Eucalyptus Lane in Montecito next to a gated mansion and ask a surfer loading his board into his car where to find a restaurant. He grins at me, still stoked from his session in the waves, and tells me he has no idea, he doesn't live around here, and points to the public stairway to the beach he's just come up. You don't have to be rich and live in La Jolla, Malibu, Montecito, Pebble Beach, Sea Cliff, Sausalito, or Belvedere to enjoy easy access to California's beaches. Public access along with a natural and scenic coastline and healthy coastal habitats can largely be attributed to a generation of 1960s and '70s activists, progressive politicians, and public servants including Sylvia McLaughlin, Phil Burton, and Peter Douglas. They and others like them held the line on sprawl and turned the tide of public opinion and policy, creating a network of parks and a coastal commission to ensure that California's golden shore remains a resource for all its people rather than transforming into another Jersey Shore, Miami Beach, or Waikiki.

Cities came late and unplanned to California. The San Francisco Bay Area was created by the gold rush and expanded with World War II. Much of that expansion took the form of infill into the bay. By the end of the 1950s the bay was an industrial eyesore with less than six miles of public access. Cities used it to dump their garbage or else gave tax credits to private dumpers for filling in tidelands for new subdivisions and shopping malls. Folksinger Malvina Reynolds wrote a 1962 song "Little Boxes" (made famous by Pete Seeger) about the cookie-cutter developments springing up in Daly City next to the bay south of San Francisco.

San Francisco Bay itself was a third smaller than it had been during the gold rush and also shallower thanks to all the sediment from nineteenth-century hydraulic mining in the hills. In most places less than eighteen feet deep, the bay was just too easy to fill. The lower bay was diked off for salt ponds; flying into San Francisco today you can still see the big Cargill commercial salt evaporation ponds colored red, orange, brown, and purple by different algae—though some are now being restored as wetlands. The North Bay was reclaimed for agriculture and the Sacramento Delta dammed off for big farm islands. These lands were made of rich peat that over time got used up and compacted, subsiding up to twenty-five feet below the level of the dams and the waters they hold back. Today these more than century-old earthen levees represent a worst-case scenario in which a major earthquake could breach them and the resulting mass flooding could drain off delta surface waters bound for bay cities, the Central Valley and Los Angeles and also back up into downtown Sacramento, putting the state capital under ten feet of water.

In 1959 the Army Corps of Engineers came up with another seemed-to-make-sense-at-the-time idea on how to manipulate nature, putting out a study recommending that 60 percent of what remained of San Francisco Bay be filled in to accommodate future growth, a plan that would have transformed the bay into a wide spot on the Sacramento River. This marked a turning point in how area citizens viewed their world-famous estuary.

In 1961 three women from Berkeley, Sylvia McLaughlin, Esther Gulick, and Kay Kerr, wife of University of California president Clark Kerr, formed a group called Save San Francisco Bay. With the support of radio personality Don Sherwood, Save San Francisco Bay quickly grew in strength and popularity, halting the corps' plans and prompting the state to establish the San Francisco Bay Conservation and Development Commission (BCDC) in 1965. "The biggest part of our whole effort has been creating awareness about the bay and its connection to everyone around it," Sylvia McLaughlin told supporters at the age of ninety-four just before the fiftieth anniversary of the Save the Bay group in 2011.

Along with the Corps of Engineers' 1959 fill plan, the 1960s saw numerous other coastal mega-projects proposed. Some were completed. Most, like developer David Rockefeller's idea to take the top off San Bruno Mountain in Daly City and use it to fill in twenty-seven miles of the South Bay for a new city, did not.

By 1969 the state had empowered the BCDC to regulate development on and around the bay and its shoreline. Today, along with reclaiming historic wetlands and preventing new fill, BCDC is opening waterfront parks and trails, working on issues of waterborne recreation and commerce, and developing plans for how to respond to a projected three- to five-foot sea-level rise by the end of the century.

In the South Bay the Santa Clara Valley rapidly transitioned from peaches and pear orchards to computer chips as Fairchild Semiconductor, IBM, Hewlett-Packard, and other early tech firms based around Stanford University began receiving military contracts that helped transform the area from an agricultural community into an economic engine of national and global innovation, first referred to as the Silicon Valley in 1971. That was the same year seventeen miners died in a water tunnel explosion as the California Aqueduct neared completion. Part of the California State Water Project, the aqueduct was a system of canals, pipes, and tunnels designed to pump massive amounts of water from the Sierra Nevada and Northern California's Bay Delta to San Joaquin Valley farms, the Central Coast, and the booming cities and suburbs of Southern California.

In Southern California real-estate speculation had been a driver of economic development going back to the post–Civil War boom set off by "The Associates," California's four railroad barons: Collis Huntington, Leland Stanford, Charles Crocker, and Mark Hopkins. The dry desert towns of Los Angeles and San Diego were particularly prone to real-estate booms and busts starting in the 1880s, but with sufficient water diverted, stolen, or acquired, the post–World War II boom proved unprecedented in its duration. Disneyland, a symbol of the region in its merging of the escapist and commercial, was founded in the city of Anaheim in 1955 in the midst of an explosion of freeway construction and housing sprawl, including a building boom across the eighty square miles of the Los Angeles basin that left less than 8 percent of the city with parkland, one of the lowest ratios of green space to cement in the nation. By contrast, San Francisco has 18 percent and San Diego almost 23 percent. Even the Los Angeles River was encapsulated in concrete as a flood-control measure from its headwaters forty-eight miles to the port of Long Beach, increasing polluted runoff from storm drains and roads. While the environmental implications of a concrete river may be disturbing, Southern California's founding escapist industry Hollywood discovered it made a great location for shooting car-chase scenes, including one in which a cyborg pursues a terminator who later transforms into the state's governor (from 2003 to 2011), Arnold Schwarzenegger).

Coastal change and development north of Point Conception would not come so easily. In 1962 President John Kennedy signed bills establishing both the Point Reyes National Seashore north of San Francisco and the Warm Springs Dam on the Russian River that would impound water for urban development in the same area. Water has always been a challenge along California's coast. Much of the water that feeds the coastal redwood forests and grass forage between Santa Cruz and the Oregon border is not easily retained as it comes ashore in the marine layer. I remember many years ago going to sleep on a star-spangled golden hillside in Sonoma County between live oaks and the Pacific with a young woman from Germany who commented on how *"Wunderschön"* California nature was, and then our waking at dawn, soaked to the bone and shivering in our tent in a thick pea-soup fog that had crept up from the sea.

Behind the coastal range, inland development along the drier 101 highway corridor spread rapidly north from San Francisco in the 1960s to San Rafael, to the "Egg Capitol" of Petaluma, to Rohnert Park, a planned city modeled after Levittown, New York, the original postwar suburb, and on north through the soon-to-be city of Santa Rosa that would quench its thirst from the Russian River's impounded water.

Megaplans for the shoreline region included a series of four-lane freeways or "laterals," that were supposed to connect 101 to an expanded four-lane Route 1 on the coast and facilitate its development. Water would be piped in from dams on the Mattole, Eel, Trinity, Klamath, and Smith rivers of Northern California, and cheap abundant power provided by a "super system" of dozens of coastal nuclear power plants according to Pacific Gas & Electric company projections.

Just north of the Golden Gate Bridge the Utah Construction Company planned to fill in part of Richardson Bay, a sparkling arm of the larger bay blessed with houseboats, sailboats, fishing boats, and sea lions chasing herring in the waters off Sausalito, Tiburon, and Belvedere. The company expected to build thousands of new housing units, a commercial district, and marina where today there is only a waterfront park and Blackie's Pasture with its life-sized statue of Blackie, the horse that used to graze there. Beyond Sausalito's hills, Gulf Oil and Caldwell Banker were planning to put fifty seven-story apartment towers and five thousand houses on the Marin Headlands by the Golden Gate and call their new city Marincello.

In rural West Marin a boat marina, heliport, restaurants, and hotel were planned to fit inside the Bolinas Lagoon next to a "Golden Gate parkway" paralleling a ridge top freeway that would link up together at the town of Bolinas near Stinson Beach. I recently drove around the rural lagoon and spotted about one hundred harbor seals hauled up on its mudflats.

With the Point Reyes National Seashore not delineated or purchased, the Marin general plan of 1967 envisioned 150,000 people living in gateway (park-entry) communities outside the national seashore with schools, shopping centers, and sewage plants dumping their treated effluent into the narrow fifteen-mile-long Tomales Bay. Today the bay is best known for its oyster farm, meandering creeks, and occasional visiting sea turtle. If you visit the park's present-day gateway community of Point Reyes Station (population 848), I'd strongly recommend the almond croissants at the Bovine Bakery on A Street.

Back in the 1960s Caltrans, the state's transportation agency, anticipated expanding Route 1 to a four-lane freeway running from the Golden Gate Bridge past Bodega Bay. There, Sonoma developers were drawing up schematics for a city of more than a quarter million people adjacent to Pacific Gas & Electric's "Atomic Park," which included the nuclear power plant that in 1962 the company began digging a foundation hole for on Bodega Head (a granite headland that sits astride the San Andreas Fault). In the end only Bodega Harbor, a development of 725 vacation homes and a golf course, was built. North of Bodega Bay, more than twenty retirement and second-home developments were planned to offer scenic views, coastal shopping, and other amenities from Jenner (and its imagined harbor resort) past the second nuclear plant PG&E planned for Point Arena (also located atop an earthquake fault), and on to the 5,000-unit golf resort development at Shelter Cove on the nearly inaccessible Lost Coast and a similar "Pacific Shores" subdivision by Lake Earl on the Oregon border.

In the end the lateral freeways were never completed, only the Russian River was dammed for water diversion, and only three coastal nukes were built, at San Onofre in Southern California, Diablo Canyon on the Central Coast, and a small Humboldt Bay reactor in far Northern California, which operated from 1963 to 1976.

Of course, big oceanfront real-estate schemes had a better chance of success in the already developed southland. In 1965 one of L.A.'s last salt marshes was filled in and a breakwater constructed for Marina del Rey that quickly became the largest recreational boat basin and swinging singles pool scene in the nation. The Irvine Company spent the 1960s transforming an Orange County ranch into a sixty-six-square mile planned city built around a new U.C. campus. As Southern California boomed, however, there was also growing resistance to the idea that growth automatically equaled progress. A plan by the L.A. Department of Water and Power to build a nuclear power plant at Malibu failed to get off the ground, as did a freeway through Topanga Canyon, in part because real estate developers like comedian Bob Hope joined local residents including actress Angela Lansbury in arguing this would actually diminish their property values.

In the Ocean Beach section of San Diego, an Army Corps of Engineers plan to build a jetty and replace the beach with a Marina del Rey–style complex built around a large boat basin and hotels hit resistance from a different demographic. As mentioned in chapter four, surfers rallied and fought the police on the north end of the beach in 1970, bulldozers were blocked by nonviolent protestors, and the first democratically elected community-planning board in the state was voted into power to kill the plan and save the waves, which it did.

Back in Northern California, Marin County activists helped elect supervisors who created a new zoning map dividing the county between the western two-thirds, which would remain coastal, recreational, and agricultural, and an eastern urban corridor that, despite spiraling property values, also retained a lot of green space. Later the private Marin Agricultural Land Trust was established to provide support for west county ranchers and dairy farmers who wanted to stay on their lands by trading conservation easements for tax relief, permanently preserving more than forty four thousand acres of agricultural land in one of the most expensive real-estate markets in the United States. Today west Marin produces some of the best organic dairy products, grass-fed meat, and farm-raised oysters in the nation.

Still, until the voters passed Proposition 20 in 1972, opposition to unwise growth and development was all local and scattershot, guerilla armies of environmentalists and coastal residents, fishermen and farmers fighting off endless waves of real-estate speculators and corporations used to having their way. Among the many grassroots leaders of the emerging coastal protection movement were Dr. Martin Griffin of Audubon, Dr. Edgar and Peggy Wayburn of the Sierra Club, and Republican State Senator Pete Behr of Marin.

In 1968 the Point Reyes National Seashore fell $38 million short of the money needed from Washington to finish its land purchases. The National Park Service considered selling off fourteen square miles of the peninsula for subdivisions to help raise the shortfall. Outraged, Behr, then running for his state senate seat, formed Save Our Seashore (SOS), which collected half a million signatures on a petition sent to President Richard Nixon. Former Hollywood actor and Republican Senator George Murphy of California told the president that his support on this issue would help get Murphy reelected. In early April 1970, Nixon released $38 million from the federal Land and Water Conservation Fund (generated by offshore drilling revenues) to complete the park purchase. Two weeks later, the first Earth Day protests took place. Eight days after that, Nixon sent U.S. troops into Cambodia in an invasion that set off massive and violent protests.

One of Nixon's major foes, antiwar Congressman Phil Burton of San Francisco, was a tough-as-nails Democratic leader and strategist who knew how to knock heads and get things done. He was a vodka-drinking, cigar-chomping, steak-eating, take-no-prisoners bundle of aggression who, through some genetic quirk, fought his major battles on behalf of the elderly, the poor, peace, and the environment. Along with expanding Redwood National Park on the north coast, taking on the state's then-powerful timber industry, Burton thought there ought to be an urban park to connect his constituents and young inner city-residents with the new Point Reyes National Seashore thirty miles to the north. With lots of grassroots support, he became the driving force behind the Golden Gate National Recreation Area (GGNRA), whose parts would stretch from San Mateo County through the city, including Alcatraz, Fort Mason, Cliff House, and the Presidio, across the Golden Gate to Fort Baker, the Marin headlands, Muir Woods, Muir Beach, Stinson Beach, and beyond.

In his book *A Rage for Justice,* Burton biographer John Jacobs recounted how at one point the Sierra Club's Ed Wayburn took maps of the proposed recreation area to Burton. "Is this what you want?" Burton asked. It would be nice to add eight thousand acres in Marin's Olema Valley, Wayburn suggested.

"Why didn't you present that to me?" Burton said.

"I didn't think it was politically feasible," said Wayburn.

"Get the hell out of here," Burton exploded. "You tell me what you want, not what's politically feasible, and I'll get it through Congress," which he did. In 1972 President Nixon signed the GGNRA into law during his own reelection campaign. Today it encompasses more than seventy-four thousand acres stretched along twenty-eight miles of coastline with more than sixteen million visitors a year, including many who drive to the Marin Headlands to look out over the Golden Gate Bridge and the city by the bay from a wild, windy headlands where the city of Marincello never got built.

Congressman George Miller, one of a generation of California Democrats mentored by Burton, including party leader Nancy Pelosi, told me of going up to the headlands with Burton after the GGNRA was established. Burton stepped out of their car onto gravel in his black patent leather shoes and business suit and said, "It's beautiful isn't it?'

"I was surprised because he wasn't normally into nature like that."

Miller smiled at the memory. "And I said something about what a gorgeous stretch of coast it really was, and he gave me an odd look and said, 'Not the view, the deal! The deal we put together. It's beautiful.' "

Burton died of an aneurysm in 1983 at the age of 56. His wife, Sala, was elected to his seat and fought against offshore oil and for AIDS funding. After she died of cancer in 1987, Nancy Pelosi ran for and won their seat.

One big coastal project that was completed in the 1960s would prove to be both visionary and transformative, though perhaps not in the way its developers intended. That was Sea Ranch.

In 1968 Sonoma County supervisors approved an application from Castle & Cooke to build a subdivision for 5,200 homes (later limited to 2,400 of which 1,800 have been built) along the spectacular coastline 109 miles north of San Francisco. Inspired by landscape architect Lawrence Halprin with help from the MLTW architectural firm, Sea Ranch homes and condominiums, built on an old sheep ranch, were designed to blend with their natural setting along the coastal bluffs like weathered barns or seabird nests. Each uniquely modern building used a simple timber frame sided with unpainted Douglas fir and redwood, selectively placed on unfenced trails next to solar-heated pools and a Scottish-style golf course that reflected the natural drama of its setting. Sea Ranch was soon being hailed in architectural digests and mainstream media as the new global standard for environmentally sensitive design excellence, though some locals saw it as a stalking horse or perhaps a Trojan horse, the gold standard that would open the coast to silver, brass, and lead.

Alan Sieroty was a newly elected state assemblyman from Beverly Hills at the time and had just hired U.C.L.A. law graduate Peter Douglas as his aide. Douglas had emigrated with his family from Germany when he was eight and had been raised in Southern California and in Monterey. Sieroty was also a friend and colleague of Sonoma state assemblyman John Dunlop, "and we were called upon to visit Sea Ranch that ran along ten miles of the Sonoma Coast," the now white-haired Sieroty recalls. "And these houses they'd built were beautiful and the coast was beautiful except you couldn't see it unless you owned a home there, so we tried to pass some protection for the rest of the Sonoma coast. Then (L.A.-based environmentalist) Ellen Stern Harris suggested, 'Don't just defend that area, take on the entire coastline.' So, since no one had ever done that, we threw the coastal commission drafting problem at Peter," he recalls, "and if it failed in [the state capital of] Sacramento we'd go to the initiative process."

By 1971 Peter Douglas had drawn up a bill to assure public access to and scenic protection of the coast but saw it stymied in the statehouse.

"My boss [Sieroty] got it through the assembly," he recalls, "but the day the senate was to consider it, our key senate vote didn't show. I ran into a lobbyist in the hallway who said the state senator was flying to his ranch to take delivery of a racehorse he'd gotten from another lobbyist who worked both for the Racing Association and several oil companies [that opposed the coastal act]. I called the press and they sent TV cameras to his ranch. The horse truck approached, and when the driver saw the cameras he did a one hundred and eighty-degree turn."

Frustrated by the legislative process, Peter, his boss, and his friends put coastal protection on the 1972 ballot as Proposition 20. COAST, Californians Organized to Acquire Access to State Tidelands, the grassroots group that had battled Sea Ranch for public access to the beach (now in place), helped launch the Coastal Alliance of more than one hundred statewide groups, including the League of Women Voters, the Sierra Club, and Longshoreman's Union, which backed Proposition 20.

Even though the state homebuilders association, oil companies, PG&E, Southern California Edison, and other opponents outspent Prop 20 supporters 100 to 1, they were unable to counter the state's nascent environmental movement or the public's memories of the Santa Barbara oil spill three years earlier.

"We won not with money but press coverage of coastal damage that was taking place at the time," recalls Congressman Sam Farr. "We only had a staff of three—Peter, Bill Press, who went on to CNN's *Crossfire*, and me. I led a bike group from San Francisco to San Diego, and all along the ride we'd stop and explain to people why we needed Prop. 20." The bike riders were shadowed down the coast by limousines belonging to public relations firms hired by the opposition.

Former California League of Conservation Voters CEO Warner Chabot recalls how in Los Angeles, some one hundred anti-Prop. 20 billboards reading "The beach belongs to you. Don't lock it up. Vote NO on Prop. 20!" were altered by activists too poor to buy their own billboards but who could still afford paint to read "Vote YES on Prop. 20!"

On November 8, 1972, the coastal initiative won with 55.2 percent of the vote. To prevent the commission from becoming the tool of any single politician or agency, the initiative's language required that voting membership come from different parts of government, with four commissioners appointed by the speaker of the assembly, four by the senate rules committee, and four by the governor. The commission, in turn, required every coastal county in California to develop and periodically upgrade a plan to guarantee local protection and access to the coast. This was codified in law by the legislature with passage of the 1976 Coastal Act, also penned by Peter Douglas, which gave the commission power to grant (or deny) building permits within the coastal zone, an area defined as ranging from a few hundred yards wide in urban zones to several miles deep in rural areas such as Big Sur and the Redwood Coast of Northern California.

"After the initiative passed, speculative subdivisions came to a grinding halt—dozens of ranches like Sea Ranch had been bought up. You had a lot of wealthy speculators who'd invested in these second-home subdivisions and now realized we wouldn't approve them," Peter Douglas recalled. "So they went to [then-Governor] Reagan and said, 'Help us sell them off.' So there was a huge upswing in purchases of parks along the coast. State money became available to buy these lands, since they were buddies of his [Reagan's] and he helped push that."

Under Reagan the state added 145,000 acres of coastal land and two marine reserves to the park system. This from a man who had opposed Prop. 20 and during his campaign for governor told the redwood logging industry, "You know, a tree is a tree—how many more do you need to look at?"

Today the California Coastal Commission occupies the nineteenth and twentieth floors of a downtown San Francisco high-rise at 45 Fremont Street. It's here I first met Peter Douglas. Bald, gray-bearded, and avuncular, with a couple of sartorial flourishes including a bola tie and brown cowboy hat, he worked for the California Coastal Commission from its early days and as its executive director from 1985 to 2011 when he retired following a long battle with cancer.

"There's no doubt our state has the most accessible coastline in the country because of the public's activist and outspoken concerns," he told me. "Without strong coastal commissions and local plans, you see these urban seawalls, these endless miles of waterfront high-rise hotels and condominiums in states like Texas, Maryland, and Florida."

Among many example of why this hasn't happened in California: When the Army decommissioned Monterey Bay's Fort Ord in 1993, the California Coastal Commission worked out an agreement so that its four miles of beachfront west of Highway 1 became Fort Ord Dunes State Park, part of a planned 1,100-mile coastal hiking trail rather than another billion-dollar private development.

The refusal of the commission to allow new developments that threaten public access, ocean views, and habitat has also been the driver behind a number of public-private conservation deals for coastal sites that elsewhere would have long gone to condos and casinos.

In December 1957, the family of publisher William Randolph Hearst gifted his unfinished Castle at San Simeon to the state park system while retaining surrounding ranchland on the Central Coast halfway between Los Angeles and San Francisco. A million visitors a year now get to see how this famed Californian was, more than eighty years ago, able to merge the media vision of a Rupert Murdoch with the architectural subtlety of a Donald Trump.

In 2005, after failing to get permits for a major resort development, the Hearst family agreed to keep their 128-square-mile coastal ranch undeveloped and transfer thirteen miles of shoreline to the state in exchange for $80 million cash and $15 million in tax credits. Peter Douglas thought this "was a raw deal for the public," in terms of the amount paid and the public-use restrictions grandfathered into the agreement. It very well could have been, but only by California's standards. Much of the purchase money came from a $2.6 billion "clean water, clean air, parks and coastal protection act" voters had passed in 2002. The only time California voters have not approved parkland and coastal bonds was in 2010, two years into a major recession that saw state unemployment hit 14 percent and state revenues crater.

In June 2011 the California Coastal Commission voted eight to four to deny a permit to U2 guitarist the Edge, who wanted to build a secluded compound of five large eco-friendly mansions and a few swimming pools on a Malibu ridgeline with a great ocean view. Commission staff claimed the compound would scar a ridgeline visible from much of the Malibu coast, cause geological disturbance, and destroy native vegetation, which is better adapted to brush fires than to pool parties. "You can't be serious about being an environmentalist and pick this location," Douglas scolded.

While consistently popular with the public, the commission and its outspoken leader generated more than a few enemies over the years. As a result its staffing has been slashed from 212 to around 120 people since the 1980s while its budget has grown only marginally from $13 to $16 million—well below inflation, which grew 150 percent. The commission was almost scuttled back in 1996, when Republican governor Pete Wilson and the Republican-dominated state legislature packed it with real-estate developers and property rights activists, then asked Douglas to hand them his letter of resignation.

"What happened is they came to me and asked me to recommend building nine hundred units of housing in Bolsa Chica [an Orange County wetland being developed by the Koll Corporation], and when my staff said they wouldn't recommend building homes in a wetland, Pete Wilson's secretary of resources became furious."

Douglas's recollection was confirmed by reporters from the *Los Angeles Times*. He then asked for a public hearing. By the time the California Coastal Commission met in Huntington Beach, there had been an outpouring of support for Douglas and his staff. Angry editorials appeared in every major newspaper in the state, and editorial cartoonists portrayed the state's political leadership as either pirates making Peter walk the plank or else sharks (though some shark advocates objected).

Hundreds of his supporters, including Alexandra Paul, one of the stars of *Baywatch,* packed the Huntington Beach meeting, calling the prodevelopment commissioners "cowards" and big-money "shills" until Douglas had to stand up and plead for calm. Amid boos and catcalls, the commission voted to postpone its decision. In the wake of that meeting, Sara Wan, a liberal holdover commissioner, helped organize Vote the Coast, which targeted ten races in that fall's election, supporting winners in eight of them. This put Democrats back in control of the state assembly and with that, the balance of power among the twelve commissioners shifted so that with seven now in his favor Douglas kept his job.

Coastal protection again became a big issue in the 1998 election, when Vote the Coast candidates won all their races and Democrat Gray Davis made it a top issue in his run for the governorship. When he was later fighting a recall campaign to replace him with Arnold Schwarzenegger in 2003, one of the first things Davis did was call a press conference by the shore to brag about his coastal protection efforts. After becoming governor, Schwarzenegger showed his respect for coastal voters by signing eight marine conservation bills, including one establishing a cabinet-level Ocean Protection Council (OPC)—one of the key recommendations that had just been put out by the Pew Oceans Commission, chaired by Monterey's Leon Panetta. Today, under Governor Brown, the Ocean Protection Council includes the lieutenant governor, secretary of resources, head of the state EPA, and a former mayor of San Diego. While facing an economic crisis that has led him to slash funding for all state agencies including the California Coastal Commission, Brown has also signed bills banning the sale and possession of shark fins (used in shark fin soup), strengthening the state's oil-spill response system, and supported a federal EPA action in 2012 that banned ships from flushing sewage within three miles of the California coast.

"California is a place where you can still get elected running against offshore oil and for protection of the coast," explains Congressman Farr, who has done it himself.

Meanwhile, the Bolsa Chica wetlands in Orange County that almost got Douglas fired, was sold to the state as a coastal wildlife reserve through a cooperative agreement between the developer, environmental activists, and a land trust. Still, in the fall of 2011, the California Coastal Commission denied another developer a permit to build 111 housing units on the upper wetlands. The commission's need to revisit this issue seemed to confirm Douglas's oft-stated belief, "The coast is never saved. The coast is always being saved."

In 2003 Douglas fought a strong judicial challenge to the California Coastal Commission brought by the Pacific Legal Foundation, a Sacramento-based probusiness nonprofit law firm that regularly sues the commission. The following year began Douglas's long personal fight against cancer, a battle he carried on with far more Buddhist grace and equanimity than he ever showed any politician or developer. Former Surfrider lawyer Mark Massara, who won a major Clean Water lawsuit against a Louisiana-Pacific pulp mill for polluting Humboldt Bay back in 1991, remembers running into Peter at a San Francisco Beach cleanup years ago when Mark's son was four years old. "Is that the man who owns the coast?" his boy asked. "No," Mark told him. "That's the man who protects the coast."

In the fall of 2011 a retirement celebration was held for Peter at the Aquarium of the Bay at Pier 39 with some four hundred of his closest friends and admirers. He arrived in a wheelchair, deathly thin but in good spirits and wearing his brown cowboy hat. In our last interview, during which he'd had to lie down on his office couch, he'd told me how consultants from the World Bank had just visited him after they'd toured the state "and they concluded we had the strongest coastal protection program in the world," he said with pride.

Peter credits public engagement for the commission's success. "People come to the commission and they're listened to, get inspired and they fight because they know they can make a difference."

"But new challenges like climate change still face the coast," I point out. "There's going to be ocean wind farms—more aquaculture offshore, wave energy, desalinization [plants for fresh water]. All that technology is very challenging, but that will be part of the future in terms of coastal management," he says. "This is still a place people identify as being theirs, it's a precious treasure and our job is to protect it for them."

At the aquarium celebration a proclamation passed by the State Assembly that day was read, comparing Peter Douglas to John Muir, Rachel Carson, and Ansel Adams. When the commission's new executive director, Charles Lester, promises to carry on his conservation legacy Peter gives him a friendly warning: "Don't screw it up."

"We won't," Charles swears. Fifty commission staff then go to the front of the room, some with guitars, put on bolo ties—that gets a teary grin out of Peter—and lead the crowd in an adaptation of one of his favorite Woody Guthrie songs:

This sand is your sand, this sand is my sand
From the first big ridgetop, to the Channel Islands
From the redwood forest, to the Mexican border
This coast was made for you and me.

On April 1, 2012 Peter Douglas passed away at his sister's home in La Quinta, California. He was sixty-nine years old. In the months before his death he'd left Hospice care, returned to a cabin he owned on the Smith River to write, and gone on a "vacation," touring the coast to revisit some of the places he loved and helped save.

While Peter Douglas played a pivotal role in protecting the coast, a comment quoted in a *New York Times* obituary that without him the coastal commission might collapse seemed overwrought. "Peter's strengths came from the fact he had a strong law behind him and it's a tragedy Peter is gone but the Coastal Act hasn't gone," the commission's legislative director, Sarah Christie, told me. "It's still strong and the agency he built is still strong, and public support for the Coastal Commission and its mission is stronger than it's ever been."

The spiritualist center of Summerland is today a small wealthy hillside community above 101 with views of the Pacific that might inspire anyone to thoughts of heaven. I've stopped at Lookout Park, just south of where they tore down the community séance room when the highway went through back in the 1950s. From here you can admire the ocean, a few offshore oil rigs, and the Channel Islands. There's a bronze plaque on a jagged granite boulder reading "To the west, within sight of this monument the first off-shore oil production on the Western Hemisphere was developed. . . . By 1899, twenty-two oil companies were operating wells on a total of twelve wharves.—Dedicated September 23, 1978 by the Petroleum Production Pioneers, Inc."

It's a surprisingly sultry November day with the air temperature in the mid-seventies, not a hint of a breeze, and the ocean flat calm. No wharf timbers remain visible on the narrow sandy beach, though I'm told you can see some stumps at low tide. It's almost like these restored bluffs, beach, and offshore kelp beds have been this way, unchanged and natural, for time immemorial.

We need to begin seeing our victories in the things that aren't here any-more and the bigger sprawling things that might have been had people not taken a stand. A squadron of brown pelicans cruises by just as something breaks the surface and goes back under beyond the kelp. It could have been a seal, but I'm not sure.

What I do know is that in helping restore the coast and the shore we've also helped protect what's offshore, that greater part of our blue planet that remains a wild frontier whose secrets marine scientists have only begun to uncover, to understand, and to explore, though for longer in California than most other places.

CURRENTS OF DISCOVERY

It's like living in Hawaii and working at Harvard.

—Dr. Steve Palumbi on doing marine science in California

C alifornia has some outstanding ocean features that have piqued the interest of scientists and their patrons for more than a century and made California a global center of oceanographic exploration and discovery.

These include deep submarine canyons leading to a steep continental shelf, one of the world's great upwelling zones, extensive seamounts, coastal islands, sandy beaches and rocky shores, a major south-flowing current and seasonal countercurrent, a marine layer north of Point Conception that helps define its coastal ecology, and a mind-boggling amount of biological diversity that alters north of Point Conception and again at Cape Mendocino.

The California Current was recently called "the Serengeti of the ocean" for all the migratory animals, including whales, sharks, seals, seabirds, turtles, and tuna it attracts each year. It carries cold water from northern latitudes along the shore from British Columbia to Southern California, where it flows through the Channel Islands, past L.A. and Catalina, and on to Baja. Early each spring westerly winds drive the state's surface waters offshore. These waters are replaced by the upwelling of deep, cold waters flowing vertically along the face of the continental shelf, carrying dissolved nutrients from the decay of organic matter that has sunk to the ocean floor—everything from fish scales to dead whales. These in turn act as the feedstock for great blooms of phytoplankton that create the nutritious marine pasture on which California's abundant sea life feeds.

The ocean also generates a marine layer of fog each summer. The inland sun heats the Central Valley, creating low atmospheric pressure. At the same time a mist of fog forms over the surface of the sea. Out on the ocean there's a high-pressure area known as the Pacific High that, because air masses like to equalize pressure, is drawn toward the hot low-pressure areas inland. This generates wind that pushes the fog ashore, where it's trapped between the water's edge and coastal mountain ridges, providing vital moisture to grow California's redwoods, Douglas firs, and seaside forests except where there's a geological gap at the Golden Gate and the fog pours in and over the city of San Francisco, covering it in a romantic, fast-moving blanket of white—if you find hypothermia romantic. I spend part of each summer morning looking across the bay as the fog rolls through, over and around the Golden Gate Bridge and Marin Headlands, covering the city in a lumpy sheet, blanket, and pillow of white, sometimes with the tops of the Transamerica Pyramid and Sutro Tower sticking out like errant goose quills.

The upwelling season lasts until September when the winds die down, the cold waters begin to sink, the fog and blue whales go away, and the elephant seals and white sharks return to mix with resident pods of dolphin and sea otter. In winter, atmospheric changes bring southwesterly winds along the coast, pushing surface currents northward inside of the California Current. This counterflow is called the Davidson Current and generally lasts through February when the oceanic and atmospheric circulation of water that drives the circle of life begins anew.

However, every few years the pattern is disrupted by the El Niño (Southern Oscillation [ENSO]) phenomenon. A slight warming in the mid-Pacific brings wild soaking winter storms and warm, nutrient-poor waters into coastal California, disrupting food webs and causing phytoplankton production to drop, generating famine among seals, seabirds, and sometimes salmon. Flooding, erosion, and property damage to the people of the coast also occurs as it did in the winters of 1982 to '83, 1997 to '98, 2006 to '7, and 2010 to '11.

El Niño is often followed by ENSO's cooling phase, called La Niña, which brings more snowfall to the East Coast while drying out the West. However, with additional ocean warming due to the burning of fossil fuel, there's been a measurable increase of El Niños and decrease of La Niñas over the past fifty years. There is now the expectation that we'll see stronger and more frequent El Niño activity in the future. Warmer water is also more expansive water because its molecules move faster (if you don't believe me boil a pan full), so sea levels will also rise and rise more rapidly as glaciers and polar ice continue to melt. The ocean's sequestering of excess anthropogenic (human-generated) carbon is also changing its ph balance, making it more acidic and impacting its oxygen levels.

One of the challenges for marine scientists is sorting out the natural variability and patterns of our living seas from the human impacts of overfishing, habitat alteration, and pollution when there are few or no historic baselines of information to work with. For most oceanographers it's like doing crime scene investigations on a vast and lawless frontier significantly less than ten percent of which has been mapped with the accuracy and resolution we've used to map 100 percent of the moon. One exception is California, which has completed high-resolution hydrographic mapping of its three-mile-wide by 1,100-mile-long state waters. Still it remains incredibly difficult to conduct research in an environment made up of an unbreathable, corrosive, and often frigid liquid medium with low to no visibility and crushing pressure that doubles every thirty-three feet down. These waters are also full of living creatures, many that sting and bite, and are constantly altered by waves, currents, eddies, and gyres, while both driving and interacting with the atmosphere in ways that can suddenly turn violent and deadly.

Oceanographers' investigative tools include long-used standards such as weighted lines and sampling nets, manned submersibles, divers, and boat-deployed canister samplers called CTD (conductivity, temperature, and depth) rosettes that are lowered on a cable to measure the water's temperature, salinity, and density. Newer late-twentieth- and early-twenty-first-century tools include multibeam side-scan sonar, multispectrum satellite surveillance, pop-up tracking tags, DNA sampling, and remote-operated and autonomous underwater vehicles and gliders.

Most of what we know about the ocean is what we've learned in the last few decades and the last few years. California-based marine scientist and ocean explorer Sylvia Earle likes to say we've learned more about our ocean planet in the last twenty years than in the previous twenty thousand. Still, the effort to scientifically understand the ocean off of California has a compelling history going back more than a century.

About eighty years after Ben Franklin identified and described the Gulf Stream as a "river in the sea" and only a few years after Charles Darwin's discoveries about finches and corals aboard the HMS *Beagle,* Congress approved the U.S. Exploring Expedition of the Pacific that lasted from 1838 to 1842. This was a wild combination of oceanographic science and violent encounters with Pacific Islanders and turbulent seas from Fiji to Antarctica to Oregon's Columbia Bar. Although an expedition party explored the San Francisco Bay watershed, it did not greatly contribute to the mapping or understanding of California's ocean wilderness.

It was in 1843 that Franklin's great-grandson Alexander Dallas Bache took charge of the U.S. Coastal Survey originally established by President Thomas Jefferson. In 1850 he dispatched a survey crew to the West Coast under the leadership of British immigrant and geographer George Davidson. There they began charting the shape of the continental shelf, which they found to be deeper, steeper, and far stranger than the gently sloping Atlantic's. Davidson soon became California's leading ocean scientist and astronomer as well as coast pilot of the survey that he oversaw for fifty years, charting the West Coast, identifying locations for lighthouses, and studying Pacific currents including the one later named after him (along with a seamount). He also surveyed a possible canal route across Panama, surveyed Puget Sound, reported to the president on Alaska's resources before its purchase, became president of the California Academy of Sciences in 1871, became the first professor of geology at the newly created University of California at Berkeley, and was a charter member of the Sierra Club.

West Coast oceanography's first patron, Leland Stanford, was a fierce-looking bearded man who arrived in California during the gold rush and went on to become both a governor and a senator but most important, one of California's "Big Four" railroad barons. In the course of doing business he oversaw the driving of the last spike on the transcontinental railroad at Promontory, Utah, in 1869, race-baited the Chinese workers whose track-laying labor he'd exploited, practiced bribery and corruption, hired gunmen to carry out land seizures, and inspired a shootout that left half a dozen San Joaquin Valley settlers dead after they got in the way of the Southern Pacific Railroad. This in turn inspired a poem by Ambrose Bierce that ends:

These mounds are green where lie the brave
Who fought and fell at Hanford:
O point me out, I pray, the grave
Of Leland Stanford.

After losing his own son to typhoid while traveling in Italy, Stanford decided he might want to leave a more favorable legacy and so in 1891 he founded Stanford University at his Palo Alto stock farm. He hired Frederick Law Olmsted, the landscape architect who'd created New York's Central Park, to design it. Its first president, David Starr Jordan he recruited from Indiana University. A Harvard-trained ichthyologist, Jordon opened Stanford's Hopkins Seaside Laboratory at Lovers Point in Pacific Grove the following year, 1892, which became America's third marine station. In 1916 the lab was moved from Lovers Point to China Point (after the Chinatown that had been there was burned out and its residents displaced). By 1923 the renamed Hopkins Marine Station had expanded to eleven acres. John Steinbeck and his sister Mary took classes there. Today Hopkins Station, just an urchin toss from the Monterey Bay Aquarium, appears little changed from that era with its stone and wooden buildings, outdoor saltwater tanks, old boathouse, and West Beach, where hundreds of harbor seals haul out.

In 1891, the year Stanford University was founded, Harvard-trained zoologist William Ritter was appointed instructor of biology at the University of California at Berkeley. The next year he led a summer class in marine biology to Pacific Grove and the summer after that to Catalina Island. He believed the best way to study marine life was in its natural setting and that scientists should look at whole organisms and their relationship to their environment, a field of study he called "the unity of the organism," that was later named ecology. He spent the next decade trying to find funding to set up a field lab and had found some supporters in San Pedro when Dr. Fred Baker in 1903 convinced him to come down to San Diego and meet with newspaper publisher E. W. Scripps and his sister Ellen Browning Scripps.

The Scripps family made their fortune establishing a string of Midwestern newspapers in Detroit, St. Louis, Cincinnati, and elsewhere, but E.W. and his sister Ellen would spend much of their wealth in the out-of-the-way, undeveloped California border town of San Diego where they settled in part to escape from the industrial urbanism, class struggles, and family struggles that had disrupted their lives to date. In his successful pursuit of great wealth, E.W. had alienated many in his extended family but now hoped to right that. He soon bought a large ranch overlooking La Jolla Point. In 1891 E.W. and his brothers started building a ranch house on his extensive Miramar estate that would become a lovely landscaped Spanish-style family compound and castle, though Ellen eventually relocated to a cottage in the seaside hamlet of La Jolla.

On their first meeting to talk about marine biology, Bill Ritter and E.W, both sons of farmers with a fascination for science and society, became fast friends. Ellen was interested in biology and education and no doubt impressed by Bill's wife, Mary, who was both a medical doctor and the first dean of women at Berkeley. They agreed to form the Marine Biological Association of La Jolla that summer and Fred Baker found Ritter lab space in the boathouse at the Hotel del Coronado. From 1905 to 1910 the lab moved to a bluff above La Jolla Cove. In 1907 the Scripps helped purchase land and began building facilities farther up the shore at its present location, then transferred the land to the University of California. Ellen gave it a huge endowment of $400,000. In 1925 Ritter renamed his marine station the Scripps Institution of Oceanography. Its growing reputation would help establish oceanography in the mainstream of American science.

Back in Monterey, a wild and wildly innovative biologist named Edward F. Ricketts had set up a small biological collection lab in a wooden cottage at 800 Cannery Row (it can still be visited by arrangement) and also began to introduce the idea of ecology to the Depression-era study of the coast and ocean. His 1939 book, *Between Pacific Tides,* would emphasize the need to comprehend not only individual species of marine plants and animals but also their interactions in the near-shore environment, where much of the ocean's productivity occurs. In 1930 he met and became friends with an aspiring writer and future Pulitzer- and Nobel Prize–winning author named John Steinbeck. Ed Rickett's casual, party-friendly lifestyle and philosophical musings would inspire Steinbeck's character Doc in his

1945 novel *Cannery Row*. In 1940, following the end of a painful affair between the biologist and a married woman, Ricketts and Steinbeck traveled together to the Sea of Cortez to collect marine samples aboard a chartered fishing boat, *The Western Flyer*. Steinbeck's chronicle of their six-week journey of discovery became *The Log from the Sea of Cortez*, published in 1951. In 1948 Ricketts was driving his car across railroad tracks a few blocks above the lab when it was hit by a train. He died in the hospital three days later. I wonder if his other friend and former lab assistant, American mythologist Joseph Campbell, saw elements of the "hero's journey" in Ricketts's death. Today the Monterey Bay Aquarium Research Institute (MBARI) has a 117-foot vessel named *Western Flyer* from which they launch the Remote Operated Vehicle *Doc Ricketts*, so in a sense he's still exploring.

Up until 1941 marine science in California and across the nation was largely focused on the sea's living resources—fish, plants, invertebrates, and marine mammals—and their interactions in the water and along the shore. That all changed with the December 7 Japanese attack on Pearl Harbor, after which the nation rapidly mobilized its military and civilian resources for total war. Scripps helped organize the University Division of War Research at the Navy submarine base on Point Loma, overseen by Scripps geologist and navy lieutenant Roger Revelle, a tall, personable man in his early thirties with sea gray eyes who would soon become the first oceanographer of the navy. Among his colleagues were the physicist Carl Eckart (who would take over the Division of War Research) and a young Austrian-born graduate student named Walter Munk. "Now physical oceanography, the study of acoustics, water temperature, currents, the bottom structure, visibility, all things that might affect submarine or ship operations, came into their own," Munk recalled.

While Revelle's people worked on acoustics for sonar, Munk and Scripps director Harald Sverdrup taught the navy how to predict swell and surf conditions for amphibious landings from North Africa to the South Pacific to D-Day at Normandy. Back east at Woods Hole, the focus was on underwater sound location, weather forecasting, mines, and explosives.

Toward the end of the war Revelle began to see new postwar work possibilities for his colleagues. He organized what would become Scripps Marine Physical Laboratory (MPL) an acoustics lab that functioned as part of the university but also conducted top-secret antisubmarine warfare research for the navy. Eckart became its first director. Other university-based navy weapons labs were established in Washington, Maryland, Pennsylvania, and Texas.

The end of World War II quickly segued into a cold war with the Soviet Union and atomic bomb testing in the Pacific. In the winter of 1945 Revelle was put in charge of oceanographic studies during the testing of atomic weapons at Bikini Atoll. "A lot of people from Scripps and Woods Hole came out. We had most of the oceanographers in the country out there. There weren't so many in those days." He half smiled, recalling the scene for me decades later. "One thing we did that was kind of fun, a simple way to measure the height of the waves from the explosion, was to put up poles on the beach with empty tin cans at one-foot intervals on the poles. Where the water filled up the cans you could figure how high the waves were." He went on to observe a number of nuclear bomb tests and later helped MPL's chief scientist, Al Focke, choose a deepwater site some 450 miles southwest of San Diego for Operation Wigwam, a Navy test-firing of a nuclear depth charge in 1955. The blast was not supposed to break the surface, but it did. Two days later a spike of radiation passed over San Diego. Twenty-five years after that an investigative team contacted thirty-five of the 6,800 people who'd been aboard thirty navy ships on scene at the time. Fourteen of the thirty-five had contracted leukemia, lung and thyroid cancer, and other diseases associated with radiation exposure. Three of them, two ship's officers and a scientist, had died. "I didn't have any knowledge of this, but I wouldn't be surprised," Revelle told me. "The Atomic Energy Commission was really very high-handed about radioactivity. The worst experience we had was the big hydrogen-bomb test at Bikini, which was a huge blast, really horrendous. Those bomb tests made an antiweapons man out of me. . . . No one who's seen one of those things go off ever wants to see another one."

Still, the nation's leading oceanographers, meeting at Woods Hole in 1956, helped the navy develop a submarine-launched nuclear missile that became part of America's "strategic triad" of air force bombers, land-based missiles, and navy "boomers" or missile submarines. For the next thirty-five years the navy would be dedicated to protecting its boomers while going after Soviet subs with the help of America's marine science centers.

This collaboration had started immediately after the war when President Harry Truman signed a bill in 1946 establishing the Office of Naval Research (ONR), which became the funder for a broad range of basic science of interest to the navy. Under Vice Admiral Harold Bowen, Revelle became director of ONR's geophysics branch, which oversaw oceanography, and he helped create the contract language for its university research grants before returning to Scripps in 1948.

By 1949 ONR's $43 million in contracts represented 40 percent of the nation's total science spending. ONR also provided surplus ships to Scripps, Woods Hole, and other institutions and university labs it was helping expand, allowing them to do more offshore "blue water" research, particularly in areas such as mapping and acoustics, which gave the navy a key advantage in tracking Soviet submarines. Biologists were brought along to study the deep scattering layer, the false bottoms Navy sonar picked up that were actually composed of snapping shrimp, small fish, and other oceanic noisemakers migrating through the water column. The navy's only other use for biologists was to work with the marine mammals including dolphins, sea lions, and a few whales that they kept.

"The physical oceanographers became the directors of all the stations, and the marine biologists felt like they were now second-class citizens," recalled Deborah Day, longtime senior archivist at Scripps.

Although Congress established the National Science Foundation in 1950 as an alternative source of research funding, the navy continued to provide two-thirds of all federal spending on marine science into the 1970s. Marine stations became top-heavy with folks like Scripps longtime director Bill Nierenberg, a former assistant secretary general of NATO and Woods Hole director Craig Dorman, a retired navy admiral who'd been in charge of antisubmarine warfare. Munk became a leading expert on tides, waves, and acoustics with top-secret access to navy sound surveillance system (SOSUS) hydrophones. "We had a kind of treaty with ONR, where if we didn't identify the location or aperture [of the SOSUS arrays] we could use the information we collected," Munk told me. "Still, some science journals turned our work down, saying if you can't identify your sources of information, we won't publish your work. . . . In retrospect, we would have been better off without such heavy security."

Many programs were dual-purpose, with both civilian and military applications. One that fired the public's imagination was the Navy's Sea Lab work between 1964 and 1969 in which navy divers lived in undersea habitats to better understand the limits of saturation diving and of prolonged isolation. Dozens of undersea habitat projects were taking place at the time. They'd started with Jacques Cousteau's flying-saucer-shaped habitat *Conshelf*, placed in the Mediterranean off of France in 1962. In 1965 *Sea Lab II* at two hundred feet down in La Jolla Canyon off San Diego was the most high-profile of the U.S. experiments, where teams of Navy divers spent fifteen days each living in a fifty-foot-long tubular steel habitat that they could enter and exit through a moon pool—except for navy astronaut turned aquanaut Scott Carpenter who got to spend twenty-eight days in the habitat. A Navy bottlenose dolphin named Tuffy ferried tools and supplies between the aquanauts and the surface. Navy dolphins based out of San Diego and Hawaii would later be sent to Vietnam and secretly used to kill enemy divers and plant mines. Still later they'd be deployed to war zones in Central America and the Persian Gulf.

In 1969 *Sea Lab III* went to six-hundred-foot depths off the Navy's San Clemente Island but was plagued by problems from the onset and canceled after aquanaut Berry Cannon died of carbon dioxide poisoning due to his rebreather's scrubber missing a key chemical. Reports of possible sabotage, faulty equipment, rushed deadlines, and too few resources committed to the program left unanswered questions about the circumstances of Cannon's death. Unlike astronaut deaths associated with NASA's manned space program, however, Cannon's loss marked the end of the navy's Sea Lab program. Today the NOAA-run *Aquarius* off the Florida Keys is the world's last underwater research station and is itself facing possible closure due to budget cuts. Most of the jobs in energy, defense, and exploration that were once imagined being carried out by bottom-dwelling aquanauts are today executed by ROV robot submarines, remote sensing systems, and automated observatories.

Revelle, a key figure in twentieth-century oceanography, would go on to become director of Scripps, president of the American Association for the Advancement of Science, and adviser to Secretary of the Interior Stuart Udall during the Kennedy administration. His wife, Ellen, whom he met as a grad student in La Jolla, was the grand-niece of Ellen Browning Scripps. They settled in a comfortable house hidden behind a stone wall on one of La Jolla's twisting oceanfront streets with a patio view of tide pools and blue water.

Broad ranging in both his thinking and his work, Revelle made other contributions most significant of which was his linking of rising levels of carbon dioxide in the atmosphere to industrial greenhouse gas emissions. He coined the term "greenhouse effect" in a paper he coauthored with chemist and physicist Hans Suess in 1957. Later he served as professor of population policy at Harvard. Among Revelle's more attentive students was a young man named Al Gore. Along with a U.C.S.D. college named in his honor, in 1996, five years after his death, Scripps Institution of Oceanography took possession of a new 274-foot navy-owned research vessel named *Roger Revelle.*

While not all of marine science was militarized during the Cold War, ongoing work in oceanographic biology, marine ecology, and the land-ocean interface was badly neglected even as the ocean came under increasing stress from human activities. One exception was the California Cooperative Oceanic Fisheries Investigations (Cal COFI), funded by the state of California in 1949 following the collapse of Monterey's sardine fishery. Since then it has provided ongoing data on the California Current and is today one of twenty-six U.S. Long Term Ecological Research sites off California helping assess the impact of different factors such as climate change, El Niño, and fishing on California's ocean.

In 2011 the Tagging of Pacific Predators (TOPP) project, part of the global Census of Marine Life, also found the California Current to be one of the world's great wildlife migratory corridors. For a decade TOPP deployed more than four thousand electronic tags on twenty-three marine species, including sharks, tuna, turtles, and seabirds, and studied their movements around the Pacific into and from the current, tracking them by satellite. The findings were then published in the journal *Nature*. The lead authors were Barbara Block of Stanford's Hopkins Marine Station and Daniel Costa of U.C. Santa Cruz's Long Marine Lab at the other end of Monterey Bay, the bay now being a world center of marine science.

California's postwar population boom and expanding university systems, both private and public, saw a rapid increase in marine research programs and stations beginning in the 1960s and included labs linked to the University of Southern California, Long Beach, Santa Barbara, Santa Cruz, Berkeley, U.C. Davis, San Francisco State, and Humboldt State University. Humboldt State, the most northern of the state campuses, became particularly popular among students who wanted to get back to a natural setting in the 1960s and '70s as well as the sons and daughters of local fishermen and loggers and as a result has generated large numbers of the state's senior working fisheries' scientists and biologists. Today its expanded focus on environmental studies and undergraduate oceanography courses keep it a viable option for students interested in marine studies in a setting where they can live in a redwood forest and work in a relatively pristine stretch of ocean.

Along with boasting the greatest number of marine science labs of any state in the nation, California also saw the emergence of the densest concentration of ocean research facilities in its midstate region along the spectacular forty-eight-mile crescent of Monterey Bay and its underwater Grand Canyon. Like a photographic negative of Arizona's Grand Canyon, instead of being shaped and scoured by the waters of the Colorado River, California's largest canyon is shaped by vast amounts of scouring rock and sediment avalanches from the land that settle into a debris fan at its abyssal mouth about one hundred miles out and two miles down.

The West Coast's submarine canyons are extremely active geologically and continuously experience underwater quakes and tremors along with slides of sand, mud, and gravel that put terrestrial landslides to shame. Longshore currents carry tons of beach sand, mudstone, and sediment down the canyons, to the deep ocean on a daily basis. More than three million cubic yards of gravelly sediment tumble down the Monterey Canyon every winter and spring. The canyon itself is thought to be the ancient outlet of either the Colorado River or some primordial great river that drained the Central Valley. In either case the San Andreas Fault has moved the huge canyon system north from its original location near where the Channel Islands of Santa Barbara now reside.

In 1970 former Moss Landing Marine Lab director Gary Greene took his first dive into the Monterey submarine canyon aboard a small sub called *Nekton*. Greene, a graduate student in geology at the time, lay on his belly by the forward observation porthole, his legs sticking between the feet of sub pilot Larry Headley. "We'd detected a deep hole we wanted to investigate. It turned out to be the bottom behind where a massive underwater landslide had filled in part of the canyon," Greene recalled.

We landed on the side of this steeply inclined mud and sediment dam about one thousand feet down, at the sub's maximum depth. Then as we tried to cruise along our tail began to drag. We assumed it was tangled up in a cable or something. You could unscrew the Nekton's tail section and float free, but between me having to crunch up in the bow and Larry wiggling around with the wrench, our movement must have set off another slide. I was looking out the porthole and everything suddenly went black from this big mud cloud, and we could see the pressure and depth gauge rising as we were pushed downslope beyond the sub's limit. We were trying to blow ballast (with compressed air from a pair of scuba tanks), but nothing was happening. The prop was making a loud clanking noise, and then something fell out of the rudder. Then it started to get lighter outside and we were rising and I could see the mud cloud below us as we broke free.

They dove again later that day, though in a different place. Another reminder of how dangerous working in the marine environment can be: A week later Headley was killed and a second *Nekton* crew member injured on a salvage job off Catalina raising a Chris-Craft powerboat when the line securing the boat broke and it sank back through the water column and hit *Nekton,* imploding its glass, flooding it, and sinking it to the bottom 260 feet down. Rich Slater, the survivor, was unconscious, cut by glass and with his eardrums blown out when they found him near a kelp bed on the surface. Headley had been wearing rubber boots that had filled with water and wasn't able to make it to the surface.

Fifteen years later in 1985, marine biologist Bruce Robison got to pilot a Deep Rover, a far more advanced design of a one-person submersible into the canyon. His interest was not in geology, the sides or the bottom of the canyon, but the water column itself and the little known animals that live there.

"At between five hundred and six hundred meters [close to 2,000 feet down] I set the trim to neutral buoyancy and turned out all the lights and waited fifteen minutes adjusting to the dark. And even at that depth once I had adjusted I could still perceive not light, but that it was less dark above me and more dark below and so I could tell the difference between up and down. And I could see patterns and displays of light in the darkness and they'd make sense these patterns and then there'd be these ripples of luminescence like heat lightning that you'd see in a cloud and then more sharp and distinct flashes of light. It was mind-boggling, like certain hallucinogenic drugs that people took in college . . ."

"Like an acid trip?"

"Yes, but real with these perceivable patterns, and I could see phosphorescent light all around me. These were from gelatinous animals and fish, and the odd thing is while this is the biggest habitat of life on earth, no one is following these sensory paths of exploration." Actually, as senior scientist at the Monterey Bay Aquarium Research Institute (MBARI), Robison still is a generation later.

His 1985 dive helped spark the interest of another patron of California ocean science, the late David Packard, cofounder with Bill Hewlett of HP, the Hewlett-Packard Company and creator of MBARI. Still, the possibility of carrying out cutting-edge marine science in the cold deep waters of Monterey Bay Canyon had its limits even in the 1980s.

Beginning in 1983, right after President Reagan declared a two hundred-mile exclusive economic zone for the United States, effectively doubling the nation's size by claiming a vast new 3.4 million square mile ocean territory, NOAA, the National Oceanic and Atmospheric Administration, began mapping the Monterey Canyon using multibeam sonar ships including the RV *Mount Mitchell*. It turned out the canyon was hiding more than just rockfish and luminescent jellies. "What we did was so accurate the navy submarine community felt threatened, so it was all classified," recalls Skip Theberge, a NOAA corps officer involved in the mapping project. It was only with the end of the Cold War and collapse of the Soviet Union almost a decade later that accurate maps of the more than two-mile-deep canyon system were declassified, civilian exploration and research rapidly expanded, and the Monterey Bay National Marine Sanctuary was established.

One sign of the changing geopolitical map of California's ocean came in 1990 when the navy and State Department approved a visiting cruise to Monterey by Soviet scientists who brought a pair of Russian MIR submersibles aboard their 401-foot mother ship, the *Akademik Mstislav Keldysh*. They explored the canyon with Gary Greene and other scientists from four local research centers and the U.S. Geological Survey. The three-person submersibles visited cold hydrocarbon seeps on the deep ocean floor surrounded by colonies of bacterial mats, clams, tubeworms, sea snails, crabs, and other critters that contain hydrogen-sulfide-burning bacteria that can convert a chemical deadly to humans into amino acids to sustain life. The first chemosynthetic (as opposed to sun-powered photosynthetic) life-forms on the planet had been discovered in 1977 living off boiling-hot water vents eight thousand feet below the surface near the Galapagos Islands; but cold seeps are a whole other kind of chemosynthetic deepwater ecosystem, and perhaps, scientists speculate, among the first communities of life on earth. Today Monterey Canyon's hundreds of cold seep communities include Mount Crushmore, Tubeworm City, Tubeworm Slump, Clam Field, Clam Flat, Invert Cliff, and Axial Valley, the first discovered back in 1990. That same year the Russians helped the Americans look for visible changes in underwater slide areas and boulder fields that might be associated with the 1989 Loma Prieta earthquake.

The post–Cold War political tide was also turning at Scripps, which began to experience a slow retreat from purely physical navy-oriented oceanography to a more integrated approach to ocean science. This evolution culminated in 2001 with the creation of the Center for Marine Biodiversity and Conservation (CMBC) under the founding leadership of outspoken marine ecologist Dr. Jeremy Jackson and his wife, coral reef expert Dr. Nancy Knowlton. Working with more than one hundred associated U.C. faculty members, CMBC helped return parts of Scripps to the ecological perspective that its founder, Bill Ritter, had pioneered a century earlier.

Still, by the 1990s Monterey had displaced Scripps and its fleet of globe-spanning research vessels as the new center of gravity for California ocean science (some people in La Jolla may disagree). With day boats that could get you into deep ocean water before your morning coffee cooled and a diversity of labs and programs studying everything from land-based nutrient loads and estuarine processes to climate, weather, and newly discovered deep-sea animals, Monterey Bay was soon drawing grad students and post-grad researchers like chum draws sharks.

Today there are more than twenty institutions in the Monterey Bay Crescent Ocean Research Consortium (MBCORC) that work together to promote marine science, education, and policy, among them the world famous Monterey Bay Aquarium, which itself draws some two million visitors a year.

Back in the 1970s the city of Monterey was still in decline following the collapse of its fishing industry a generation earlier. A few postgrad students working at Hopkins Marine Lab used to party in the abandoned and decaying Hovden Sardine cannery next door at the south end of Cannery Row, among them Nancy Burnett, daughter of industrialist David Packard. Her sister, Julie, was also studying marine biology and in 1977, when David and his wife, Lucille Packard, were looking for a new project for their foundation, Nancy suggested they convert the cannery into an aquarium focused on the marine life of the bay. In the course of the next seven years and the $50 million it took to build the aquarium, Julie Packard became its executive director, a job she still holds. Her engineer dad designed the wave machine for its multistory kelp tank, which remains the centerpiece of the famed aquarium if you don't count its outdoor overview of the bay's actual kelp forest. The David and Lucille Packard Foundation has also gone on to become one of the nation's leading funders of marine science and conservation work.

A corporate innovator and engineer, David Packard was both a conservationist and a staunch conservative at a time when the two terms were not mutually exclusive. Deputy secretary of defense from 1969 to 1971 under President Richard Nixon, he responded to massive antiwar protests with a memo arguing that the military should be exempted from the Posse Comitatus Act, which limits its use for domestic law enforcement. He was a key player in such right-wing bastions as the American Enterprise Institute and the Hoover Institution at Stanford, his alma mater. He was also a personal friend of former President Herbert Hoover.

While HP grew from the seminal Palo Alto garage electronics startup into a major defense contractor, Packard, its longtime CEO, maintained his integrity in both his business dealings (exempting himself from any accrued profits during his public service) and his family life. By the time his daughters' aquarium was up and running he'd had his own curiosity piqued.

"Dad was very excited about the bay's deep water," explains Julie Packard, a tall, slender elegant woman with penetrating brown eyes. "He wanted to do something major as an engineering challenge; the challenge of getting down there really intrigued him."

In 1987 he founded the Monterey Bay Aquarium Research Institute. With HP's experience in the development of robots for manufacturing and leadership in the computer industry, he decided to focus on engineering that could advance oceanographic research, including developing remote-operated underwater vehicles (ROVs) in lieu of manned submersibles like Woods Hole's deep-diving *ALVIN.* He also advanced instrumentation for sampling in the ocean and computer science and information technologies to speed and facilitate scientific understanding, returning not just samples but usable data from the sea. In 1988 MBARI purchased a converted oil-field supply boat, the *Point Lobos,* as their first research vessel and outfitted it with *Ventana,* their first ROV. The following year they started building their dock and marine facilities at Moss Landing, a rustic fishing community twenty miles north of Monterey near the local power plant.

Within a decade MBARI's main complex on the beach had grown to more than two hundred thousand square feet and it employed more than one hundred scientists and engineers including CEO Marcia McNutt, who would go on to head the U.S. Geological Survey under President Obama. By then they had also purchased a twin-hulled $22 million ROV mother ship the *Western Flyer* and were discovering at least five new species of animals a year in the canyon's waters including *Calyptogena packardana,* a clam named after David Packard, who certainly contributed enough "clams" to the effort. Early scientists involved with the privately endowed institution were particularly thrilled with Packard's unique approach to exploring the bay.

"Dave Packard said, 'I don't want you to waste your time writing grant proposals. I want you to decide what you want to study and reach as far as your imaginations will let you and don't be afraid to fail,'" Bruce Robison recalls.

By bringing scientists and engineers together to stretch their imaginations, MBARI became a leader in the development of ocean-observing systems, including autonomous underwater vehicles (AUVs), buoys, fixed long-term observers such as MARS (the bottom-wired Monterey Accelerated Research System), mechanical crawlers, and new software to better comprehend geo-biological processes.

Its sprawling two-story green-and-gray facility is located across the street from the fishing harbor in Moss Landing that used to be an active whaling port. Moss Landing was also the site of an aluminum plant during World War II and later the planned site of another of those 1960s nuclear-powered waterfront development schemes. It's located halfway between Monterey and Santa Cruz exactly where the submarine canyon comes ashore one hundred yards off the beach.

In one of MBARI's engineering shops I'm shown their big ROV *Doc Ricketts,* which is being worked on for its next expedition aboard the *Western Flyer.* Stripped of its crush-proof yellow syntactic foam hull that makes it look like a giant SpongeBob, its twelve-by-seven-by-seven-foot metal frame is a Legolike construct of waterproofed motors and electronics, sampler tubes and seven big thrusters (directional propellers) tops and sides, video and still cameras, and lights and a big robotic manipulator arm up front. In another shop with a building-length water tank they're working on a benthic rover, a one-ton bottom crawler/sampler, and in a nearby garage a pair of torpedo-shaped ten- to fifteen-foot Dorado-class AUVs are broken down on dollies.

We go into a lab with computer workstations, workbenches, a drill press, and a new AUV named *Daphne* on a rack. Researcher Thomas Hoover is monitoring another AUV that's swimming out in the canyon. They launched it on Tuesday off a Boston Whaler and will retrieve it next Monday. Meanwhile the six-foot self-directed vehicle will look to find and follow a plume of nitrate and chlorophyll while popping to the surface every forty-five minutes for a GPS fix and to receive messages and new instructions. Hoover shows us its track on his computer screen. He can also download it onto his iPhone.

"Did you find a phytoplankton bloom last night?" Jim Bellingham asks, entering the room with a few Silicon Valley visitors in tow. Jim—thinning reddish hair, plaid shirt, tan pants, and an almost creaseless face—started the first autonomous underwater vehicle program at MIT before Marcia McNutt recruited him to MBARI. "The work here is less fundamental than MIT and more applicable," he explains. "You give a system to someone and they go with it. Like right now we're looking to follow algae from bloom to bust, find a patch and then stick with it. Water columns move so to understand ecosystems you have to follow them around." Among other potential uses this could help scientists better understand the increase in harmful algal blooms. "We want every scientist to have one of these," Bellingham smiles boyishly, indicating the AUV in the center of the room.

Back out on the shop floor I'm shown a twelve-foot triangle of metal and Plexiglas with baffles and pumps that let it unfold on the deep ocean bottom to a length of thirty feet. Then for nine months they put sea urchins and other animals into the rig's central test chamber, increasing the carbon dioxide inside the chamber as a real-world test of how an increasingly acidic ocean will affect the growth and development of animals two thousand feet down. At Hopkins in Monterey, U.C. Santa Barbara, the U.C. Davis Marine Lab at Bodega Bay, and other U.C. labs they're also working with urchins, mussels, and abalones to see how ocean acidification, which makes it harder for shell-forming animals to extract calcium carbonate out of seawater, will impact California's diverse marine species and habitats.

I interview MBARI's CEO, Chris Scholin, a young-looking exec with floppy blond hair, a $40 million budget, and a Ph.D. in biological oceanography from Woods Hole. He tells me he grew up in St. Louis but was inspired to become a marine biologist watching Jacques Cousteau specials on TV. Today he's inspired by the day-to-day work going on around him. He tells me of a whale fall (dead whale remains on the ocean bottom) where there's a brooding octopus with a clutch of eggs that Bruce Robison discovered with his ROV. "He found her a thousand meters [over three thousand feet] down sitting on a rock and occasionally has gone back to see if she's hatched them and its been four years and she's the longest-brooding animal ever encountered." He smiles like a proud father to be.

He's less sanguine about the work they're doing on ocean acidification. "We have naturally acidic water here with the upwelling, but with experiments we've done we're seeing declining oxygen and an expanded oxygen minimum zone [science speak for less oxygen in the water column]. "We're seeing a decline in ocean pH and no one knows what will happen with the upwelling systems. Climate models see an increase in coastal winds so we may see more upwelling [as the winds moves more surface water out of the way]. The ocean is going to be different, more acidic and with an expansion of the oxygen minimum zone. Maybe we'll see the California Current become more like Peru's, with a dead zone below a certain depth, a simplified ocean, but maybe off this coast it won't be so bleak. We already have a low-oxygen area, and most animals here have learned to tolerate broad changes in temperature, oxygen, and nitrogen so perhaps we've got more rugged grizzled veterans of the battle with the environment [tougher urchins and abs more able to adapt]. From our perspective we have a job to do at MBARI because you can't manage what you can't measure."

Six months later I leave home at 4:00 A.M. and arrive at the MBARI docks at 6:15 A.M. There, the 110-foot *Point Lobos,* not so affectionately known as the Point Puke, is getting ready for its final cruise before it's retired and replaced with a new boat, the 137-foot *Rachel Carson,* another converted Louisiana oil-field supply vessel.

On the aft deck they're getting the ROV *Ventana,* a big orange beast about eight by six feet with its own crane and yellow cable spool, ready to dive. The tool sled on its front includes a suction nozzle for sampling, underwater lights, a big HD camera in a dome, smaller pilot cameras, D-sampler boxes made of clear acrylic that can be gently lifted over animals during collection, and a powerful pair of hydraulic arms. It's the unmanned equivalent of Woods Hole's *ALVIN* manned submersible in that it's done more underwater science work—almost fifteen thousand hours to date—than any other ROV in the world. Today will be its 3,668th dive.

A short time later Bruce Robison arrives. He has a white beard, bushy brows, unruly hair, lively gray-blue eyes, and long large ears that give him more the look of a grizzled nineteenth-century sea captain than the twenty-first-century scientist he is.

He recently sent me one of his peer-reviewed reports on how large, aggressive Humboldt squid four feet and bigger (also known as diablo rojo or "red devil" in Mexico) are expanding their range north into California's waters. He links this to climate-related oceanographic changes, including warmer, less oxygen-rich waters—two conditions that favor the squid—along with a decline of their top predators, including the overfished tuna and billfish. The inky squid, which got a lot of TV coverage in 2010 when Southern California sports boats started reeling them in, have also been killing off juvenile hake, threatening the largest stock of groundfish caught by commercial fishermen on the West Coast. Everything, as they say, is connected to everything else.

Soon we get under way, heading out the harbor entry past the last abandoned dock pilings covered with preening black cormorants and white gulls. There are sea lions and a couple of cute sea otters frolicking around our bow as we clear the channel past the MBARI complex and the sleek wood-and-glass Moss Landing Marine Lab on a sandy bluff to its south. Operated by a consortium of seven Cal State schools, the original lab buildings located on the spit were destroyed in the 1989 Loma Prieta quake. The replacement lab on the bluff opened in 2000.

Common murres, with their poor takeoff skills, flap across the surface of the water to get out of our way and a whale rises and dives off our starboard side as we head into the teeth of a 28-knot wind with white capped six- to eight-foot seas rising up around us. Bruce tells me we're headed to his sampling site fifteen miles out to do transects—"mowing the lawn" back and forth for some hours—taking HD video at different depths, then counting all the critters to be found when they review the videos back at the lab. He tells me their work over the last sixteen to eighteen years has documented that the oxygen minimum zone is expanding. "What's happening is some animals are being pushed closer to the surface because of their intolerance for hypoxia [lack of oxygen]. And these are animals that migrate down during the day to avoid visually cued predators [bigger fish above] and this could be very disruptive to them [to rise up and be eaten]."

One of the animals that might be affected is the barreleye fish that he and his crew have videotaped more than two thousand feet below the surface. It's got a transparent fluid-filled head shield that looks like a fighter jet's canopy. Most of the time its big green eyestalks are looking up for falling food and predators, but it can also drop its eyes forward toward its mouth when feeding. Its canopy skull also protects the eyes when it's stealing food from the stinging tentacles of jellyfish. In the past its clear fluid head tended to implode when nets were used to collect specimens. The ROV video of the bizarre but not untypically weird deep-ocean fish was posted on YouTube and has received more than six million hits. This is just another example of how we're discovering new and amazing life in the ocean even as we're putting it at risk. I'm also reminded of the more typical challenges of carrying out science at sea by today's seas sloshing back and forth across the rolling deck as I foolishly partake of a glazed apple Danish down in the galley.

Bruce says his research site's been worked since 1928 when Henry Bigelow of Harvard started taking water samples there. As the sun rises over the golden shore, gulls and pelicans and long-winged albatross start circling around the boat, which is pitching and yawing in a way that's giving me a familiar headache and making me queasy enough to want to stay out on the open deck and stare at the horizon, looking for a fixed point. This is easy enough since even as we arrive on site in more than four thousand feet of water, the arc of the bay shows rock steady coastal landscapes on three sides of us.

Bruce, the captain, and the chief ROV pilot huddle and decide that though it's too rough to launch now they'll hang out awhile to see if the seas settle enough to put *Ventana* over the side.

A few minutes after their decision we're surrounded by a huge pod of white-sided dolphins who suddenly appear, dozens of them rolling all around us in twos and threes, creating their own chop amid the whitecaps with their heads, backs, and dorsal fins breaking the surface and their white bellies flashing just below the gray-green water. They keep coming back to the boat, sparking excitement as a few hundred yards away a bait ball of forage fish is attracting a frenzy of diving birds, cormorants, gulls, guillemots, and pelicans. The spray off the bow is refracting the color spectrum as I stagger to the rail and start throwing up over the side, surrounded by grinning dolphins and majestic albatross and rainbows, if you can believe it, and it's the worst and the best the sea has to offer. After another two hours conditions improve enough to deploy the ROV.

One of the crew sits on the crane while Mike Burczynski, one of the ROV pilots, comes on deck wearing a headset radio and guides the deployment operation. The second pilot, D. J. Osborne, is in the ROV control room in front of the galley and below the bridge, where there are several padded chairs, control panels, and a dozen video screens, including several flat screens where they can watch what's in the water through the ROV cameras. From there they can relay the images live to "the beach," at MBARI and to the aquarium, where the public can regularly join in the exploration, sometimes with a live-running commentary from Bruce, who can also answer their questions.

Two cable handlers stabilize the ROV as the crane lifts it and lowers it over the side. They then let out yellow cable and every 13.5 meters (forty-four feet) clamp on a football-shaped orange float that gives the cable slightly positive buoyancy so it floats above *Ventana,* which is useful when the ROV is down in the canyon flying among steep walls and slopes and rocky spires.

It does its first open-water run at 50 meters for a length of 300 meters and then goes deeper to 100 meters, 200 meters, 300 meters, and so on down to a depth of 1,000 meters.

I go into the control room to watch Bruce and D.J. fly the ROV while Mike handles the manipulators. A few other folks from Bruce's team watch the screens and various monitors and take notes as the ROV cuts through the deep gray-green water. The water is full of small, raggy, gelatinous critters and stinging colonial siphonophores that can grow more than 150 feet long, as well as some smaller fish and jellies and marine snow, or detritus, that some scientists record as "schmutz." It's warm and cozy and rolling steadily in the control room and people are drinking hot coffee and after a bit I go back out on deck and get sick again.

Pretty soon I've found a more comfortable spot to take my notes—lying flat on the galley table bench. I get up when the ROV is being retrieved and watch them remove a D sampler (a Plexiglas tube with a sliding trap door) in which they've captured a pelagic octopus, a *Japetella* about a foot long with orange-and-white speckled skin and large button black eyes and place it in the wet lab trailer secured on deck.

Back at the MBARI dock, some forty to fifty people, including Chris Scholin, have turned out to celebrate the vessel's final voyage, and I'm offered a Budweiser from an ice chest and immediately begin to feel better. The *Western Flyer* is across the quay, its captain having decided not to venture out in the weather. Bruce is grinning. "We had to launch," he says, explaining their decision to dive the *Ventana*. "For the last trip we were not going to come home with our tail between our legs and"—his grin widens—"the fact that the big boat didn't go out because of the weather makes us hold our heads just a little higher."

Back at his lab office overlooking the beach, Bruce lists the reasons for the expanding oxygen-depleted zone beneath the surface "One, warm water holds less oxygen [and the ocean is warming], acidic water also holds less oxygen and diminished or increased upwelling and stratification of waters could mean less oxygen so there are three or four factors at play here."

"The common element being added carbon dioxide?"

"That's right."

"And the largest wildlife migration on the planet is the vertical movement of fish and marine mammals up and down through the water column every day, so if there's an oxygen-depleted zone in the middle of that?"

"That could be a problem."

I tell him about a talk I had with a skeptic who when I described the scientific consensus on climate change replied that scientists also claim we're related to monkeys.

"All we can do is all we can do," Bruce says with a resigned shrug. "Scientists build the best case we can present to society about what's happening in the world. Our job is finding things out for society. We don't have a vested interest. We're not looking for bad news. We're just reporting what we find."

As we talk I notice a live feed from the MARS observatory nine hundred meters (almost three thousand feet) down in the canyon playing on a small TV monitor in the corner of his office. It shows a sable fish swimming past the sand-colored bottom, and again I'm struck with the idea that we're discovering amazing things even as we're threatening their existence.

Bruce, who grew up in Southern California swimming, surfing, and diving believes Californians are more committed to protecting ocean resources than most people. "It's part of our heritage for everyone," he says.

Certainly a positive measure of applied ocean science and the state of our seas may be what's returning to California's waters after a long absence, their barking and breaching, squawking, thrashing, and sinister silhouettes partly a reflection of our ability to use the best available science to inform policy in ways that can help restore sea lions, otters, whales, seabirds, sea turtles, salmon, sharks, and other marine wildlife.

It's these other prodigal tribes of Californians I've come to greatly admire both for their inherent wildness that we're only beginning to understand as well as for their complete disinterest in our ongoing human dramas.

RETURN OF THE
BEASTS

*If there's not something bigger and meaner
than you are out there it's not really wilderness.*

—EDWARD ABBEY

t was in the 1950s that Al Giddings, Paul Dayton, David Powell, and a
handful of other frogmen, in homemade wool and rubber wet suits, with
U.S. Divers air regulators designed by Jacques Cousteau and newly purchased (or homebuilt) compressed-air tanks, became the first humans to
experience California's underwater wonders free swimming below the surface carrying their own air supply. Before that there were only hose-fed
hardhat divers with weighted shoes.

Giddings would go on to become a leading underwater cinematographer, shooting *The Deep*, *The Abyss,* and countless documentaries before retiring from Oakland to Montana. Paul Dayton would become the respected Scripps scientist introduced earlier, and David Powell a founding fish collector for Marineland of the Pacific and later the Monterey Bay Aquarium.

Giddings recalls one of his early and scariest dives, "It was 1962, about eleven A.M., boat diving off the Farallons. There were maybe half a dozen divers spearfishing in deep water. I was putting my camera back onto the boat when I heard this woman screaming. I began to swim back out. I stopped to look around and right in front of me was [Al's buddy] Leroy French, screaming, 'Please God, Al, don't leave me.' I didn't know what was going on. I thought maybe he was having an air problem. Suddenly this huge white tail rose out of the water behind him. I thought it was a killer whale it was so big.

"All Leroy could see were my glazed eyes and he heard this splashing behind him as the tail went under and then he was yanked under and this six-foot ring of blood bubbled around me. I put my head down and began swimming through this pool of blood when he popped back up, thrashing and wild, his mask gone. I dove under him and turned him around, began dragging him back toward the boat one hundred yards away.

"I wasn't going to let go if it tried to pull him under again, and he was still screaming. Don Joslin met me about halfway back to the boat. There was this panic, people trying to climb the anchor chain, and we got him up over the high side of the boat but we're still in the water ourselves, in this blood trail waiting for the next strike, which, thank goodness, never came."

French survived his ordeal with five hundred stitches in his arms, hands, calf, and buttocks. At the time people didn't know that white sharks frequented the waters off the Farallons or that there was such a thing as "the red triangle," at the apex of which they'd decided to go spearfishing. The term would later become popular when referring to the ocean waters between the Farallons, Big Sur to the south, and Bolinas to the north, which see more human encounters with white sharks than anywhere else on earth, averaging about one bump or bite every year and a death every ten or twelve years. All they really knew in 1962 was that there were big sharks off California.

Years later, following the 1975 release of the movie *Jaws* based on the novel by Peter Benchley, there were bloody competitions among sport fishermen to kill trophy "man-eaters" for display, including five white sharks killed at the Farallons in a single summer. Southern California used-car salesman Cal Worthington even offered a bounty for a (dead) great white to use in one of his TV commercials.

Californians' attitudes about ocean ecology and wildlife were also evolving. One of the key turning points involved a small white shark named Sandy. Caught in a fisherman's net off Bodega Bay in August 1980, the young three hundred-pound female was trucked to the Steinhart Aquarium in San Francisco's Golden Gate Park, where she was kept in a large tank for seventy-two hours. While there, Sandy, named after the fisherman's ex-wife, was visited by the mayor, the national media, and forty thousand tourists. CBS anchor Walter Cronkite dubbed her "the darling of San Francisco." Unable to get the shark to eat, the Steinhart staff decided to release her back into the wild, which they did from a charter boat near the Farallons. Today the Monterey Bay Aquarium periodically catches and releases white sharks when they either outgrow their display tank or start eating their co-attractions.

In 1993 California passed the White Shark Protection Act, which makes it illegal to kill or capture great whites off California except for scientific or educational purposes (an exemption won by Anheuser-Busch, the company that owns SeaWorld). That act, in combination with a ban on gillnets that trapped young sharks and the Marine Mammal Protection Act, which helped boost the population of their main prey, also helped the white sharks make a comeback. John McCosker of the California Academy of Sciences, one of the first and leading researchers to study white sharks, told me their return was "good for the ecosystem but problematic for recreational users."

It became problematic for Eric Tarentino on October 30, 2011, when the twenty-seven-year-old surfer went into the water at Marina State Beach on Monterey Bay for an early-morning session.

"Five minutes after I paddled out I caught one small wave and then I paddled back out and kind of parallel to the shore. I don't remember seeing much wildlife. It was still kind of dark, the sun wasn't over the hills yet. Suddenly I just felt something hit me. It was like getting hit by a moving wall and I don't know if I was knocked out. It was from my right side and below and there was a full bottom-jaw print on the bottom of my board so it probably hit me with its mouth open and its upper jaw hit my neck and closed down on my right arm. I don't know if my inside rail sank and I sank toward it, but somehow it caught my arm and the first time I saw it was underwater and everything was silent and I felt my body being pulled down and saw the shark. I was almost inverted as it was pulling my arm across my body so I didn't see its mouth but right behind its mouth—and that's when it suddenly struck me and I went Oh, shark! and just thought I have to get away so I kicked it and pulled my arm out of its mouth that was partly open so I got its teeth scraped across my arm. It looked like it was going down into deeper water but I just surfaced and grabbed my board and dashed for the beach yelling 'Shark!' and I didn't feel anything, which was the scariest part because I could see my arm bleeding pretty bad and it was a long way to shore with no waves coming and thinking if that shark wants to hit me again there's nothing I can do, you just feel so vulnerable."

Eric and his surfing buddy, Brandon McKibben, soon caught a wave into shore and got help in the parking lot, where other surfers stopped the bleeding using a beach towel as a tourniquet for his arm and another to staunch the bleeding from his neck till an ambulance arrived and took him to the hospital. "The doctors in the emergency room were relieved my neck wasn't gushing blood," he tells me.

"He's one of the luckiest unlucky kids I've ever met," one of the doctors told his mom, noting the bite to his neck came within two millimeters of his carotid artery.

"So that's good," Eric agrees, "plus it's always nice to still have your arm. I know I had thirty staples in my arm and then surgery a week later on my neck because the shark severed a muscle in my neck so there's layers of stitches. There's about ten to twelve on the outer cut right now and lots of internal stitches."

He tells me he should be better in about a month and of course he'll continue surfing, "but maybe not so early in the morning."

Oddly, four years earlier Eric's friend Todd Endris was attacked by a twelve- to fifteen-foot white shark off that same beach within yards of where Eric was hit. That shark bit Endris three times trying to get a firm hold, peeling away the skin on his back before it got one leg and Todd was able to kick it away with the other. At that point—no kidding—a school of bottlenose dolphins that had been playing in the waves came over and formed a protective circle around Todd, allowing him to climb back onto his board and catch a wave into shore, where he was stabilized and taken to the hospital with severe injuries.

"You tell yourself there are no sharks out there just so you're not think-ing 'shark' all the time, but with Todd and me people are complaining we've ruined that beach for everyone," Eric says. Then he laughs, "at least for a couple of months."

In 2008, a sixty-six-year-old veterinarian Dave Martin, training for a triathlon off Solana Beach in San Diego, was killed by a white shark. The previous death was also of an open-water swimmer who got hit swimming alone without the protection of even a surfboard or dive gear (some say wet suits act as their own pressure bandages).

Since 1952 there have been more than one hundred white shark attacks recorded off California's coast, but fewer than one in ten has proven fatal. It seems the sharks don't target humans as prey but will strike humans they mistake for prey. One clear example of this visual cue confusion is how white sharks in the murky waters around the Farallons—where as many as forty big sharks gather each fall when young elephant seals return to the islands—consistently strike researchers' surface targets whether they're shaped as seals or as surfboards. White sharks will also mouth things out of curiosity. In the mid-1990s a shark in La Jolla Cove near San Diego at-tacked a kayak from below, knocking the paddler into the water. It then came around slowly and mouthed her head before deciding she wasn't anything of interest. At the hospital they removed a tooth from the woman's sinus cavity, gave her some stitches and codeine, and sent her on her way. I was interviewing a number of people who'd been bitten by great whites at the time for a *Men's Journal* article. She was the only one too freaked out to return my calls. More typical was Marco Flagg, an unflappable German diver who had his whole body in the mouth of a shark off Point Lobos south of Monterey. Luckily it bit down on his tank and up on a metal navigation device strapped to his chest, making him something of a metal sandwich that the shark then spit out after shaking him around like a chew toy. "After that [attack] I had people who said to me 'Let's go kill the sharks,' and I thought that was really stupid," Flagg noted. "But on the other hand I don't feel so bad about eating fish anymore."

Judging from the two-inch puncture wounds in his forearm, upper leg, and abdomen, his doctors figured the shark's mouth was about 2.5 feet across, which would make it around fifteen feet long and three thousand pounds. Adult males typically grow to about thirteen to sixteen feet and females fifteen to twenty feet and more than two tons.

White sharks are the subject of countless books and Discovery Channel "Shark Week" documentaries and, along with Navy SEALs and aircraft carriers, are one of three things off California that the media, with its remorseless appetite, can't seem to get enough of.

California's white sharks, *Carcharodon carcharias,* likely breed in the Pacific and give birth off Baja or Southern California, though neither event has ever been recorded by humans. After birth the pups, 1.5 to four feet long, make their way into the Southern California bight, where they mature chasing fish and gaining some two hundred pounds a year. As they bulk out they become less adept at catching fish, and at around twelve feet in length, they transition into ambush predators. That's when they stop lurking around the L.A. harbor entry at Angels Gate and off of Malibu and move to the rockier waters north of Point Conception where there are more seals, sea lions, and dead whales to provide bigger, juicier, or at least fattier, energy-dense meals.

Shaded grey and black above and white below, they're perfectly camouflaged as they cruise rocky coastal bottoms and point breaks now stalking their victims from below. When ready to attack, they beeline for the surface like sub-launched cruise missiles, striking their prey with tremendous force that can drive seals and sometimes the shark itself out of the water. At the last moment before it strikes, the shark rolls a thin membrane over its eyes to protect them, depresses its lower jaw, and detaches and thrusts its upper jaw forward. With its mouth open wide, it impales its victim on its serrated lower teeth and may also saw off chunks of flesh as it closes down with its upper triangular-bladed teeth, which come in replacement strips seven to nine deep. It will then back off of larger prey items and wait for them to bleed out before returning to feed more leisurely at the surface.

Today our knowledge of white sharks—the fact, for example, that the adults will swim out to an area halfway to Hawaii dubbed the "white shark café" for six to nine months of the year where they'll feed or breed or both—has only recently been discovered thanks to dedicated researchers with modern acoustic and pop-up satellite tags. Typically a shark will be darted with a lightweight electronic tracking device (to measure depth, time, temperature, and location) attached to a small float. After some days or weeks the tag breaks free and pops to the surface, and its recorded information is transmitted to a space satellite. California's white shark experts range in experience from John McCosker, who's been at it for more than thirty years to U.C. grad student Taylor Chapple, lead author of a recent paper. There's Peter Klimley, Scot Anderson, Barbara Block, Ken Goldman, Salvador Jorgensen, Burney Le Boeuf, Scott Davis, Sean Sommeran, Chris Lowe, and many others, including Dr. Michael Domeier of San Diego whose tagging technique, highlighted on the National Geographic TV show *Shark Men* includes line hooking sharks and reeling them aboard an elevator platform on the side of a large ship, then lifting them clear of the water, aerating them with a hose through their gills while taking blood and DNA samples, cutting off their capture hooks, and drilling and bolting satellite transmitters onto their dorsal fins before releasing them back into the water. When NOAA allowed this operation to take place in national marine sanctuary waters off the Farallons, a number of other shark researchers (and conservationists) pointed out this was already one of the most studied populations of white sharks in the world and such invasive tagging techniques were not needed there. In April 2012 a twenty-year-old South African bodyboarder was killed by a white shark close to where three days earlier the *Shark Men* crew had been chumming the waters with bait to attract sharks to tag and film. By then National Geographic had canceled a second season of the show.

While white shark research is advancing rapidly there are still many unanswered questions, some very basic, such as the actual number of sharks off California. Estimates range from 219 adults and subadults—an estimate based on photo id of dorsal fins and a math algorithm—to fewer than a thousand but significantly more than at any time in the past fifty years.

"I think anyone who gives you a number is pissing in the wind—methods used to identify numbers of sharks are problematic—some sharks may not be counted if they don't visit known areas [such as Ano Nuevo and the Farallons] or rise to the surface to strike at a target," says Professor Chris Lowe of the University of California Long Beach, director of the U.C.L.B. Shark Lab, which got its start in 1969.

"Gillnets killed lots of baby white sharks before Proposition 132 banned them [the fishing nets off of central and southern California, beginning in 1994]. Also you see the prey fish: white croaker, black sea bass, halibut, leopard, and soupfin sharks coming back [due to improved fisheries management and reduced fleet size] so much of the juvenile white shark diet has recovered and much of the adult food base has also returned thanks to the Marine Mammal Protection Act. The last five to ten years we've seen increased numbers of sea lions coming up dead or with shark bites on them—also harbor seals and otters on the central coast."

Lowe says he and his grad students also have no problem finding and studying younger sharks off Southern California. "In the summer we just go out to the western end of Santa Monica Bay by Will Rogers Beach at

Malibu. You'll see them there cruising the surface, four- to eight-foot juve-
niles. On one stretch of beach we counted twelve in a mile and a half just a
couple of hundred yards off the beach. It's like Stinson Beach (in Northern
California) except you don't have the big boys and girls here. Still, there's
always some level of public concern and I remind people we don't see adults
down here. The good news is we're the nursery."

It's like native Californian Ken Kelton, whose kayak was lifted out of
the water and shaken like a rattle by a white shark once told me: "The
ocean is a dangerous place, but it's also a place you can go and have to yourself, a place that's clean and yes, wild. If you go into the ocean you're making a choice. You need to know you can drown, you can get lost, or you can
be eaten by great beasts."

Three people roll her 215-pound body onto the metal dissection table. She
was brought into the hospital alive two days ago after being found wounded
on an isolated beach but died within hours from a gunshot wound. It seemed
to be a crime of passion. Now, with a running green hose, galvanized
bucket, scalpel, and yellow rain gear, Dr. Frances Gulland goes to work in
the necropsy (animal autopsy) room of the Marine Mammal Center, a nonprofit research, rescue, and education facility. The confident, sun-reddened,
blond, British-born veterinarian begins tracing the bullet track through the
animal's neck and body, cutting away tissue and fat in a messy but precise
manner as bloodstained water from the running hose sloshes off the table
and down a drain in the room's cement floor. Soon Frances switches to
surgical pliers to extract the copper-colored rifle slug. NOAA enforcement
agent Joe Koczur takes it from her and rolls it in his palm with grim satis-
faction. It will be used as ballistics evidence to help convict the fisherman
who shot this sea lion and several others like her, criminal violations under
the Marine Mammal Protection Act.

Fifteen years later I return to the newly refurbished mammal center
with its hilltop view of the cloud-shadowed silver sea by Rodeo Beach, part
of the Marin Headlands/Golden Gate National Recreation Area. Below me

a group of middle-school students and their teachers are hiking past a whale skeleton display on their way to Rodeo Lagoon.

Inside the entry to the largest ocean animal hospital in the world, past a display of wildlife sculptures made from plastic debris found along a beach, a few sea lions are barking and a few splashing in their fenced-in concrete pens and pools although most of today's thirty patients are just lazing through their treatment and recovery, waiting for their next feeding time. Given that they can consume forty pounds of fish a day, there's plenty of incentive for the center staff to get them well and back out in the ocean as soon as possible.

Despite losses from both natural (shark) and anthropogenic (human) causes, California's pinnipeds are making an impressive recovery from past centuries of slaughter, mostly by sealers and later by a few commercial fishermen who still see these "fur bags" as competition for their livelihoods.

Sea lions are actually pretty innovative poachers. They've learned to remove salmon from fishermen's lines, leaving only the head attached to the hook. Years ago a pair of sea lions outsmarted my friend Jon Christensen when he was sling spearfishing and had a string of fish he was carrying by his side while he swam underwater. When a pair of sea lions first approached he poked at them with his spear and they swam away. A few minutes later one of the big animals charged straight at Jon through the water. He instinctively pulled the fish behind him, where the second sea lion was waiting, and the animal grabbed them, taking off as the first one gracefully barrel rolled away from him.

Based on island counts on San Miguel and other breeding colonies, aerial surveys, and extrapolations from math algorithms it's estimated California today has more than 35,000 resident harbor seals, more than 125,000 visiting elephant seals, and 300,000 California sea lions that won't go away.

Frances Gulland attributes this to "a combination of protected pupping sites on the Channel Islands, Ano Nuevo, and the Farallons, plus legal protection they've gotten under the Marine Mammal Protection Act. So, if you give them a place that's protected to breed and legal cover [don't kill them] and they still have a good food supply in the water, they'll come back." She explains this in her cluttered office on the second floor of the main building overlooking the open-air recovery pens. "Now we're seeing new problems, including cancer and brain damage and domoic acid poisoning, plus congenital defects in harbor seals," she says, "but so far those numbers are small so they don't impact these [upward population] trends."

Still, she's worried about new and exotic pollution-related problems. In 1998 she saw her first sea lion suffering seizures from domoic acid poisoning, domoic acid being a natural neurotoxin that's linked to red tides, which turn algae and the fish that eat the algae toxic. Now she calls this "the new normal." The day before my visit in late 2011 she'd seen her first elephant seal suffering domoic seizures at Ano Nuevo State Park near Santa Cruz. Still, she can't think of a better place in the world to be studying these problems than in California.

Frances Gulland was raised in Italy, where her father worked as a fishery scientist for the U.N. Food and Agriculture Organization. She loved going to the beach "and like many girls, I wanted to be a vet." She grins. She attended veterinarian school at Cambridge and later worked at the London Zoo before getting her Ph.D. studying the relationships of parasites and wildlife. She did fieldwork on feral sheep on Saint Kilda Island off Scotland, lemurs in Madagascar, wild dogs on the Pampas of Latin America, and lots of herd animals on the Serengeti plains of East Africa before agreeing to take a one-year fellowship at the Marine Mammal Center in 1994. "What kept me here is how everyone in California cares about the animals and brings them in when they find them sick or in trouble, and also in the Bay Area there was the money to fund the work in contamination [studying the impact of pollutants on marine mammals]. Plus, it's gorgeous here and there are intelligent people interested in linking up science with policy. So you can go check out a dead whale and cut it up to see if it's been killed by a ship strike and then report to people who actually make the rules on shipping and ship speeds."

Still the challenge of playing Dr. Dolittle to the ocean's wild creatures is enormous. "There's nothing in vet training to prepare you for marine mammals," she admits, having gained most of her knowledge on the job, knowledge that's since led to a presidential appointment to the U.S. Marine Mammal Commission, a small agency that oversees the animals' protection under the law.

"In vet school you learn about organs and tissues, but you soon realize how important feed and the environment and social structure is to the health of these animals."

Unfortunately five of her center patients won't make it today. There's a female adult sea lion the media has dubbed "Broadway Bound" that was rescued yesterday crossing Highway 101 just below San Francisco Airport. She had an old bullet wound to the back of her head that had also fractured her jaw. She was also having seizures and so will be euthanized the next morning.

"So why did the sea lion cross the road?" I ask.

"Domoic acid, probably," Frances replies. "It binds to hippocampus cells, and their spatial sense is lost as the hippocampus atrophies, so an MRI will likely show shrinkage as well as damage from the bullet wound."

While toxic algae blooms and red tides are naturally occurring, there's been an unnatural increase in harmful algal blooms (HABs) worldwide, along with the resultant poisoning of sea lions off California during the last fifteen years.

"There was a story with a headline Zombie Sea Lions," Frances recalls. "Increases in red tides also mean increased closures for shellfish and die-offs of mussels." There's a major die-off of abalones off the Sonoma coast as we talk, shutting down the ab diving season and hurting the local economy. In areas off Monterey it could be associated with agricultural runoff from the Salinas River, but it's also associated with upwellings offshore, so the jury's still out on this.

Three other sea lion patients will die from leptospirosis, which causes kidney failure. It's a not uncommon infection from bacteria found in stagnant pools of water or water exposed to infected urine. Also known as "mud fever," leptospirosis often afflicts people in Asia, who contract it from working in rice paddies. In the United States it's found most often among surfers and slaughterhouse workers. That may say something uncomfortable about what's happening to coastal water quality as well as to regulatory oversight of the meatpacking industry. Of course, if you're a California sea lion splashing around with your mob mates in some sun-warmed rocky coastal pool or water-filled depression turned green and brown by your own fecal waste and urine, as I've seen them do, you're also at high risk.

The last center patient not to make it is a small male bottlenose dolphin stranded on Ocean Beach and so named "Lil' Surfer" who died on arrival this morning, the result of blunt trauma. Seeing no markings from nets, blades, or bullets, but many teeth scrapes consistent with his own species, Frances believes he was beaten up and killed by larger dolphins.

While most people think of bottlenoses as the hippies of the sea, they're really more like Hells Angels, fighting, having gang sex, and sometimes beating small harbor porpoises to death for no apparent reason other than that they can. There's even been a scientific paper about the practice titled "Porpicide in California." And don't get me started on the southern sea otter, a cuddly but voracious forty- to eighty-pound marine weasel into rough sex.

The Marine Mammal Center has treated more than ten thousand sea lions since it first opened in 1975, as well as more than six thousand harbor seals, elephant seals, dolphins, and sea otters. The great majority have been rescued and released in good health. Trained volunteers respond to reports of and collect sick and injured animals and bring them back to the center where others volunteers feed and clean up after them, educate the public, and help the vets, nutritionists, and other specialists treat them.

Jogging near my house the day after my visit, I spot a sea lion lying on the small beach at Richmond Marina's Vincent Park, something I've never seen before. A woman is sitting nearby with her two dogs having already called the Marine Mammal Center on her cell phone. She is waiting to make sure no one bothers the supine animal until the rescuers arrive with their hoop nets, plywood shields, and cage, she explains. People do care.

While most releases of rehabilitated animals go well, there was one in September 2002 that will live on as perhaps the worst nonprofit fundraising event in history. A number of center volunteers and high-end donors had been invited aboard the whale watch boat *Salty Lady* for the release of two sea lions that had been successfully treated and were ready to return to the wild. Just off the Farallon Islands the first animal, named Edog, was released from his carrier, which had been lifted to the side of the boat. After hesitating a few seconds, he jumped into the water and beelined for the nearest island, where a dozen other sea lions were hauled up on the rocks. Next, little Swissy hesitated on the edge. She'd been treated for a small wound and parasites and was now in good health. She dropped into the water and leaped through the air one time before diving back under the dark green water about fifteen feet from the boat. Suddenly the surface of the water exploded as an eighteen-foot great white shark came shooting up with Swissy in its mouth. There was a furious splashing, a blood slick, screams from the donors onboard the *Salty Lady,* and then after some more thrashing it was over, the shark having quickly fed on its small prey and returned to the depths. The center no longer does animal releases off the Farallons.

Frances Gulland recalls that dramatic moment as one among many she's experienced as a California marine vet and researcher. "When I first got here I realized the breadth of issues is just amazing," she says. "You have all these newborn pups you try and hand rear [during harbor seal birthing season] and that's very intensive and then you'll have trauma gunshot wounds with sea lions so that's like an ER clinic, and then what do you do when a dead whale is on the beach so you have to deal with logistics—like I've become good friends with these folks who own a landing craft for towing whales off beaches. Also, if it's a floating whale, you might have to search its ears [to see if the eardrums are ruptured] for [navy] sonar damage, but maybe you have trouble getting a rope on it without getting eaten by the great white sharks feeding on it. It's always challenging." She smiles demurely her eyes bright with anticipation of her next encounter.

We're heading out under the Golden Gate Bridge aboard the *Starbuck,* a forty-foot sailboat captained by John Wade, a member of the Farallon

Patrol, volunteer sailors who run people and supplies to and from the islands every few weeks. It's damp and gray with low clouds, patchy fog, four-foot swells, and everyone is bundled up against the cold, typical July weather for San Francisco. Onboard are Wade's two-person crew, along with a couple from the Point Reyes Bird Observatory (PRBO), the research group that's been working on the islands since 1968, and Adam Fox, a young field biologist who'll be spending the next six weeks tagging and tracking seabirds on their largest nesting colony south of Alaska. Sometimes called California's Galapagos, the Farallons are best known for the white sharks that feed on the islands' juvenile elephant seals each fall.

Adam has just finished two years on the Northwest Hawaiian Islands of Midway, Laysan, and Frigate Shoals following a failed romance, living in a tent on coral sand studying monk seals. Like war reporters and big-wave surfers, field biologists tend to go to extremes.

The waters outside the Golden Gate are dotted with pelicans, cormorants, murres, and a few shearwaters flitting about. Two hours later, halfway to the islands, we pass the sea buoy on which several sea lions have hauled out. Until recently the Coast Guard's rescue swimmers used to practice out here, dropping a dummy called SpongeBob into the water, then either jumping or being lowered on a winch cable from a rescue helicopter to retrieve it. One swimmer was halfway down the cable when the pilot reported, "A big fish just came up and took SpongeBob under." Since then they've done their practice rescues off Ocean Beach. Later we spot the spray, rolling dark back, and broad tail of a humpback whale.

I'm at the wheel as we approach the jagged granite spires and barren humps of maintop and lighthouse hill that mark the islands known as the Devil's Teeth. We can hear breaking surf, squawking birds, and barking sea lions that are soon crowding the waters around us. I'm reminded of my approach to Palmer Station Antarctica years earlier, only this ominous cloud-shrouded, salt- and guano-spattered wilderness has a San Francisco zip code.

Off East Landing we hook up to a mooring buoy where we'll later see urchin-diver-turned-photographer Ron Elliot in the cold murky waters fixing the anchor chain before shark season begins. Years ago Navy SEAL trainees from Coronado used to take night swims through these waters to prove, I guess, that they could act less bright than actual seals.

We are met by PRBO program manager Russ Bradley in an eighteen-foot rigid-hull inflatable with U.S. Fish & Wildlife Service emblazoned across its orange floatation collar. The islands are a wildlife refuge while their surrounding waters are part of NOAA's Gulf of the Farallons National Marine Sanctuary.

We climb onto Russ's small boat and motor to the edge of the cove below the landing. A big metal crane, its bull wheel anchored on a concrete pad halfway up the rugged cliffs, begins rotating our way. The original crane was made of redwood. One hundred fifty years of coastal logging and shipping have made Californians expert at building cliff-mounted cranes and pulleys. The hook is lowered to where Russ can attach four boat-secured cables to it. We're then winched fifty feet off the water ("Going up"), swung above a landing platform ("Going in"), and lowered onto a homemade cradle of algae-stained wood and old truck tires ("Going down"). The crew has a permit that allowed them to chase seventy sea lions off the platform and crane earlier so they could bring us up here.

We load our gear onto a pair of tracked carts and roll them down a narrow rail, scattering a few dozen among twenty thousand squawking Western Gulls who occupy the island's marine terrace and hills along with mobs of equally loud sea lions by the water's edge. This is the largest Western Gull breeding colony in the world, although this season has been the worst in forty years for reproduction with fewer eggs laid and fewer chicks surviving. Some were even eaten by adult gulls, suggesting a severe food shortage.

There are two old nineteenth-century light keeper houses on the flats below the 360-foot-high Lighthouse Hill with its steep switchback trail. The guano-stained buildings are surrounded by more gulls and this season's brown-and-black-spotted fledglings, most of which have grown almost as large as their parents. I watch a couple of them, now able to fly and feed themselves, pull their necks in and drop their heads, trying to make themselves look smaller as they approach their moms, hoping for an extra feeding. One fledge who's wandered off his ten-foot territory is getting badly pecked and bitten by several adults till he manages to escape. Later I spot an adult gull eating a dead Cassin's auklet, getting the smaller bird half down its gullet then upchucking it and shaking it about before trying again. William Leon Dawson, author of *The Birds of California*, once wrote: "Much that is good and all that is evil has gathered itself up into the Western Gull." Every year at the height of their breeding season, when the researchers have to wear hard hats to keep from getting whacked and shat on by pissed-off gulls, they watch an old VHS copy of Alfred Hitchcock's *The Birds* (filmed in nearby Bodega Bay) to remind themselves it could be worse.

During my visit there are one hundred thousand birds on the islands and ten thousand sea lions, elephant seals, Steller sea lions, harbor seals, and northern fur seals. The fur seals began recolonizing the islands in 1996, the first to return since the Russians exterminated more than one hundred thousand of them in the nineteenth century. On a low rise near the houses is the stone foundation of a Russian hunter's hut. Across the water on Saddleback Island thousands of cormorants and black-and-white murres make it look like someone's poured pepper over the big guano-stained rock. During the bird breeding season just past there were a quarter million common murres in residence, seabirds that look like a cross between a cormorant and a penguin and play the same role in the Northern Hemisphere as penguins do in the southern, except they can also fly. Gold rush eggers reduced the murres' numbers from one million to six thousand before the egg collectors were banned from the islands in 1881. Near North Landing at the other end of the island the collapsed rock walls of an egg company collection house stands as mute testimony to the birds' near extermination.

Today tens of thousands of birds litter the seventy acres of Southeast Island, the forty acres of the adjacent West End Island that's connected by a zip line and several nearby outcrops. To the northwest are the smaller, steeper Middle and North Farallon islands and five miles to their west the precipitous edge of the continental shelf where the water suddenly drops from four hundred to more than four thousand feet deep and nutrient-rich cold, deep water flows up the ledge almost every spring as offshore winds displace the warmer surface waters. That's when the feeding frenzy begins for all creatures, great and small. Offshore Central California is one of the world's few upwelling zones that are among the most biologically productive places on earth.

Along with Russ, a big gregarious Canadian from Vancouver with square black glasses, PRBO's second on-island biologist is Pete Warzybok, a lanky upstate New Yorker with a light red beard, red hair over his collar, and a casually friendly manner. They supervise two to six seasonal volunteers, often graduate students like Russ's wife, Annie Schmidt, working seven days a week, six weeks on-island and two weeks off, a routine that can continue for months on end.

I put my gear away in the sparsely furnished PRBO house after leaving my sneakers in the front "shoe room," which functions like a mudroom to keep the pungent bird guano out of the living quarters (also the persistent kelp flies that swarm up from the island's rotting seaweed). Along with a well-worn couch and stuffed chairs, decorative flags and seal skulls, the living room has a large gray patch of boat fabric pinned on one wall from the pontoon of a Zodiac raft with a large jagged circle in its center where a shark bit through it. "In seven seasons out here I've only witnessed one shark attack," Annie confesses. "There was a blood slick in the water, a carcass floating, and then I saw the shark thrashing on the surface. I was pretty excited to see it."

Outside, the seabirds occupy all the barren terrestrial area that the seals and sea lions haven't claimed. The gulls are on the flat areas, including fertilizer flats. There are burrowing birds like Cassin's and rhinoceros auklets, which also burrow under most of the plastic recycled walkways and trolley rails, and other birds that nest in large cliff crevices, including the famously goofy-looking tufted puffins (this is their most southern breeding colony). There are small crevice nesters such as pigeon guillemots and ashy storm petrels (about half the world's endangered population of ten thousand breed here). Steep areas and cliff faces are occupied by Brandt's cormorants and murres. When a murre chick leaves the nest, it will tumble down a cliff, perhaps a hundred feet or more, before hitting the water, where its dad will take it out to sea and teach it to fish. After a few weeks playing penguin underwater, dad will teach it a new trick, how to fly.

Southeast Island's highest crags are home to a pair of peregrine falcons, the first breeding pair since 1933 (the lighthouse keepers used to shoot them). Then there are transiting birds such as dusky shearwaters and albatross, and odd visitors including pelicans, geese, ravens, mockingbirds, bats, owls, and hummingbirds. Leaving the house, we spot a resident gray whale surfacing just off the marine terrace.

"One day last week we saw fifteen blue whales and forty humpbacks from the island," Pete tells us as we hump up the hill to the lighthouse, whose nineteenth-century glass Fresnel lens has long since been replaced by a small automated coil that looks more like something you'd use to zap mosquitoes than to signal ships at sea. A few miles out we can see a massive Hanjin container ship on its way to the Port of Oakland.

In 1984 the tanker *Puerto Rican* exploded in the Gulf of the Farallones, releasing more than half a million gallons of oil. Aerial video from the time shows how the tides providentially drove the oil in a two-pronged band around the islands without any coming ashore. Earlier, in January 1971, two Standard Oil tankers had collided under the Golden Gate Bridge, spilling eight hundred thousand gallons of oil that spread in the bay and out to sea but again missed the Farallons.

While the Farallons twice avoided serious oil impacts, some disasters remained hidden. In 1953 the SS *Jacob Luckenbach*, a freighter bound from San Francisco to Korea with half a million gallons of bunker fuel onboard, collided with another ship and sank in 180 feet of water. It began leaking oil, but slowly over the years and decades. Researchers later determined that between 1990 and 2003 oil from that single shipwreck killed more than fifty thousand seabirds and eight sea otters.

Then there are the tens of thousands of barrels of radioactive and toxic waste dumped into the deeper waters of the gulf between 1946 and 1970 by the navy and the Atomic Energy Commission. They have been the focus of occasional ROV studies, but no real risk assessment or plan of action has been drawn up other than to leave them where they are.

From the top of Lighthouse Hill there are spectacular views of the islands, current-driven foam lines, a whale-watching boat arriving offshore, and rock formations around Fisherman's Bay that make me think of pirate treasure. These big jagged rocks include Sugar Loaf, Chocolate Chip, Arch Rock with its tall keyhole with sky showing through, Finger Rock, and Aloun Peninsula, covered by more than one thousand lounging sea lions scattered up to 150 feet above the sea. Out at Shell Beach I can see the more tawny coats of lazing Steller sea lions, some elephant seals, and a few dark-haired fur seals with their big rear flippers. In the fall, PRBO volunteers do two-hour shifts up here looking for blood slicks in the water in order to record shark attacks on the seals.

Heading back down the trail, we find the small black eviscerated body of a dead pigeon guillemot taken out by a peregrine. Over the constant cacophony of sea lions and gulls we can also hear the high-pitched wasplike whine of another guillemot hidden in the rock face of the hill.

Back down on the flats, a science team from the U.S. Fish and Wildlife Service, Cathy Johnson and Kevin Aceituno, have set up a sampling lab in the front room of the old Coast Guard house. The PRBO crew have brought them week-old abandoned eggs from around the powerhouse, carpentry shop, and other structures that they're carefully opening with surgical scissors and whose putrid contents they're then pouring into brown bottles that they will forward to a lab to sample for lead from paint or other possible sources of contamination. Looking out the window, I spot the spray and rolling back of another whale.

The next day I follow along as Pete shows Adam how they collect and tag birds. Two stubby-winged puffins fly past us below the cliffs near Sea Lion Cove. One of them is carrying a pair of small fish in its orange lobster claw of a beak. We look up and see another clownlike face checking us out from a crevice and then more of the squat birds, all orange, white, yellow, black, and red with white tufts like Einstein's hairdo, clinging to the cliffs farther up. "They're our celebrity birds," Pete explains. "Once the tourist boats spot them they move on and start looking for whales."

We head over to a rock pile that has become a nesting site for burrowing birds and also the site of some of the bird boxes the researchers set up to make it easier to study their subjects. "We're going to see who's home," Pete explains as we scramble along the cliff edge. I look over the side to see a huge gray elephant seal in the water staring up at me with big gooey doll eyes, pupils the size of tablespoons for finding squid in dark waters up to a mile deep. They feed in Alaska, then return here to molt and breed. The big harem bulls, the beach masters with trunklike proboscis, can grow up to twenty feet and weigh four tons. These are not the animals the sharks mess with. It took nineteenth-century Yankee sealers and whalers to wipe out California's northern elephant seal population, killing them off for their oil-rich blubber. Only a single colony of between twenty and one hundred survived the onslaught far south on Guadalupe Island in Baja. Naturalists from the Smithsonian Museum spotted eight of them there in 1892 and proceeded to shoot seven for specimens to take back with them. It was from that single isolated colony that more than 120,000 elephant seals have returned to California.

A bull sea lion, more than eight hundred pounds, is on the bluff above the larger elephant seal, up on his front flippers, thick-necked head thrown back to the sun, posing like a Venice Beach muscleman, so I take his picture.

Pete lifts a board over a nest site. "One way to identify who's in is that storm petrels have a strong musky scent," he explains. He reaches in and pulls out a dark pigeon guillemot chick that smells more like a parakeet. He puts it in a red bag and weighs it with a bar scale, keeping his free hand under the bag so the chick's protected. It weighs 378 grams, just over thirteen ounces. Adam retrieves a chick that is only 254 grams. "Okay, still somewhat small. They should fledge around four hundred and fifty in a good year," Pete explains. They pull the flapping little fuzz balls out of the bags and put them back in their rock burrows.

Another downy gray guillemot chick weighs 322 grams, just over eleven ounces. "You compare growth curves and it reflects ocean productivity," Pete explains, writing in his yellow field notebook. "Productivity is not as high as last year. The krill is good. The [krill-eating] whales and Cassin's auklets are happy, but forage fish [which also feed on krill] dropped out early and all the other birds depend on the fish," he says, weighing another chick.

"So the pattern's disrupted?" I ask.

"It used to be a big krill year meant a big fish year, but things don't seem to be working out as well now. These [fish eating] guillemots can lay two eggs in a season. But the second chicks all died this year."

Adam bags and weighs another chick and we move on. Pete checks an empty nest. "He's fledged, he's gone. He was fully feathered yesterday." On the rock next to the nest is a small dead chick, flattened out where a gull got to it, one of those second chicks of the season. On the other side of the rubble pile a chick weighs in at a healthy 440 grams. "See. That's a good weight. He's been getting fed more." Pete grins like a proud uncle. He spreads its wing out to show Adam how its feathers are developing, then bands the little bird with a pliers with multiple size holes for crimping metal leg bands so there's some room left on the skinny bird legs. The biggest crimping hole, four, is for pigeon guillemots—Cassin's auklets are size three and for tiny ashy storm petrels there's size one, which looks like you could fit it around a large sewing needle. All bird bands have prefix and suffix numbers. This bird's new id is 884-02478. Guillemots live twelve to fifteen years on average, though they've recorded one that lived twenty-three years. One Western gull banded on the island has lived for thirty-four years but hasn't been spotted this year.

A pigeon-sized adult guillemot—black body, white wing patch, and vermillion legs—is standing nearby with a small Cabezon, a juvenile rockfish, in its lipstick-bright vermillion-lined beak, waiting for us to leave so it can feed its chick.

Pete weighs another chick. "Want to try banding it?" he asks Adam. Adam bands the bird. I videotape it.

"How was it?" I ask.

"It was great. He was very cooperative," he says, giving credit to the bird.

The next chick I get to weigh (I've done this before). It's 350 grams in its flopping bag. I pull it out, careful to hold its wings together in my hand, a warm fluff ball with a strong, rapid heart. I disentangle one of its claws from the bag, then place it down through the roof of its artificial burrow, where the little guy scurries back into the depths.

Next we look for rhinoceros auklets. "This one has fledged," Pete announces at a bird box nest with four thin, silvery fish out front, sardinelike saury that mom or dad must have brought home to find junior had already flown the coop.

While the bird boxes are great research tools, they are also warmer than natural rock burrows. This wasn't a problem until things started heating up. The bird observatory has documented that the highest recorded temperatures on the islands have increased four degrees Fahrenheit over the last four decades.

"We've also seen a big jump in the frequency of extreme heat events," Pete notes. "One day we had a heat triage where we could be losing birds in those boxes, so we put plywood shades on the boxes in light gray colors [to reflect heat] and built an air gap [vent] that seemed to work, so now we're looking to redesign all the boxes."

"We're really trying to figure out how climate change is impacting normal variation," Russ tells me back at the house. "Cassin's auklets, for example, are krill eaters. So eating lower on the food chain they are a key indicator for species response to things like El Niño events. In 2005 they went to zero, a complete breeding failure after thirty-five years [of being observed]. The jet stream shifted so the winds didn't drive the upwelling—they just didn't happen that year, and in 2006 they failed again.

"In 2010 there was more productivity but overall their population has declined," Pete adds. "We're seeing rising temperatures, changing ocean conditions, and more extreme variation with higher highs and lower lows. Patterns are now changing from the first thirty-five years we were here.

Krill and forage fish that tracked each other [matching patterns of productivity] now seem to be responding differently."

What they're telling me is consistent with what I've heard in Antarctica, Australia, Fiji, New York, and Florida, where scientists have shown me how climate change that's already under way is disrupting key species relationships to each other and to their habitats from polar ice to salt marshes to coral reefs and now, apparently, California's ocean upwelling zone.

That evening we form a posse, the eight humans on the island equipped with low-light orange headlamps, hand radios, towels, glassine bags, swabs, and vials full of some kind of DNA preservative. We leave the house and enter a world of darkness and amplified noise with one hundred thousand riotous birds squawking all around us. The FWS team will be taking feather samples from the gull fledges for mercury testing while the PRBO crew will be taking DNA samples as part of a new screening process that can test for the presence of thousands of avian viruses all at once. The San Francisco State lab that described the SARS virus is involved, and seabirds are an unknown vector for viruses so this could be pretty interesting research—*CSI Farallons.*

"We'll be swabbing the birds' cloaca with large Q-tips," Russ explains.

"That's the bird's butt?" I ask.

"Yes, bird butt."

Of course as soon as we've left the trail people start telling ghost stories—mainly about the Aleut slave woman whom the Russians brought here during the seal hunts and who's been seen about the houses or else felt when people wake up with a heavy weight on their chests. At the carpentry shop they throw a towel over the first of fifty birds to be sampled and plucked. The gull fledge is wrapped securely and held bottom up so the researchers can take some white poo-like sample from his cloaca. They then break the swab tip off in the small vial and seal it. The fledge is then taken over to Kevin, who plucks four feathers from his chest and hands them to Cathy for bagging. Then the bird's released where it was caught. "We might say none the worse for wear," Cathy claims, though the bird might not agree. Soon they've got five birds processed and move on toward the greenhouse. Pete shows me a Cassin's auklet (already sampled on another night) and a rhinoceros auklet in its burrow that, sure enough, has a distinctive horn on its beak.

The group is starting to break up in the dark with two people heading upslope with a flashlight and towel, their voices fading into the squawking cacophony of thousands of gulls, some now taking flight.

"This is bad. This is what the birds want us to do, to separate," I warn Kevin and Cathy, who give me an odd look.

"He's the size of an adult," Russ complains, trying to get a struggling fledge wrapped up in a towel. It poops on his pants leg, then calms down. Soon seven more birds have been sampled. With seven working researchers and one reporter flashing a camera in their faces, things soon take on a production-line efficiency. I can see how the gold rush eggers with their multipocketed vests would have been able to sweep an area quickly and move on. We head north past the houses and down the trail to capture more fledges by Sea Lion Cove, where the loud pinniped party never ends.

Gulls are flying all about and one brushes my hair with its wings at the same instant a rhinoceros auklet slams into my ankle, rushing across the trail. The bird captures continue in rocky fields and up steep hillsides with some slipping and sliding involved.

The FWS team has its forty samples, but the PRBO crew would like fifty, so they start grabbing adult gulls. Some birds fly off as the towel wranglers try to corral them. The last three gulls are caught and the count completed just as we get back to the house. Inside, Annie shows off the black-and-blue mark on her left arm where a gull bit her. Volunteer Jen Aragon has her leg up on a chair in the kitchen with an ice pack on the bump where she fell diving after a fledge. I mention how it started to feel like a hunting party toward the end. "But fair," Pete insists. "I'd like to see some elk hunters throwing towels over their prey."

Before calling it a night, the PRBO staff take their seats around the kitchen table as Russ brings out the daily journal. Along with scientific data the bird observatory has been collecting anecdotal evidence of changes on the islands every evening since 1967.

Tonight's comments from the researchers include the fact all the first fledges from the Western gulls are now able to fly. Steller sea lions, harbor seals, fur seals, and a gray whale were seen today. Pete reports seeing fifteen Risso's dolphins and also a sport fisherman reported seeing a leatherback (the largest of all sea turtles) over by the central island, which sparks everyone's interest. Among transient or unusual birds seventy-four sooty shearwaters and sixty-three pelicans were sighted, also one peregrine, two elegant terns, an oriole, a robin, and a mockingbird.

Russ asks if there were any boat incidents.

"We keep track of sightseeing and sportfishing boats that come around," Pete explains. There was no unusual boat activity today.

Tragically there will be a major boating incident the following year during the annual Full Crew Farallones Race around the islands, a race that dates back to 1907. On a rough spring day, April 14, 2012, with ten- to fifteen-foot seas and 25 knot winds, a thirty-eight-foot sailboat, *Low Speed Chase,* coming close around Southeast Island was hit by two waves that knocked seven of its eight-person crew into the water and drove the boat ashore, putting it over on its side. The Coast Guard rescued three of its crew and retrieved one body while four others were lost to the sea. In a disturbing coincidence, two weeks later four sailors were killed when their thirty-seven-foot sailboat was destroyed when it struck the rocks on one of Mexico's Coronado Islands off San Diego, during the annual Newport to Ensenada Race that's been going on for more than sixty-five years. There's an old sailor's saying that seems appropriate: "What the sea wants the sea will have."

"Any island dreams?" Russ asks his compatriots around the table. No one's had any.

"Island dreams usually have two common themes," he later tells me. "One is the island is being invaded—houses are floating ashore or kids running around suburban streets or else wolves or some other predator that could mess up the ecosystem show up. The second kind are anxiety dreams of messing up the data and fieldwork as the volunteers who make it out here really want to do good studies."

Before leaving the next day, I take a walk past Sea Lion Cove with Russ.

Down where they tore out the old rail line three sea lions are paddle walking along the sandy track like they're on their way to an afternoon tea and sardine party. Suddenly a sea lion on the edge of the cliff looks our way and starts to panic though we're well clear of him. A wave of anxiety ripples through the mob as Russ and I crouch down low on the path so as not to cause a stampede to the water during which animals could get crushed. A couple of hundred sea lions on the cliff are now bobbing their heads up and down together to see what's going on. After a few minutes of mass bobble heading and nervous barking the mob settles back down. Still keeping low, we make our way over a rise and behind a rock ledge where they can't see us.

The ride back to the mainland proves unusually calm and clear so that I can see both the islands behind us and the Golden Gate ahead and below us tens of thousands of sea nettles, big brown jellyfish sliding past.

Going under the Golden Gate, I keep an eye out for harbor porpoises that have begun to resettle the bay, the first time they've been seen here in more than sixty-five years. Despite findings by marine scientists about the impacts of pollution and climate change on California's living seas, days like this still give me hope. Exhilarated by my Farallons encounters, I look forward to my next adventure traveling the length of California's golden shore.

THE URBAN COAST

Walk there all day you shall see nothing
that will not make part of a poem.

—"Point Joe" by Robinson Jeffers

C hoosing whether to head up or down the coast of California, my first instinct would be to head out, beyond the shore break to the best surf, around the points for the good winds, and below the surface for the best dives. I've got a friend, Roz Savage, who twice headed out the Golden Gate in her twenty-three-foot rowboat—brought back the first time by a Coast Guard rescue helicopter—before becoming the first woman to row solo across the Pacific and the Indian Oceans (having already rowed the Atlantic). Another friend, Margo Pellegrino, paddled her small outrigger canoe from Seattle to San Diego in the summer of 2010 and got to see California from the sea, although much of it appeared to be made of fog, she says. Still, she and June Barnard, her land-support truck driver, had some great stories to tell by the end of their journey. "One goes not so much to see as to tell afterwards," John Steinbeck once claimed. So why not start at the bottom of this story and work my way north?

About two hundred feet short of where the old U.S.-Mexican border fence reaches the Pacific Ocean, its top beam has fallen away, leaving just a picket line of upright steel poles marching into the sea. Some of them are twenty feet high; others have sunk deeper into the sand but are still tall enough for the seagulls to perch on. The bottoms of the last forty or so beyond the high-tide line are encrusted with barnacles, seaweed, and mussels. I walk up to the fence. On my side there are miles of empty curving beach running along the Tijuana Slough National Wildlife Reserve, a kind of DMZ with shorebirds including snowy plovers, least terns, a rookery of brown pelicans, and an H-60 military helicopter circling overhead.

It's just another Sunday at the beach in Playa Tijuana, with hundreds of beachgoers enjoying the blue-sky day, parents taking their kids into the two-foot shore break, a girl in a wet suit heading out with a bodyboard. Someone's playing a boom box. A couple of guys kicking a volleyball around watch me curiously as I take photographs while other folks kick back with beers and snacks at shoreside cantinas below a string of condominiums.

A green-and-white border patrol jeep comes charging down from a bluff and across the sand, pulling to a stop next to me.

"Sir. Would you please stay north of the secondary fence," the agent behind the wheel suggests authoritatively. I tell him I thought this was still U.S. territory and he agrees it is but says he'd still like me to stay behind the newer $700 million fence line that terminates above the beach by a paved patrol road. On the older fence they've hung metal signs in English and Spanish reading "Danger, objects underwater." They'll soon begin construction on a new waterfront fence extending three hundred feet into the surf.

"Makes you wonder who's afraid of who." my friend Jon says when I return to where he's waiting for me a few hundred yards up the beach. It has taken us several hours to get here. We started about three miles north at Seacoast Drive in Imperial Beach, a scruffy border town with cheaply built condos and an unobstructed view of the Tijuana bullring just past the border fence.

We walk along a sand berm onto the beach, where dead crabs and lobster tails are scattered among the windblown wrack of dried kelp and plastic. Offshore, dozens of pelicans were diving on a bait ball. Some years ago the United States gave Tijuana a sewage treatment plant to deal with the raw sewage that was flowing through the slough here. That plant, like San Diego's, does not use secondary treatment systems (San Diego has operated under an EPA waiver for more than thirty years). Instead it dumps its human waste offshore. San Diego's pipe dumps its waste 3.25 miles offshore in six hundred feet of water. Tijuana's pipe goes out 2.5 miles and dumps in 250 feet of water. Add to that Tijuana's rapid population growth, and the result is high fecal coliform bacterial counts and frequent beach closures along the border.

A mile short of the border we hit the Tijuana River on a fast outgoing tide. Jon wades in to midcalf but the cold, surging water threatens to knock him off his feet. We decide to backtrack and approach from the old Border Park. We drive along tarmac and dirt roads past horse ranches and stables, dusty sheep, dried-out sage bushes, and nurseries selling palm trees. We stop at the main Border Patrol station, where an agent tells us the park is closed and we should call the sector commander and arrange to come back tomorrow "if you don't want to get harassed by the agents down there."

We keep going through more scrub, coyote brush, oak, and pinion pines till we hit a dirt parking lot and locked gate where a U.S. Fish and Wildlife agent in a four-by-four truck tells us the park is only closed to vehicles. Hikers and horses are still allowed. He gives us a map. I notice he has a shotgun and M4 assault rifle in easy reach of the driver's seat. It's 1.5 miles to the beach past the old abandoned glass-and-cinderblock state park kiosk where they used to collect $5 per vehicle. We walk under tall surveillance towers with arrays of video, low-light imaging, and other sensors, part of a high-tech "virtual fence" that a 2010 Government Accounting Office (GAO) report said was mostly a waste of money. We then get onto a horse trail that takes us down to the beach and the fence by the bullring.

On our way back we climb up the bluff to the picnic area, its rusting barbeque stands now fringed by dry scrub and weeds breaking through its cracked asphalt. Unchanged is the sweeping coastal vista north to Imperial Beach and Point Loma jutting out into the Pacific like a prow at the top of the bay that's bracketed by Interstate 5 on its east side and the Silver Strand to the west. The Silver Strand is a narrow shale uplift that stretches north to Coronado Island on the harbor and includes some upscale gated communities, navy boats, and a SEAL compound. A second Border Patrol jeep shoots past us, leaving a rooster tail of dust while two more helicopters circle loudly overhead.

I remember when the border was much more porous with sections of fence full of cut-and-rewired man-sized holes and other sections made from old Vietnam surplus landing pads that you could scale with a painter's ladder. As the border has tightened up much of the action has moved east to Arizona. Some has also gone offshore with people being smuggled up the coast by small boat. The following night I go out on a Coast Guard migrant patrol, something more commonly associated with their Caribbean operations.

We meet at their air station on Harbor Drive near downtown at 1:30 A.M. The last time I was here I was working on my Coast Guard book, *Rescue Warriors,* and they were practicing "aerial use of force." We flew a couple of H-60 Jayhawk helicopters offshore to the navy's rugged San Clemente desert island where they did live-fire training from the hovering helos, both daylight and night-fire with M14 rifles equipped with laser sights and night-vision targeting systems. In between we landed in a whirlwind of dust and I accompanied their trainer through the rocky landscape of cactus, sand, and creosote to the silhouette targets that needed replacing, checking ourselves for cactus sticklers before reboarding the aircraft.

This time I'm boarding a thirty-three-foot Defender boat with Lt. JG

Sean Groark, the bearded and shaven-headed coxswain BM2 Omar Rose, BM3 Kenneth Hall, and BM1 Chuck Ashmore, whom I first met when he was running a security patrol on San Francisco Bay six months after 9/11. There's been a dramatic increase in maritime people smuggling along the border, they tell me, with more than seven hundred interdicted at sea in just the last year. "With the land clampdown you see a big increase in water-borne smuggling," Sean explains. "It's like a balloon where if you squeeze one end another expands. So now we're seeing more offshore pangas [small Mexican boats]."

We pull off the dock, then return ten minutes later for the night-vision goggles someone forgot. I grab one of the four cushioned hydraulic chairs in the cabin while Omar gets on the radio to report we're on an LE (law enforcement) patrol.

"Roger," their sector command responds.

They go through their GYR, Green, Yellow, Red safety brief for the patrol that will run between the border and Torrey Pines State Park in North County, giving agreed numbers for supervision, planning, environment (foggy with two- to three-foot night seas), crew selection, and mission complexity. They come up with a total of fifteen, meaning they're good to go. Any number greater than twenty-five becomes a challenge. They're told there is a "Mike" boat being run by Immigration and Customs Enforcement (ICE) on patrol along with some possible targets but no air cover tonight. There's a report from a National Guard vehicle ashore of a vessel DIW (dead in the water) off Torrey Pines Beach.

"Be hard to find in the fog," Omar predicts. "Coming up," he adds, pushing the throttle forward and bringing the rigid-hull boat's triple-three hundred horsepower outboard engines up to 35 knots as we speed across the harbor and past Point Loma lighthouse with its beautiful keeper's house where the sector commander gets to live.

Outside we hit those two- to three-foot seas and start bumping and bottoming out, at one point going airborne as we surge north. While the Defender can do more than 50 knots Omar opts to wind it back and spare us a bruising.

"Getting FLIR (forward-looking infrared radar) on it. It's unlit two miles west of Torrey Pines," Sector radios, relaying field intelligence from the National Guard truck.

"We've got a close contact on radar without lights," Ken Hall reports.

"Could be the Mike," the immigration enforcement boat, Chuck notes just as they light us up with a high-intensity spotlight.

"Nice going," Omar mumbles. It would be hard for an observer nearby to miss the distinct profile and orange color of a Coast Guard special-purpose boat when it's floodlit like this. They turn their light off as we approach. There are three of them in an open go-fast boat with a cloth Bimini top in lieu of a cabin, very *Miami Vice*, but not where I'd want to spend a cold foggy night offshore. They tell us they'll patrol south since we have this one covered. To our right half a dozen bottlenose dolphins surface next to us, a curious clan gamboling by our boat, before we surge away from them.

I can see why there have been a number of migrant drop-offs at Torrey Pines, home to the last few thousand wind-sculpted trees of the same name. It's the only dark stretch of coast along the lit-up beach and cliff-top communities north of La Jolla.

"Actually we've been finding people doing landings at Del Mar, Solana Beach, this whole area," Sean tells me, "all the way up to L.A. and Dana Point even."

Within a few months the smugglers will move farther out to sea and land people (and drugs) farther north to avoid detection. This will include fifteen Mexican migrants found stranded on Santa Cruz Island off Santa Barbara. At four times the size of Manhattan, Santa Cruz is the largest of the Channel Islands and the smugglers may have mistaken it for the mainland.

We begin searching for the mystery vessel with little luck. Sector reports the FLIR has lost it. The crew searches with a night-vision scope and lets me look through it at what becomes a bright emerald sea with green buildings and flaring land lights by a beach and coastal road but no boat. We spot a flashing light that turns out to be a NOAA science buoy. Sector says we're a mile southwest of the boat we still can't locate.

"No joy, huh?" Chuck asks ninety minutes into our search.

"Nah, nothing on radar," Ken replies. The land unit has a scope on the boat and is trying to vector us into it via Sector Command.

We're less than six hundred yards offshore at this point.

"Keep heading northeast," Sector directs.

"We want to inform you there's not a lot of east left us," Ken responds.

"They [the land unit] want to know where you are. Is there a landmark you can give us?"

They give Sector longitude and latitude while Chuck pulls out his iPhone and uses its GPS to determine our position. "We're off 10th Street by that shopping strip in Del Mar."

"Head due south," we're instructed. "You're on a good line right now."

Soon we spot a glow low in the water and then a twenty-five-foot dory-type open boat that appears to be empty. As we approach we can see two rubber boots propped up on the gunnels. The Coasties energize their flashing blue lights and turn on a spotlight and a sleepy couple, a man and his wife in full rain gear and boots, groggily stand up. They're licensed commercial fishermen with several poles in the water waiting for dawn to see if they've caught any white sea bass. After a brief conversation the crew reports to Sector. It's now 5:00 A.M.

"What's your intention?" Sector wants to know.

"We'll patrol the area and intercept any northbound traffic," Omar replies wearily. It took us more than two hours to locate a boat that had already been spotted, wasn't trying to avoid us, and wasn't going anywhere. This crew is looking for fast-moving needles in a liquid haystack, I think. It's hard for people who don't spend a lot of time at sea to realize how vast it really is. The Pacific alone covers one-third of the planet. This favors smugglers and pirates. If you don't want to get caught, move by night and cover your boat with a blue tarp during the day. Omar shows me the FLIR on his console that can display a ghostly white image of the seas but only for three-quarters of a mile out.

I go out on the back deck for some cool air and listen to the water lapping on our hull before we get under way again. We thump up to Cardiff-by-the-Sea and then turn around. Omar plans to be at the harbor entry at dawn to see who might be trying to get in while the morning fishing boats are heading out.

"Excellent plan. Shows you're being aggressive," Chuck declares with a barking enthusiasm designed to at least keep us awake if the sliding and thumping of the waves doesn't. We bang our way south. I brace my legs to lift out of the chair without hitting my head on the metal roof each time we bottom out. We finally slow down in the predawn gray by the harbor entry.

"There's someone trying to sneak in." I point to the navy's 844-foot amphibious assault ship *Boxer*, headed into the harbor with a Harrier jet on its flight deck. "It doesn't have a [security] escort," Chuck notes before we make a quick run around the vessel, staring into its massive open fantail.

As dawn breaks over the city skyline, a string of recreational fishing boats heads out to sea. The crew spots an older boat coming in from a night's fishing with a white-bearded guy at the controls and hit their lights, calling over to let him know they're going to do a standard safety boarding. "Lot of one-man, two-man operations where they'll fish at night off Mexico and then come in when the others are going out," Omar explains.

"Do you have any weapons on you?" Chuck calls out, always the first question. He and Ken go out on the port side as we approach, but the waves are rocking the two boats so the fishing captain is instructed to get moving and we come up beside him so they can do an underway boarding. Ken is the first one to jump onto the other vessel. After going through their inspection and finding nothing wrong they climb back aboard and we head into the harbor, stopping at a fuel dock where a big sea lion is swimming around barking loudly. We fill up and are back at station just after eight in the morning.

I head back over the hill to Ocean Beach. San Diego's Point Loma (the peninsular "hill" I head over) has million-dollar views of the ocean and bay and some multimillion dollar homes from which to view them. Just north along Sunset Cliffs is Ocean Beach or O.B., the surfer town where I spent a lost decade one endless summer.

There's O.B.'s famous surfing pier and dog beach. Across the San Diego River and dredged out Mission Bay with its tourist hotels, SeaWorld theme park, Over the Line tournaments, and incessant fireworks is Mission Beach. Its boardwalk begins at Belmont Park, built by John Spreckels in 1925, with the Giant Dipper wooden roller coaster, a reminder of beach amusements before the age of Disney and Magic Mountain. A small family-friendly park today, in seedier times it had more of a cotton candy and quaalude ambience with midway riots on Cinco de Mayo and exiled Saigon bar bands playing cover tunes of dead American rock stars. Of course similar things could be said about the restored waterfronts of Long Beach, Venice, Santa Monica, and Santa Cruz, although, to be fair, Venice still retains much of its scabbed-over urban crustiness.

San Diego's Mission Beach is still full of students, youth hostels, music bars, and crowded stucco apartments. Pacific Beach to its north is more residential and has some good surf spots, while La Jolla, "the Jewel," is pretty much Aspen with a cove. The Marine Room on La Jolla Shores is a great place to get a drink, watch the joggers on the beach, and enjoy photos of storm waves washing through the bar during the El Niño winter of 1982. La Jolla's long-running controversy has been about harbor seals taking over the "children's pool," a small cove behind a breakwater. I figure when your big battle is over seals, kids, and sand you're leading a pretty good life.

North County San Diego retains some of its laid-back 1970s hang-loose feel, including the naked folks and hang gliders at Black's Beach. Battles here in towns like Solano Beach tend to revolve around the illegal shoring up of cliffside homes with boulders, Riprap, and spray-on Gunite. Some 10 percent of the California coast is now reinforced in this manner, although armoring shoreline to fight erosion is like battling fall foliage with a leaf blower. Armoring can actually accelerate the loss of beach sand in front of and adjacent to unyielding walls and is generally illegal under the California Coastal Act. Still, it's hard to make that argument to some homeowner whose cliff-top mansion or condo is teetering on a clumpy sandstone ledge. I remember a three-story pink apartment building that was evacuated a block down from us in Ocean Beach at the end of a street slowly crumbling away until a third of the building hung suspended sixty feet above a narrow rocky beach and then one night, more than a year later, gave way with a crackling jumble and roar of collapse that left the beach littered with stucco and woody debris. The ice-plant-covered fifty-foot drop behind our own cliff house once had a street running in front of it. Now our entry was on "Ocean Front Street," actually a back alley. After the pink apartment collapsed, the city brought in bulldozers, cranes, and dump trucks and spent six months piling up boulders for a breakwater and then backfilling tons of dirt, creating a planted slope and seawall to protect our house and a dozen others hanging on the edge, starting work at 6:00 A.M. every morning. We objected. I'd personally enjoyed the way the house would shudder during winter storms and our plateglass windows vibrate and rattle as winter rains mixed with salt spray pelted the living room glass. The deep reverberations of the waves were like your mother's heartbeat, rocking us to sleep. Of course, we were renters.

Mudslides and erosion are common along the California coast, with the town of Pacifica south of San Francisco generating regular evening news stories each winter as cliffs are shored up and apartments evacuated during the heavier storms. The TV cameras are weather wrapped and locked down on their tripods waiting to catch an apartment collapsing down a sloughing cliff. Still, most California towns and counties haven't even begun serious planning for the additional impacts of sea level rise and intensified El Niño storm surges linked to climate change. Towns along the Russian River, which lets out to the sea at Jenner seventy-eight miles north of San Francisco, have seen three "storms of the century" in the last thirty years. What are now listed as hundred-year flood events along the California coast are projected to be annual occurrences by 2100. At the other projected weather extreme, once-in-a-decade droughts may be happening every other year. I hope like sea urchins and abalones we coastal Californians, rugged veterans of the battle with the environment, will be able to adapt.

I continue north through San Diego county on historic 101, with its surf shops, taco stands, car lots, Subways, Burger Kings, Swami's ashram and surf beach, and on past Cardiff's waterfront parks to the town of Oceanside, which marks the southern border of Camp Pendleton, a Rhode Island–sized U.S. Marine impediment to coastal sprawl. Until recently Oceanside was a pretty rough town, but it is gradually morphing into another homogenized beach town with upscale family and retirement condos along Harbor Drive and by the pier where you can no longer get a patriotic tattoo, a cheap drink, or a professional come-on, except from real-estate agents.

Then there's the Marine Base itself, sixteen miles of coastline and desert scrub up to the Orange County border. Driving through on Interstate 5, I watch cobra gunships maneuvering overhead and combat training operations taking place in the dunes as I'm waved through an immigration checkpoint by green uniformed Border Patrol agents where northbound traffic is periodically stopped and searched for undocumented workers from Mexico just short of the double-domed guano-covered containment vessels of the San Onofre Nuclear Power Plant. Next to the nukes runs a service road that leads to state camping sites full of RVs and to Trestles whose waves are full of surfers. Marine Corps surfers have their own gate to enter (at "Churches" just above lower Trestles) where Military I.D. is required. A few miles farther on is the beach town of San Clemente, where President Nixon retreated to his mansion, "La Casa Pacifica," after his resignation in 1974 and where the Surfrider Foundation has its headquarters.

North on Interstate 5 is the Mission town of San Juan Capistrano, famous for its small seasonal birds (as Pacific Grove is for its monarch butterflies). If you stick to the Pacific Coast Highway you'll hit Dana Point with its big maritime museum, yacht harbor, wide streets, and bland plazas, as well as Laguna Beach, a once quaint village with a two-screen theater, bak-

eries, cafés, art galleries, and old waterfront motels now reclassified as resorts. A place where middle-class families once came for quiet beach
summers, it's turned thick with tourists and traffic on PCH, the Pacific
Coast Highway, one of the many names Highway 1 claims in its serpentine
meander north. Still, I stop to enjoy a quick break at Crescent Bay Point, a
flowering pocket park at the north end of town above Shay's Cove and just
south of Emerald Bay. There's a life-sized bronze statue of "Laguna Locals,"
a sea lion and cormorants. Just offshore—in clear turquoise waters unique
to this stretch of Orange County coast—three stand-up paddlers have
paused to watch four in-the-flesh sea lions hauled up on Seal Rock barking
conversationally. Half a dozen pelicans launch off the rock and drop into
single-file patrol over the water's kelp beds and black cormorants.

Farther on, the coast wanders through sandstone defiles to Newport
Beach (boats and money), Huntington Beach (surfers and money), Seal
Beach (old navy weapons bunkers and affordable housing), and on to the
city of Long Beach, mostly poor except along its revived waterfront where
the Aquarium of the Pacific, one of the anchors of its urban renewal, includes an urban oceans program. "We have the largest ocean economy in
the nation here in Southern California," notes aquarium president Jerry
Schubel. "We have more than twenty million people and lots of ocean uses,
including the two largest container ports in the nation, the largest small
boat marina, the best surfing and surf culture in the U.S. We discharge 1.2
billion gallons a day of treated wastewater, but we're still seeing growth in
tourism and recreation because we use our knowledge and technology cor-
rectly and when we do so we can protect the environment and enhance
the economy." He suggests that California state regulations need to be
adapted—without adulterating their environmental standards—to allow
for the development of clean offshore energy and ocean aquaculture in the
Southern California bight, perhaps in a designated research and development zone to encourage entrepreneurship. "This is the urban ocean you see
in most of the world and we could be the model," he argues. "It's not like
Northern California, where there's almost nobody living north of San
Francisco."

Beyond North America's largest port complex and the town of San Pedro, with its working-class soul where the Industrial Workers of the World once fought it out in the streets with the Ku Klux Klan, is the gerrymandered shoestring of L.A. real estate that has become the Harbor Freeway corridor linking the City of Angels to its port, one of its major sources of revenue. L.A. has always been good at reaching out for new wealth, be it trade revenues to the south or freshwater to the north and the east, including Owens Valley, Mono Lake, the Colorado River, and the Sacramento Delta. Owens Valley farmers' water became San Fernando Valley water after L.A. mayor Fred Eaton and his land speculator buddies, including Harrison Grey Otis of the *Los Angeles Times,* diverted much of the flow as portrayed in the Roman Polanski film *Chinatown.*

However, I'm jumping ahead of my car, which now takes the long jog around the Palos Verdes Peninsula with its irrigated green parks and botanical garden, its high-end ranch and mission homes, and venerable golf courses—also Donald Trump's golf course, also tons of DDT mixed into the sediment on the marine shelf offshore (locals are divided over which is the greater environmental insult). Palos Verdes gives the impression some crazed geologist wrenched Pebble Beach and its seventeen-mile drive from Monterey and tossed it down atop a Southern California bluff, then gave it that slightly bleached-out look common to sun-scored coastal deserts and canyons including Topanga and Malibu, where the wildfires burn. To the north of Palos Verdes are a string of beach cities, including Redondo, Hermosa, and Manhattan before the big oil refinery complex at El Segundo that keeps the L.A. freeway traffic creeping along with some of the highest gas prices in the nation.

I stop for the night at Marina Del Rey, where I put up with my friend Mike Shuster, an NPR reporter. This trip is not exactly Smeaton Chase's as recounted in his early-twentieth-century classic *California Coast Trails: A Horseback Ride from Mexico to Oregon,* setting up camp, starting a beach fire, and tying up his horse Chino each night during the months of travel (and travail) it once took to ride to Oregon. Or so I reflect, sitting on Mike's balcony at the Dolphin Marina with a cold beer in hand, overlooking the yachts and sailboats moored along the channels of the largest recreational marina in the United States with its more than four thousand boat slips.

With my black Honda Fit parked downstairs, a tent, sleeping bag, pad, pillow, beach towel, bodyboard, wet suit and snorkeling gear in the rear, trail mix, water bottle, reporter's notebook, and audiobook in the front passenger seat, I'm not exactly roughing it. Perhaps my road trip is as good a reflection of twenty-first-century California coastal travel as was Smeaton and Chino's giddyup and whoa saunterings of 1911. More significant, I believe much of what was wild when they passed through still is.

The last time I sailed out of Marina Del Rey was with the Santa Monica Baykeeper (now Los Angeles Waterkeeper), one of California's hundreds of marine conservation groups. Within ten minutes we'd stopped the boat to watch a bait ball, a concentration of sardine, anchovy, or other forage fish being fed on by wild dolphins, sea lions, and diving pelicans, a scene of savage predation befitting the Serengeti plains but taking place less than half a mile off the urban coastline of the second most populous city in the United States. Recently, humpback whales began feeding on anchovies less than half a mile off the Santa Cruz boardwalk, almost knocking over kayakers and paddleboarders who flocked around them till the Coast Guard was forced to set up separation zones. One video widely seen showed two feeding humpbacks, mouths as wide as steam shovels, rising up amid leaping fish directly in front of a two-person kayak and woman on a surfboard who barely had time to react before the great leviathans dropped back below the surface and dozens of gulls swooped in to feed on the stunned fish left in their frothing wake.

The day I leave Mike's I'm stuck in stop-and-go traffic on the Pacific Coast Highway just past the Santa Monica Pier. Looking between the boxy multimillion-dollar waterfront homes I see a pod of bottlenose dolphins cruising past, making better time than I am.

From here Malibu runs up the coast for twenty-seven miles, much of it gated waterfront mansions and home colonies on coastal bluffs overlooking palm trees and wide white-sand beaches that can still be accessed by the public thanks to the Coastal Act and despite some strong resistance from a few locals, including Barbra Streisand and media mogul David Geffen. One local Malibu conservationist makes the argument that the Coastal Commission insisting on installing a public bathroom on an isolated ocean cove may not be the best environmental practice even if it is done in the name of public access.

I continue north past steep sand dunes towering above the highway, past Point Mugu and its naval air station and Port Hueneme with its commercial docks and surfing pier where Highway 1 bends inland and a road diversion takes me through Oxnard, a major agricultural hub filled with cheap housing tracts, strip malls, taquerias, check-cashing stores, and brown dust from the nearby strawberry and bean fields, Carey McWilliams's *Factories in the Field,* now with factory outlets.

I continue north through Ventura with its shopping centers running down to the water where they morph into crowded tequila bars and marinas. Shortly highways 1 and 101 merge by the coast and run by the unincorporated town of Seacliff hanging on to a lip of land next to an artificial island. From Mussel Shoals you can see the first offshore oil platforms, also surfers off Carpinteria by a rocky point where several Mediterranean-style homes are clustered. Its downtown is more mission-style, with red-tiled restaurants, whitewashed walls, and palm trees dead-ending on the beach. Then there's Summerland and the wealthy enclave of Montecito, with its mansions nestled into rocky points by wind-sculpted pines and Montecito's Butterfly Beach, with its afternoon strollers and paddlers and sailboats heeling gently over in a breeze and a green verdant park above a sugar white-sand beach and blue water so perfect you wonder when the mermaids and sea unicorns will show up for happy hour.

Which brings us to the ultimate red-tiled, whitewashed enclave of Santa Barbara, population eighty-eight thousand, nestled between the brown San Ynez Mountains and the blue sea, the rugged Channel Islands and oil platforms to its south. Its architectural style, like its service industry, is predominantly Spanish. A visit here is like a dose of MDMA, but just as ecstasy can deplete your serotonin I've always feared that extended exposure to

Santa Barbara might dampen my ability to feel social outrage or any other strong emotion not associated with surfing, sailing, fine wines, or western-saddle trail riding. This is where Prince William came to play polo after he married Kate and where Ronald Reagan had his 688-acre Western White House, Rancho del Cielo, where he used to tell reporters the old saw that there's nothing for the inside of a man like the outside of a horse.

I stop in Goleta Beach for lunch with my friend Jesse Altstatt, a marine biologist and professional science diver who also surfs and owns a sailboat. Lithe and athletic, she wears her straight chestnut hair loose and has lively brown eyes behind aqua frame glasses—basically your classic California water woman.

Raised in Palo Alto, Jesse visited the state beach at Montara and went clamming on Tomales Bay when she was little. "My job was to keep the bucket from sloshing on the drive home," she recalls. Her dad also took her deep-sea fishing and she caught a shark as big as she was when she was twelve. "But I also remember going out one time with my dad where we didn't catch anything and he said, 'Well, I guess the fish are all gone,' and that stuck with me. But it was really Mrs. Coen, my seventh-grade ocean-ography teacher, who changed my life. I remember how she took us on field trips and biological sampling on San Francisco Bay." She smiles as she recalls this. It was then that Jesse began volunteering at the California Academy of Sciences aquarium, where she also swam after hours with the harbor seals and two white-sided dolphins that would crowd the front of the tank when they knew the young volunteers were about to jump in with them. She did her first dive in the aquarium tank and later got scuba certified at Monterey Bay, where she met her first wild seal and fell in love with the otherworldliness of the California kelp forest. Since then she's spent more than 1,500 hours underwater mostly working, including re-storing sea grasses off Anacapa, one of the Channel Islands. She got her bachelor's in aquatic biology at U.C.S.B. and started surfing her junior year. Later she got a master's in marine biology. She's continued living in the Santa Barbara area except for some extended work trips, including one to Palmer Station, Antarctica, where she was bitten by a leopard seal that came up over an ice edge and grabbed her, no doubt thinking penguin. They had a momentary stare off and it let go. At that point her excited colleagues grabbed hold of her as the large predator swam away. Luckily she was not badly injured. The New Zealand newspapers ran several stories on the unusual incident, including one headlined "Seal finds biologist unappetizing."

After her first field trip as a grad student she'd called up her old junior high school to thank Mrs. Coen. It turned out she was in a nursing home suffering from Lou Gehrig's disease. Jesse went with Mrs. Coen's daughter to visit her there and tell her how she had helped determine Jessie's new life as a marine biologist. Her former teacher, unable to speak at that stage of the disease's progression, took a pad and in a shaky hand wrote, "This is what makes teaching worthwhile."

After a short visit at U.C. Santa Barbara's Bren environmental school, I head north again, bypassing the Point Conception headland where California's oceanography, biology, and weather change dramatically. I spend the night camped out in Lompoc, then travel on through the brushy hills around Vandenberg Air Force Base, big empty country dotted with giant golf ball–like radar domes. Somewhere past the picturesque town of Orcutt, Highway 1 turns into an empty two-lane country road with few distractions except for some roller-coaster hills over one of which appears Officer E. Alarcon Jr. of the California Highway Patrol who does a predatory U-turn, pulls me over, and gives me a $300 speeding ticket.

I take a slower ride through the artichoke fields outside the town of Guadalupe past lines of trucks and old cars pulled off by the side of the road where farmworkers are harvesting the crop near the Rancho Guadalupe Dunes Preserve, part of the twenty-two thousand-acre, eighteen-mile-long Guadalupe-Nipomo Dunes Complex. Here endangered snowy plovers and California least terns can be found among the same rolling dunes where Cecil B. DeMille filmed *The Ten Commandments* and then buried the sets that have now become their own archaeological relics still lost to the sands of time. A sign at the park entry warns of mountain lions roaming the wild coastal scrub. The road ends with a sweeping overview of the Santa Maria River and its fringing riparian green swamp meandering through the dunes to the sea. Since winter storms have washed out the road to the small beachfront parking area, county rangers have staked a three-quarter-mile-long rope trail through the dunes. Cliff sparrows and gulls accompany me on my sandy hike to the wide beach with its dried kelp and gull feathers and broken shell fragments, where I take off my sneakers, roll up my jeans, and wade into the not quite bone-chilling water. Even though it's a Saturday morning in August, there's no one in sight but two wet-suited surfers catching humpy three- to four-foot waves. A squadron of pelicans flies past, wingtips into the gray-green curlers. I look back at the small fore dunes with their grass clumps that are the windy nesting sites for the terns and plovers and the rising back dunes with their denser scrub and thick underbrush able to hide a resident mountain lion perhaps waiting for a dead seal or surfer to feed on.

To the north is the Oceano Dunes State Vehicular Recreation Area, where ATVs and dune buggies are permitted to do doughnuts in the sand and the only cougars to be found are among the classic muscle cars in the parking lot.

I talk to Chris Terry, a dark-haired surfer carrying a swallowtail board as he gets out of the water. He tells me he's a fourth-generation local Portuguese from the Five Cities area (Shell Beach, Pismo Beach, Grover Beach, Oceano, and Arroyo Grande) and that the open-access dunes for the ATVs is a big tourist draw to the area for gearheads from the Central Valley. "Folks have big Thanksgivings here just to reserve spots for spring/summer permits to drive on the dunes." He thinks he's pulled a rib muscle in the surf but says he doesn't need my help hiking his board out, so we part. Two Vietnamese fishermen are hiking in through the dunes as I'm leaving, also an Anglo dad and his young boy carrying two rods and a bucket, hoping to catch some surf perch.

I continue driving north through a quilt of dunes and farm fields and stately corridors of eucalyptus trees planted against roadside erosion, passing through the small railroad town of Oceano.

In the 1930s Oceano became a mecca for nudists, artists, mystics, and freethinkers like the artist Elwood Decker, who believed the dunes were centers for creative energy. Although the "dunites" are long gone, the sensual allure of these big coastal sand hills remains.

I pass through Grover Beach and into Pismo, the onetime "clam capital of the world" (till they were overharvested) with its RV parks, long pier, and happy hordes of summer tourists in the foggy cool of the afternoon. This is the beach town Johnny Carson used to make fun of regularly on *The Tonight Show,* though it seems perfectly nice to me. It's a few miles southeast of the cove by Avila Beach where the Diablo Canyon nuclear power plant operates and where unhappy security guards once clued me in to a great investigative story on security lapses at the plant during the first Gulf War. Post-9/11 plant security has been greatly improved. Diablo Canyon has two Westinghouse reactors and more than two earthquake fault lines, one, the Shoreline Fault, was discovered less than half a mile offshore in 2008 not by PG&E's top seismologist and his staff of fourteen but by Dr. Jeanne Hardebeck, a scientist with the U.S. Geological Survey. That, along with concerns over the 2011 Fukushima nuclear disaster in Japan, delayed Pacific Gas & Electric's request for a twenty-year extension of its operating permit. Of course Diablo Canyon has always drawn controversy. Before it went on line in 1981, more than 1,900 members of the antinuclear Abalone Alliance were arrested protesting its construction.

I get back on 101 and then break off at the CalPoly college town of San Luis Obispo for the twelve-mile ride back to the shore at Morro Bay that's dominated by Morro Rock, a 576-foot-high twenty-three-million-year-old volcanic plug and home to peregrine falcons. It's the largest of the "nine sisters" of volcanic domes that stretch between San Luis and Morro Bay. While this onshore geology is impressive, 2.5 miles offshore is the Davidson Seamount, which is 7,480 feet tall, eight miles wide at its base, and goes on for twenty-six miles. It's the largest seamount in the United States and includes forests of eight- to ten-foot-high deep-sea corals at the top of the seamount (still 1,500 feet below the surface), also waters rich in a mind-boggling variety of marine wildlife.

Since the seamount is mostly out of sight and so out of mind, Morro Bay's second major attraction is the trio of 450-foot-tall smokestacks at its natural gas power plant. Like Diablo Canyon and the other electric-generating facilities along the coast, this is a "once-through" power plant, which is to say it takes in seawater at a rate of 464,000 gallons per minute to cool its condenser before discharging it directly back into the sea, having heated the water from fifty to sixty degrees to sixty-seven to seventy-seven degrees. Its seawater intakes also allow for significant entrainment and impingement (sucking in and trapping) of wildlife including many fish, larvae, and fish eggs.

On the day I visit Morro Bay, the town is swarming with tourists, seabirds, sea lions, kayakers, stand-up paddler's, horseback riders, and a few fishing boats heading out, including the *Dorado* with crab pots on its deck. The town's small fleet fishes for crab and black cod and also works its way up and down the seamount and the coast in search of additional prey items just like the sea lions.

Heading north along Morro Strand State Beach I pass the surfer town of Cayucos, pass bird rocks full of black cormorants, and Highway 1 once again becomes a lonely two-lane road winding through dry, rolling hills with wide marine terraces on its seaward side. I pass the town of Harmony, population eighteen, which suggests there aren't too many Californians living in Harmony. I stop in Cambria for no particular reason, wandering residential streets nestled among cypress, alder, and pine trees thick with Spanish moss. I stop by a doe and her spotted fawn grazing too close to the road and shoo them back into their suburban woodland by the sea.

I drive on past Moonstone Beach and San Simeon and Hearst Castle, and on to Big Sur. But first I have to pull over at Piedras Blancas by the turnoff sign reading "Elephant seal viewing area."

Right now there are just over hundred elephant seals, mostly females and young of the year, on the beach and an equal number of tourists behind a low wooden fence on a five-foot bluff above them. Many of the seals are lying in clumps of two to ten like slow-moving sofas using their flippers to throw sand onto their wide gray-brown backs.

One big bull in the water, well over two tons, rises up with his floppy elephantine trunk to challenge another who turns away and swims off, uninterested as it's not mating season and so there's really not much to fight about. It's the end of the male molting season, a kind of whole body facial peel and cleanse for the big marine mammals who haul up here during the one to two months a year they're not at sea diving after squid and other tasty treats.

This is a recent colony. Biologists first spotted a dozen elephant seals here in 1990. In 1992 the first pup was born. By 1996 more than thousand pups were born, and today more than seventeen thousand animals visit or are born here every year. Ten colonies have now replenished themselves in California including this one, one at Ano Nuevo State Park north of Santa Cruz, one on the Farallons, and one at Point Reyes National Seashore.

I chat with Tim Postiff, one of three blue-jacketed volunteers from the Cambria-based Friends of the Elephant Seal while nearby a German tourist girl feeds a ground squirrel from her hand while her friends take pictures. The air is redolent with the stink of the sea: iodine, guano, and rotting vegetation. It lingers as I head north across open rising country under gray-capped skies and onto the steeper coastal mountains that rise like fists from the sea at Big Sur. Here you're confronted by a sudden shock of elevation and dramatic vistas you can't find the words for—at least not to write down while keeping your hands on the wheel as the serpentine road twists up and back on itself climbing into three thousand-foot granite heights cut by defiles full of dark evergreens, cypress, and redwood, the aeries of golden eagles, hawks, and eighty reintroduced California Condors with nine-foot wingspans who sweep down from their mountain fastness along Big Sur's ninety miles of coastline seeking carrion to feed on, nature's bald-headed sanitation crew.

There are the turnouts and stop-and-go road crews where constant rock slides have them trying something new—a roadbed suspended above the cliff—not unlike the one or two modern houses I spot hanging off the cliffs on steel support beams and you can just imagine a kind of human cliff sparrow city having been built here if not for the challenges provided first by centuries of steep, foggy wilderness isolation and later, when the technology became feasible, by the California Coastal Commission.

I've called ahead on my cell phone to see if I can reserve a spot at Kirk Creek, a campground with cushiony native grasses on a bluff west of the road with a trail leading down to a beach and another leading up into the Ventana Wilderness. I've forgotten, of course, that it's still a Saturday in August, and the woman on the phone makes sympathetic clucking sounds and suggests I might have better luck on a weekday later in the fall.

So I keep driving past Sand Dollar Beach and the famous eighty-foot McWay waterfall plunging onto the beach at Julia Pfeiffer Burns State Park like a travel poster for Hawaii and over the Big Creek and Bixbie bridges, engineering marvels from another age when America built things, and also I stop to take pictures at various turnouts where tourists from Japan, China, Germany, Holland, Latin America, and elsewhere congregate for the famous California coastal vistas. Perhaps they'll also stop for a hot tub at Esalen or Pinot Noir at Nepenthe, a quick gander at the Henry Miller Library or to linger by the inns and cafés that make up the twisting, narrow, damp, slightly moldy village strips clinging to the side of the forested road far above the sea where hidden coves act as birthing wards for harbor seals, historic refuges for sea otters, and hunting grounds for solitary cougars and golden eagles.

Then, just as I'm getting acclimatized, Big Sur drops down through towering redwoods, forest sentinels that stretch twenty miles inland and back onto open marine terraces where some time later, on a gentle curve, I spot, like a priceless miniature, like an HO model railroad town built atop a boulder, the Point Sur Lighthouse with its keeper's house and water tower, outbuildings, and four-story-tall light building, and at the foot of the steep, curving road etched up the face of the 361-foot-tall volcanic rock, a row of seemingly tiny cars pulled over where the weekend state historic walking tours begin.

The lighthouse, built in 1889 and still functioning as an aid to navigation, was inspired by the 1875 shipwreck of the *Ventura,* a 280-foot steamship with 186 people onboard that ran up onto the rocks in heavy fog. It didn't help that the captain was drunk at the time or that eleven crew members immediately took off in a couple of lifeboats, leaving the passengers behind. Still, everyone survived. Years later on a stormy night in 1935, two of the lighthouse crew got to witness the offshore crash of the Navy airship U.S.S. *Macon* mentioned earlier.

As I drive on (intending to return for the tour someday) I see that the massive lighthouse rock is attached to its own beach and ocean inlet and farther on see that the great rock and beach and inlet have taken on the appearance of a small diorama at the end of a long sandy peninsula because this stretch of coastline exists on a scale that can still inspire awe of the natural world and reduce the works of man, our cathedrals, monuments, office parks, and shopping malls to something far less thrilling.

I drive on past Point Lobos, one of my favorite marine reserve dive spots, and Monastery Beach and into Carmel-by-the-Sea, where Clint Eastwood used to be the mayor. Along with its Monterey pines and former artist cottages now listing in the low millions, it's also brimming with high-end handbag and watch shops and gawkers on Ocean Avenue, particularly as this is Pebble Beach's Tour d'Elegance weekend, which means several blocks are lined with Teslas and Porsches, Lamborghinis and Mercedes, along with a mixed lot of Aston-Martins, Triumphs, Corvettes, and classic roadsters. At the foot of Ocean Avenue you can pay $9.50 to take 17-Mile Drive through Pebble Beach past Lone Pine and the monarch butterfly landing zone (they migrate from the mountains of Mexico) and the famed links into the city of Monterey. I opt to backtrack to Highway 1 and am soon driving into the scenic ocean canyon town, the state's first capital, with its famed aquarium and Cannery Row and network of marine research centers.

It's getting late so I keep heading north around the curve of the bay past Fort Ord and its miles of decommissioned army base beachfront now designated as park trails for the people of California. I move on through the college town of Santa Cruz (Go Banana Slugs!) and the ag fields north of town by Davenport, the recently named "Slow Coast," and on past the Pigeon Point Lighthouse, roadside fruit stands shut down for the night, through the traffic lights in the overgrown town of Half Moon Bay where the California Coastal Commission faltered, allowing construction of the first large hotel on a state beach in a generation, then on past Moss Beach with its cliff-top Distillery Restaurant above the cove where they used to offload smuggler's booze during Prohibition and the adjacent Fitzgerald Marine Reserve with its popular tide pools. Here where land and ocean meet is a mesmerizing window into the sea, hundreds of yards of sloshed-over rocky reef with rushing surge channels and a sandbar where wet-eyed harbor seals haul out. During low tide the rocky depressions form natural aquarium pools full of flowery anemones, limpets, big sea stars in orange, red, brown, pink, and purple, also small blenny fish, spiny black urchins, and sometimes an elusive flounder or octopus that missed that last tide train home.

I move on past the state beach at Montara and over the steep sea cliffs of Devil's Slide where rockslides and avalanches of mud periodically shut down access to the south—sometimes for months at a time—which is why a new tunnel has recently been opened. Then it's downhill past Pedro Point into Pacifica and its storm-tossed waterfront back up the eight-lane highway hill onto 101, and into the brightly lit city by the bay, the one they say was built on rock and roll but only long after it was built on gold nuggets and greed. I cross the Bay Bridge with its new half-completed eastern span designed to withstand the next earthquake. I turn onto 80 near the Port of Oakland past Emeryville where the AMC movie complex has replaced the old Ohlone Indian shell mound, then onto 580 and home, finally home to rest in the Bay Area that everyone thinks of as Northern California, although really it's more like the top end of central California. What it really is, is a case of demographics trumping geography. People call it Northern California because as Jerry Schubel pointed out, "there's almost nobody living north of San Francisco."

THE REDWOOD COAST

Of what avail are forty freedoms without
a blank spot on the map?

—Aldo Leopold

As Margo Pellegrino paddled her outrigger from Oregon into California waters I got a call from her husband, Carl, who was flying out from their home in New Jersey with their young kids, Julia and Billy. "I think we'll meet her at the Mattole River," he told me on the phone, looking at a map.

"No you won't. You can't get there," I told him. "Let's meet at Fort Bragg."

A few days later she paddled in through the fog to a kayaking outfitters' dock up the Noyo River at Fort Bragg under the watchful eyes of a pair of

nesting ospreys before we all went to dinner on the waterfront in the small
fishing and tourist town of seven thousand. Carl couldn't get over where we
were. "This is Northern California? Where are all the cities? Where are all
the people?"

Why is it that almost half the coastline of the most populous state in the
nation, a coastline that's also arguably among the most scenic and spectacular in the world, is so thinly settled that the largest coastal city between
San Francisco and Portland, Oregon, Eureka, California, has a population
of just twenty-eight thousand? Even today, with twenty-five million Californians living in coastal counties south of the Golden Gate, the five
coastal counties north of the bridge: Marin, Sonoma, Mendocino, Humboldt, and Del Norte have a combined population of fewer than one million people and more than two-thirds of them live in Marin and Sonoma
within commuting distance of San Francisco. How come the very ser-
viceable harbors at Bodega and Humboldt Bay aren't major port towns or
at least swarming with summer tourists like you find on Cape Cod, along
the Jersey Shore, or on North Carolina's outer banks?

Part of the answer is climatic, part economic, and the rest I'd attribute
to the sprawl-preventing California Coastal Commission discussed earlier.

Northern California was not just a late frontier but also a wet one. From
Big Sur north much of this precipitation takes the form of fog off the ocean
that feeds the redwoods and the conifers but also lays a damp, cold blanket
across the coast through much of the year, particularly during the summer
months.

Farther north the coastal range becomes a temperate rainforest with the
Redwood Coast receiving an average forty to seventy inches of rain per
year, so that when it's not foggy, when the marine layer isn't trapped between the mountains and the sea, it's likely raining. This leaves the coastal
zone cold, damp, and depressing at least eight months of the year with thin
soils best suited for cord grass and other forage, sheep and cow country
where the big trees were cut down to make way for dairy farms after the
gold in the rivers played out. Here Portuguese, Italian, and other new arriv-
als began fishing offshore as the salmon in the rivers declined, the result of

overfishing and dirt fill and loss of shade from logging as anyone not ranching, farming, or fishing was soon cutting down the region's big Douglas fir and redwood trees for shipment to San Francisco, San Pedro, and San Diego.

Timber barons built settlements and mills up and down the coast, including company towns like Scotia on the Eel River and great Victorian mansions that can still be seen in Ferndale, Eureka, and Arcata, among them the massive Carson Mansion on M Street in Old Town Eureka. By 1855 nine mills and 140 lumber schooners operated just on Humboldt Bay from where they also shipped fifty thousand barrels of smoked salmon to the boomtown of San Francisco.

Through the nineteenth and much of the twentieth century the economy of Northern California, with its heavy winter rains, steep coastal cliffs, and thick foggy forests developed around its natural resources, trees, fish, and grass. Many of today's wealthy Bay Area communities, such as Mill Valley in Marin County, got their start milling redwood lumber. To the east beyond the coastal range drier warmer inland valleys such as Sonoma and Napa grew grapes and later became a world-famous wine-growing region with good rail and road connections. Along the north coast the towns used fishing boats, schooners, and cargo ships to get their goods to market from the 1850s on through the Depression of the 1930s, which saw population declines throughout the northern part of the state. For the dairy industry cheese making was essential, as raw milk would spoil on the sail downcoast to San Francisco or "Frisco," as they called it.

While there were many impressively engineered cliff-side cranes, chutes, and trapeze riggings to load logs from sawmills that dotted the northern coves onto the lumber schooners built at the Fairhaven Shipyard on the Somoa spit by Humboldt Bay, and while fishing piers and jetties were built, washed away by winter storms, and built anew in Bodega Bay, Point Arena, Fort Bragg, Eureka, Arcata, Trinidad, and Crescent City, construction of surface roads came late to the region. The first plank road out of Crescent City in 1858 connected it not with other California towns but with the Illinois River in Oregon. In 1894 a wagon road finally connected Crescent

City to Trinidad in Humboldt County and the treacherous coastal road south from there. Even the Redwood Coast's queen city of Eureka (named for gold strikes on nearby rivers) didn't have reliable ground transport to the Bay Area until the 1914 opening of a railroad link to Willits in Mendocino County. For the most part trade and travel were conducted by steam schooner. Commercially, things didn't change much till the arrival of safe auto transport with "the Redwood Highway" of the 1920s, also chain saws and logging trucks in the 1940s and '50s, which dangerously accelerated the region's timber harvest, as did corporate raiding in the 1980s. By then major timber companies, including Georgia-Pacific, Louisiana-Pacific, the Pacific Lumber Company, and Simpson had staked out much of the political economy of the north even as tourism began drawing people to the spectacular coastal wonders of the region. While the bluff town of Mendocino became a B&B tourist mecca, the Georgia-Pacific mill blocking off the waterfront in the larger town of Fort Bragg to its north limited that town's visitor industry potential and created divisions between people working in resource-based businesses such as timber and pulp and the newer tourism and recreation sector of the economy.

Environmentalists began fighting to protect the last redwood stands, establishing and expanding redwood national and state parks in Humboldt and Del Norte, which include the world's tallest trees, and later the Headwaters old-growth redwood forest in Humboldt.

At the same time "back to the land" hippies and urban refugees began seeding the rough grounds and backcountry logged-over second-growth mountains with what would become the next great harvest and economic mainstay of Northern California: marijuana.

The state estimates today's pot crop to be worth $14 billion compared to $2 billion worth of wine grapes or about equal to the retail value of all of California's bottled wines. It's certainly worth far more then the historic timber yield. It's also said to account for half to two-thirds of all economic activity in Mendocino and Humboldt counties, where many people shifted to growing pot gardens after the lumber mills closed, eliminating some of the social divisions that peaked during the "timber wars" of the 1990s.

That's when, in the summer of 1990, I got to witness 425 riot police separating 1,500 environmental demonstrators from hundreds of angry loggers, town drunks, and rowdies by the mill gates in Fort Bragg. Today the GP mill is long shut down and Fort Bragg's recession-era economy balances precariously between tourism and salmon.

The marijuana industry has also diversified over time to include older Mendocino garden growers who might produce harvests of $1 million or less, both indoor and outdoor and industrial "diesel pot" growers with large prefab grow buildings in Humboldt's back country that have high energy and water demand and due to their unregulated use of fuels, pesticides, and illegal water diversions, tend to pose an environmental threat to river-dependent salmon and other anadromous fish, not unlike the timber industry before them. Then there are the Mexican cartel growers who often farm large plots on public lands and tend to be more violent in defense of their crops. Today a number of growers with Proposition 215 permits from the state to grow medical marijuana plants—although often raising more plants than their permits allow—are nonetheless cooperating with local law enforcement to target the Mexican cartels. But that's another story and mostly upriver.

So let's start the second half of our coastal journey on San Francisco Bay during Fleet Week and its Blue Angels air show that, unlike the onetime America's Cup of 2013, has been an annual spectacle on the bay for more than thirty years. I'm getting to see it close-up with the Coast Guard, which is working hard to maintain a semblance of order on the water.

I head out with Chief Aaron Harris and his crew on their forty-seven-foot surf-rescue boat that's going to be controlling the west end of the box—the half-mile-by-one-mile safety zone in the bay over which the Blue Angels will be flying.

We stop by Sector Command on Yerba Buena Island to pick up Ens. Everett Fujii who will be the operational controller for the short end of the box by the Golden Gate Bridge. We begin to form a blue line in the water around noon with the buoy tender *Aspen,* a California Highway Patrol boat, and two 25-foot Marine Safety and Security Team (MSST) Defender boats to our left. To our right are two Coast Guard auxiliary boats, along with sheriffs and police boats.

The eighty-seven-foot Coast Guard cutter *Hawksbill* is stationed next to a temporary buoy in the center of the bay. The Blue Angels will fly their air-show formations using visual cues including the south tower of the Golden Gate Bridge and the *Hawksbill.*

As the winds and currents pick up Everett works at maintaining the line. "Have the CHP come up to us on our port and fill in this gap. Push the two RBS [response boats small, i.e. Defenders] our way."

At 12:30 P.M. with hundreds of powerboats, sailboats, tugs, and ferries coming onto the water vessel traffic system (VTS), San Francisco gets on the radio to announce that the safety zone is now in effect. The security boats "energize" their flashing blue lights and the box is cleared. One hot-shot in a speedboat cuts across the middle of the box and is chased down by a MSST team with its siren wailing.

The air show starts with a Coast Guard Dolphin helicopter flying over and deploying a swimmer who drops thirteen feet into the cold bay water, their contribution to the party. By now tens of thousands of spectators have gathered along the shoreline. The first aerobatics are performed by the Collaborators, a four-aircraft team led by Oracle's red baron biplane.

"This is where my stomach would throw up," Everett Fujii says, watching as pilot Sean Tucker stalls his biplane after a long vertical climb then falls backward, spiraling toward the water and trailing smoke before pulling out just short of disaster.

"We have a white-hulled vessel in the zone by Fort Mason," the radio crackles. "Roger. We got him." There's the sound of another siren on the water.

Four gray marine helicopters fly over the bay followed by an F-16 jet fighter accompanying a World War II Mustang, then another prop-plane performer. Next it's the Patriots: four trainer jets trailing red, white, and blue oil smoke. *Fat Albert,* the Angels' C-130 four-engine transport plane, does a flyby and a few steep climbs, like a dump truck doing wheelies.

Then the main attraction commences with the roar of the Blue Angels F-18 Hornets performing gut-churning turns, climbs, and wingtip-to-wingtip formations leading to their trademark six-plane delta formation. They also do a series of loops and flybys close to the deck, startling at least one sea lion who jumps out of the water in front of us.

"We've got a big gap here, so I'm going to push over a little, sir," Aaron informs Everett as he works the throttle. Behind us a kite surfer is recklessly weaving his way through the crowd of spectator boats. Still, he seems a model of propriety compared to the Blue and Gold ferry with hundreds of people aboard that suddenly speeds through the crowd of vessels to find a better viewing spot.

"Hey, Coast Guard. Why don't you do something about that idiot?" someone on the radio demands.

"If you don't give that guy a citation what are you here for?" Another boater jumps in on channel 16.

Everett has pulled out a rulebook and is going through it. "I'm searching for authority to do something but just being a jackass isn't a violation," he explains to me. Just then one of the Hornets streaks by so close to the deck it creates a trailing ball of water vapor, momentarily distracting everyone. Then another Blue and Gold Fleet ferry, the *Emperor,* comes steaming full speed toward the line so that Aaron has to cut it off with our forty-seven and hits the siren, as do several other security boats.

The Blue Angels end their show with wide, looping, mile-high vapor trails at the far ends of the bay before streaking back toward each other in what promises to be a six-plane high-speed collision in the center of the bay before they zip past each other only yards apart. The blue line on the water reenergizes its lights to maintain the box after the Angels fly off to the airport.

Soon the radio tells us the box is clear and we join the anarchic parade of boats now dispersing across the water. We drop Everett Fujii at Yerba Buena and head back to Station Golden Gate in the cooling chill.

The radio announces someone's gone aground on a mud bar. A harbor seal pops its head up to check us out as we pass. The radio says the *Amber*, a thirty-foot sailboat, is reporting a head injury on board. It's just north of Treasure Island and Sector Command is responding. "If we see it, we'll help," Aaron announces, calling his crew, seamen Forrest Morgan and Grant Duenas and mechanic Isaac Allen onto the open bridge to keep watch with him.

A twenty-five-foot Defender boat with an EMT onboard reaches the *Amber*. "Not critical but recommend she go to the hospital from the Berkeley Marina," the medic reports after examining the injured boater. Cold spray splashes us as we head back to the station on Horseshoe Cove by the Golden Gate.

Heading north from the city you can go over the Golden Gate Bridge, cutting off 101 onto Highway 1 at the turnoff between Sausalito and Mill Valley, though I choose to head through Mill Valley just to get into the redwoods sooner. I climb through charming giant tree-shaded neighborhoods of wealthy celebrities and businesspeople such as actor Robin Williams, Bob Weir of the Grateful Dead, and Pixar director Andrew Stanton. Over Mount Tam past the redwoods at Muir Woods and Muir Beach, Highway 1 does some extreme twists and turns atop steep ocean cliffs before dropping back down to sea level at Stinson Beach, the first coastal town north of the bay, population 486.

I pull into the state beach on a July day as the nation is sweltering through one hundred-degree-plus temperatures. Here it's forty degrees cooler with a light drizzle under gray skies. Still, people are determined to enjoy themselves, starting up barbeques on the grass next to the parking lot. By the towering bushes at the entry to the beach a warning sign reminds beachgoers of dangerous currents. Below that is a shark advisory reading: "Great White Sharks live in these waters. A shark attack occurred here in six feet of water.

Be aware of the potential for sharks close to shore along the entire length of the beach." Still the cold, sharky waters and cool, drizzling day hasn't kept hundreds of determined holidaymakers off the wide, sandy beach.

"Oh . . . It's cold" a young teenage girl with a bodyboard and green bikini runs up to tell her mother who's sitting on a beach towel in a sweatshirt and jeans. Next to her, the girl's father has wrapped his beach towel around himself like a blanket. Two other girls run up to them in full-length insulated wet suits, making me think two of their three kids may be college material. There are a few surfers in black wet suits, like lanky harbor seals, trying to catch waves, and a couple hugging down by the lifeguard tower in a romantic exchange of body heat. As I head back to the car, the grills are getting smoky and the cool air has become redolent with the odor of pork, corn, and mesquite.

Beyond the Bolinas Lagoon and the Audubon Ranch, where hundreds of egrets and herons roost in the treetops, Highway 1 passes the Olema-Bolinas Road with its missing road sign that privacy-seeking locals kept removing till Caltrans finally gave up. Still, throngs of surfers, birders, and other visitors manage to find their way to Bolinas on weekends when the surf's good or the Pacific flyway active. There's an inlet to the lagoon between the canal homes on the sandy spit at the north end of Stinson and Bolinas beach, a place longtime Cal Academy of Sciences shark expert Dr. John McCosker does not recommend I swim. "If you want to get bitten, surf Bolinas around Labor Day," he cautions. "I won't guarantee you'll be bitten, but it's your best chance."

One of my friends, a private investigator, lives on the Bolinas bluffs off Daffodil or Pine or one of those unpaved residential roads that hasn't changed much in thirty years where she can watch a bobcat sun itself in a clearing in front of her small A-frame.

From Bolinas it's a short jog north to Point Reyes National Seashore or along the fifteen-mile length of Tomales Bay through rolling farm country, past creeks and ruminating cows and the Hog Island Oyster Farm, past Dillon Beach, a secluded, dog-friendly spot on the Pacific where a surfer got dragged under and spit out by a shark in 2006 and a kayaker got his paddle yanked two years later, then on to Bodega Bay, where Hitchcock filmed *The Birds* and the gulls and ravens still cop an attitude.

My recent trips to Bodega Bay have included visits to the one hundred thousand-square-foot U.C. Davis Marine Lab, the overbuilt Bodega Harbor resort development grandfathered in just as the California Coastal Commission was being set up, and a day offshore with Dirk Rosen's MARE group dropping an ROV off a leased fishing boat to document the area's newly established marine protected area.

The ROV is green, about six feet long by four high by three wide with cameras and prop thrusters within its metal frame, and it plugs into six hundred feet of one thousand-volt yellow umbilical power cable on a spool. After hooking the top of the ROV to a winch two members of the secience crew hold its bottom rails on both ends to steady it and slide it over the side a few miles offshore where it whirs off forty feet before Dirk dives it. They also put out a "clump weight" made of a pile of free weights linked to the ROV that creates a thirty-meter tether or ninety feet for the ROV to wander around on the bottom once the main cable's played out.

Dirk "flies" the robot from inside a small blue surplus military shipping container secured on the deck and equipped with a thinly padded bench, six video screens, and a toggle joystick controller. They've also attached a video screen to the outside of the van that allows me, from a folding chair on the open deck, to watch the ROV descend past a sea nettle and lots of tiny krill. Our fishing boat the *Donna Kathleen,* rolls and wallows in low seas. I figure this beats the warm, claustrophobic, slightly diesel-fume-flavored space inside the container as I have no desire to be seasick again.

Once on the rock and mud bottom 250 feet down, the ROV's cameras show lots of flowery tunicates and a brightly colored nudibranch (sea slug) and big white furry-topped mushroomlike anemones. Its lights catch a big lingcod, then another as it (the ROV, not the fish) moves along at a stately half knot. There's a multilegged reddish sun star and a group of juvenile canary rockfish—an endangered species now safe within this MPA. Four grad students from Cal State Monterey are taking notes and eating saltines while laser lights on the ROV size the fish for both still and digital video recording. There's an olive rockfish and sea pens and a beautiful little multifinned sculpin feeding on the krill caught in the ROV's lights, raising a little cloud of sediment as he scrambles after one and then another. "Shrimp cocktail anyone?" ex-fisherman, now MARE deck officer Steve Holz asks on behalf of the fish. The ROV moves on. There's another sea nettle and a hagfish (a.k.a. slime eel) and more cod and soon it's time to raise the robot sub. Despite some technical glitches, both mechanical and software-based, they'll deploy it two more times today.

Up on the bridge Tim Maricich, the boat's captain, tells me working with the robot sub crew is easy: "Nothing I haven't done one thousand times before putting out crab pots or deploying gear." His grandfather came over from Croatia in 1900 and started fishing off of California, as did his dad when the catches were big enough to raise families on. "I'm not a first-generation fisherman," Tim complains. "I'm the last generation."

Though I've run into my share of sea dogs, I'm bemused that Tim's family, including his wife and son, who help run the boat, have a couple of sea cats aboard, Snookums and Rocko.

Snookums, dark and tan, has come up from the galley to take some air and seems a little woozy on her paws. Rocko has joined Tim in the pilothouse where he's lying under a quilt with just one black paw showing, looking like a very queasy kitty. Later they'll both recover and eat their fish treats on the run back into Bodega's Spud Point Marina.

Heading north from Bodega Bay on a bright fall day, I spot something increasingly common along the coast, cliff-side houses losing their battle with erosion. These ones are in the small settlement at Duncan's Beach where the cliffs are covered in blue and green tarps and boulders have been illegally dumped over the edge in a futile attempt to halt the power of the sea. Electronic warning signs by the side of the road report "Abalone season closed in Sonoma County." This is due to a toxic red tide.

Just before I cross over the Russian River into Jenner I pass a large field where a herd of cattle is following a rusty pickup with its tailgate down and a cowboy kicking apart bales of hay for them to feed on. On the other side of the bridge is a sand spit where a dozen harbor seals have hauled up. This is where the old frontier meets the blue frontier.

Beyond Jenner the two-lane highway climbs fast with a few long loops around deep creek beds. Twisting up the road I see red-tailed hawks and then when I can no longer afford to take my eyes off the road, the shadows of hawks gliding across the vertical sunlit cliff face to my right. Just beyond where the road crests I squeeze off the two-lane tarmac at a gravel pullover to take a picture. The mountainside drops away precipitously on a seventy-five to eighty degree incline full of loose scree and a few shrubs down to the blue-green ocean more than one thousand feet below. A couple on touring bikes has also pulled over, dug into their saddlebags, and are eating peanut butter and PowerBars. I tell them they're close to the top.

Kelly and Emily Marcus are from Maryville, Tennessee, and six weeks into their bicycle trip from northern Washington to San Diego. They're teachers and recently spent two years running a school in a native Alaskan village north of the Arctic Circle. He's a red beard and she's tan and brunet and both are healthy and athletic looking with bulging calf muscles.

"So what do you think of California so far?" I ask.

"Pretty," he says.

"But very hilly," she amends, taking another spoonful of peanut butter.

Soon I pass Salt Point, a popular abalone dive site close to where a free diver got decapitated by a shark and a number of padlock-gated state parks and overviews, shut down due to budget cuts, before I reach my destination for the night: Sea Ranch, the converted sheep ranch that runs for ten miles along the northern coast of Sonoma.

I put up with friends from San Francisco, Steve and Pipa. Pipa, an inveterate horsewoman has just been riding on the bluffs. Due to the economy they're going to have to sell their second home here at Sea Ranch after six years. They're sad about this and I can understand why. While Sea Ranch's extensive lands with their bluff, meadow, and forest homes, all architectural gems in unpainted wood and shingle, is the reason the California Coastal Commission was created, it's also the ultimate getaway destination for those who love wild salty places where the mountains meet the sea. After decades of driving past it I'm glad to get this peek behind its low split-rail fence.

"Sometimes it feels like a Potemkin village, since most of the houses aren't occupied most of the time" Steve tells me as we hike toward the water with Pipa and their collie/shepherd mix Tango through golden fields of straw and elephant grass and scattered meadow homes along the sides of which a few grazing deer check us out incuriously. With 1,800 houses and condo units, three large pools, a community center, golf course, visitor lodge, and landing strip, its year-round population is still only 280, mostly retired pilots (from the air you can see it's one of the sunniest stretches of the coast), high-income professionals, and discreet ex-growers. It also retains a herd of sheep that are now used to keep the meadows grazed as a fire precaution. The sheepherd, likely the world's richest drover of livestock, earns around $100,000 a year.

We walk down to Shell Beach where a dozen harbor seals are bobbing vertical just offshore, checking us out from among the sea rocks and kelp. "Lone pups are not abandoned. Mom is just out feeding," a sign by the beach warns lest anyone try to "rescue" a baby seal that doesn't need their help. Steve has walked the twenty-one-mile perimeter of Sea Ranch, but today we take a more leisurely saunter past cypress windbreaks and wind-sculpted pines and a great blue heron claiming an ocean view for itself. We walk along the bluff past a state marine reserve to Walk On Beach, which has big driftwood sculptures and handmade structures and piles of kelp wrack drawing thousands of kelp flies for the shorebirds to feast on. There are freshwater drizzles down the brown stone faces of the forty-foot bluffs here that will become roaring cataracts, cascades, and waterfalls during the winter rains to come.

On the walk back to their small house and studio off Whalebone Reach, we spot some late-blooming purple thistle, huckleberry, and blackberry bushes and stop to admire a large white winged bird with gray patches that takes off from a lone sapling in the meadow.

Later we have dinner at the Lodge by Black Point Beach where the *Kenkoku Maru,* a Japanese freighter, went aground in the fog in April 1951, the month I was born. The Lodge is not as well known as the Timber Cove Inn to the south but still has great food and far fewer raccoons hanging out.

Along with raccoons, skunks, deer, hawks, herons, black bear, and buzzards, cougars get a lot of local attention. Four years earlier an older couple went hiking and a big cat attacked the man from behind and his wife stabbed it with a ballpoint pen till it took off into the woods. This generated some panic and a community meeting of more than four hundred Sea Ranch homeowners. Eventually things settled back down and now the proprietor of the Four-Eyed Frog bookstore in Gualala keeps track of all local cougar sightings.

Climbing through a high forest clearing by the landing strip the next morning, surrounded by fir, ponderosa, and bristlecone pines, most draped in hanging pale green moss, we turn around to look down across the planted and slanted roofs of the eco-designer homes far below, the golden bluffs, and the steel blue sea where the horizon is softened by morning fog. "The grass is emerald green in the winter, like Ireland" Steve tells me as I spot a couple of deer below us. "There are wildflowers in the spring with constant winds blowing out of the north. The summer is pretty foggy and gray but September, October, November like this, with these hot, dry, quiet clear days. This is the best," he says in a wistful tone. He is accepting about their imminent departure, understanding that we get our transient pleasures and then move on, but still. . . .

Immediately north of Sea Ranch is the town of Gualala just over the Mendocino county line. Across from the supermarket there's the old logger's hotel from 1901 and nearby a hardware store where they've nailed big plate-sized abalone shells to the wall with the names and dates of the divers who pried them off the sea bottom. This reminds me of trophy heads hanging in general stores and taverns in Wisconsin and Vermont although breath-hold diving for abs in California's cold, dark, and entangling under-water kelp forests makes deer hunting in lovely fall foliage seem kind of prissy.

North of Gualala is Anchor Bay and its beach where rumrunners used to drop their loads during Prohibition. Another half hour up the road is the town of Point Arena, a place author Stephen King would appreciate. There's something insular and vaguely threatening about what the tourist books call "this sleepy hamlet." I remember a night my late love, Nancy Ledan-sky, and I couldn't find a place to stay driving south down Highway 1 on a foggy Saturday night and finally we found a cheap motel here. The town was empty, cold, and clammy and the taciturn innkeeper acted insulted when we pointed out there were no towels in our room and we walked un-der the marquee of the empty theater to a café where we were the only customers and a waitress who'd been crying served us soup from a can.

Today Point Arena's population is around 450 and its local politics have turned toxic as a result of a two-year campaign to recall the mayor and city council. Main Street is a hilly affair with the only movie theater for about one hundred miles. Nearby on two different cutoffs are the historic light-house (rebuilt after the 1906 earthquake) and the harbor. There's a boat hoist and stone cobble beach at the fishing pier by the harbor and a two-story building with shops, a restaurant, and deli. Most of the earlier build-ings and the pier itself were destroyed by an El Niño storm in 1983.

I stop by the Point Arena lighthouse that is more than eleven stories high. I walk out to the edge of the Devil's Punch Bowl, a wave-eroded cra-ter now partly open to the sea, to admire some nearby sea isles with flat grassy tops. I look back up at the white column of the lighthouse set against the clear blue sky and can imagine the vertigo and think, maybe not Ste-phen King, maybe Alfred Hitchcock.

I head north through Manchester, population 120, and the coast turns gold and green with a few multimillion dollar houses of glass and wood set amid steeply rising dairy farms where brown Jersey cows graze and gaze out to sea at a few fishing boats plying the rough North Pacific. I pass a logging truck full of redwood logs headed south, a less common sight than it was twenty years ago. I drive by Irish Beach, one of those planned second-home developments that never took off after the Coastal Act, and pull over in the former logging town of Elk, population 250. Located on a bluff 135 feet above a driftwood crescent beach with rocky outcrops, this wide spot in the road was once a large mill town of two thousand producing eighty thousand board feet of timber a day that got shipped off a big wharf to San Francisco. Back then the coast was abuzz with steam mills and timber ships and the smell of sawdust, but the last mill in Elk burned down during the Depression and the redwood and Douglas fir were played out by the 1960s. Still it's a lovely and serene place with some nice B & Bs on the cliffs. There's a white church, a market, restaurant, and the 1901 Elk Garage (it replaced the blacksmith shop) on one side of the road. On the ocean side, three guys wearing camo shorts, long-sleeve Ts and bill caps are loading their black Tundra pickup full of beer and wet suits in the dirt parking lot—ab or urchin divers, I figure, since Sonoma's red tide has not spread this far north.

Just to the north of Elk is where Highway 128 comes in from 101 by way of the bucolic Anderson Valley, now full of vineyards and wine-tasting rooms, and the real tourist stretch of the Mendocino coast picks up with countless B and Bs like the Little River Inn by Van Damme State Park, fancy restaurants including Café Beaujolais and 955 in the village of Mendocino, many opportunities for cliff weddings, hot rock massages, new-age retreats, beach walks, even a "skunk train" with forty miles of track, the last of some sixty short-line logging railroads that now provides a tourist ride between Fort Bragg and Willits inland on 101 through second-growth redwood forest and small pot patches along the Noyo River that's still home to steelhead trout, chinook and coho salmon. Even with its many pricy visitor attractions, Mendocino remains one of the most spectacular stretches of blue ocean coastline in the world, with forested hilltop ridges where great horned owls can still be heard, and narrow rocky coves full of kelp and sea stars and abalone and gray sandy pocket beaches.

It's been awhile since I last visited the village of Mendocino on its 150-foot-high bluff and I'm glad to see this logging town turned artist colony turned tourist magnet of almost nine hundred souls hasn't changed, at least not in the last few decades. It has the same wooden water tower and white church with the same carved scythe-bearing angel and maiden on top near the same main street of old hotels and false-front saloons facing the bay by a giant driftwood bench where the Big River lets out to the sea. The whole New England–style town settled by gold rush Yankees has been designated a historic district of Victorian, Queen Ann, Italianate, and salt-box houses. This is where the exteriors for Angela Lansbury's TV series *Murder She Wrote* were shot, the cliff-top California town doubling for her character's village in Maine. Many of the houses are now B and Bs scattered on a few streets and unpaved lanes full of wildflowers and blackberries that terminate by a grassy open field where the last windswept pines and a lonely settler house have only the Pacific Ocean for their neighbor.

The Headlands State Park surrounding the town on three sides was established to protect the bluff from development. This was after local artist Emmy Lou Packard, a muralist and painter who as a young beauty lived and worked in Mexico with Diego Rivera and Frida Kahlo, made a disturbing discovery. Unlike Angela Lansbury's character, the death threat she uncovered was less personal than spiritual in nature in that the Boise Cascade timber company planned to develop condominiums that would have blocked the view south from Main Street on land where the old Union Lumber mill had burned down. In 1968 Emmy Lou helped found the Headlands Park Committee that eventually led to a 1972 swap of timberland for town land as well as a range of other local efforts that have preserved the village's unique historic character.

Ten miles north of California's version of Colonial Williamsburg is Fort Bragg, with its modern highway bridge over the Noyo River Harbor where the fishing docks, seafood restaurants, boatyards, Coast Guard station, kayakers, and raucous sea lions are located. Things are looking good this year because the salmon are back in the million-plus range, which not only puts money in the pockets of commercial fishermen but also draws tourists and recreational fishers. I park at the north end of town for a quick walk on Glass Beach. A sign at the head of its sandy path reads "Abalone watch—

stop poaching," and gives a Web address. The trail is lined with pink, white, and yellow wildflowers—fuchsia, yarrow, trillium, tansy, and black-eyed Susan. From below the bluffs where two kids are digging into the side of the sandstone cliff, I watch a dark bank of fog building offshore, the darkness rolling toward the coastal mountains to the north. I pick small pieces of sea glass out of the sand—white, brown and green—the sand still chill from where the waves have washed over it. This used to be the town dump where troops from the fort, loggers, and fishermen tossed out their bottles. Now nineteenth- and twentieth-century garbage has turned into twenty-first-century treasure.

I've been to a beach in Hawaii where plastic debris from the Pacific Gyre that won't biodegrade has broken down into so many tiny pieces that there's as much polymer as coral and silicate making up the multicolored "plastisand." There's also larger marine debris, including plastic toothbrushes, buckets, hunks of polystyrene foam, fishing nets, and Bic lighters. More recently I was strolling a wild beach by Davenport on California's Central Coast with a friend and we started picking up plastic trash and had filled up our arms and pockets within a hundred yards. None of our discarded plastic is or will ever be as attractive as the rounded glass fragments I'm now filling my pockets with.

Back in the car KZYX Mendocino county public radio warns there are calves loose on the road between Ft. Bragg and Westport. This is followed by a report of increased winds, rain, and four- to six-foot ocean swells on ten-second intervals.

Westport is the last town in Mendocino before Humboldt and the Lost Coast, though *town* is a pretty extravagant word for a few dozen buildings, picnic tables on the beach, a community store, and not much more. Of course once there was a great timber pier and port complex here, too, but that was back before history and nature reclaimed this fetch of the coast.

North of Westport, Highway 1 jogs inland over high ridgelines through the thirty-mile-wide band of fog-fed coastal redwood mountains that stretch from Big Sur to Oregon. The road then hooks up with 101 at Leggett.

I could continue along the coast on the Usal Road that's more of a pine-shaded dirt track, running along the high cliffs of the Sinkyone Wilderness, down to Shelter Cove, and back up into the King Range, which rises four thousand feet above the sea. It then winds through the pungent marijuana forest hamlets of Honeydew and Petrolia passing the Mattole River and its wild, driftwood-choked beach and Cape Mendocino, the most westerly point in the continental United States, before eventually emerging in the Victorian town of Ferndale on the Eel River Valley below Humboldt Bay, maybe twelve hours of driving on mostly passable though sometimes badly rutted track before the winter rains threaten to wash out big sections of it.

Instead I follow the main road, slowing down for two deer crossing 101 just south of Garberville in southern Humboldt, the farm town capital of the Emerald Triangle of weed that includes Mendocino, Humboldt, and Trinity counties to the north and east where you can explore the rarely visited Trinity Alps Wilderness, the Trinity River (a tributary of the Klamath), and find close to fifteen thousand trinity county residents, not all of whom are involved in marijuana farming. North of Garberville around Weott I cut off onto the Avenue of the Giants, which meanders for the next thirty miles through one of the "Redwood Empire's" first big tree parks.

Silent grandeur is the oft-used and appropriate term when you're among centuries-old redwoods. I remember watching my uncle Arthur from Indiana when he was in his eighties staring up at his first redwood tree in Muir Woods with a look of wonder you'd expect on the face of an eight-year-old. I began to tell him about the timber wars then taking place here in Humboldt. "Why would they let anyone cut them down," he interrupted. I stop at Founder's Grove, named after the 1918 founders of the Save the Redwoods League that helped prevent the logging of tens of thousands of acres of these giants that have been around since the age of the dinosaurs. "Ambassadors from another time" John Steinbeck called them.

I get out and walk along the open paths at the base of the rose- and brick-colored behemoths. Their needles help clear the understory except for some big ferns and saplings. Periodic wildfires help germinate their seeds. Some of these trees were already big when Jesus was a young man. There are a handful of tourists here with young kids, but everyone's amazingly quiet. It's a place of silent and respectful awe except for some discreet bird-song coming through the forest.

Judi Bari was no Tweety Bird, however. She was a loud, funny, contentious Earth First! activist who organized the Redwood Summer timber protests of 1990 in Mendocino and Humboldt. She was run off the road by a logging truck and received numerous death threats while organizing to save the last stands of unprotected old-growth forest that the Pacific Lumber company planned to cut down. I got to know her when Steve Talbot and I were working on a documentary titled *Who Bombed Judi Bari?* for the San Francisco PBS station. This was after she'd been maimed by a pipe bomb that was planted under the front seat of her car. Initially the FBI targeted her for transporting the bomb, but when the evidence showed she was the victim and not the perpetrator of the crime, the agency seemed to lose interest in the case. Having survived the near-fatal bombing, she died several years later of breast cancer. Her legacy is the 7,472-acre Headwaters Forest national preserve near Humboldt Bay that the government bought from Pacific Lumber in 1996 and that includes three hundred-foot-tall giant redwoods more than one thousand years old.

Soon I'm driving through Scotia, the Pacific Lumber Company mill town, population 850, and on into Fortuna, a city of eleven thousand at the foot of the Eel River Valley. From there I continue on up along the south end of Humboldt Bay, the second largest estuary in California, and on into the city of Eureka.

While hipsters rave about the Humboldt State University college town of Arcata at the north end of the bay with its historic green plaza, farmers' market, festive parades, and mix of environmental activists and marijuana grow houses, Eureka strikes me as the ultimate livable city if you can call a town of twenty-eight thousand in a greater metropolitan area of some seventy thousand people a city. Still, it has a lively buzz about it from its commercial and recreational boat marinas and downtown streets to its Old Town district with its nineteenth- and early-twentieth-century stores, houses, hotels, restaurants, and saloons looking across the cleaned-up bay to the

Samoa Peninsula where the old Louisiana Pacific pulp mill closed its gates in 2010. Passing a 1920s-era office building near the food co-op I spot a storefront flyer for a Buffy Sainte-Marie concert that weekend.

Just north of Arcata is McKinleyville, a sprawling suburban town of thirteen thousand with the world's tallest totem pole that has grown up around the regional airport where flights are canceled one out of three days due to fog.

I'm reminded of Southeast Alaska as I continue north through fog and drizzle and expansive rugged landscapes and seascapes that are home to fishers and martin, otter, coyote, owl, hawk and cougar, elk and eagle, black bear, sea lion, pelican, shark, and whale.

I drive into Trinidad near Humboldt State's marine lab and have a late sandwich by the hamlet's forested headland and lighthouse above a dozen moored fishing boats, a green sea isle, and a kayaker heading out from the pier. Here I pay my respects at the fishermens' white anchor memorial with its names inscribed in marble: "In loving memory to those who perished at sea—they shall live forever in our hearts." It lists the names of more than sixty locals who went out to fish and died at sea. Among other things, Northern California is a long time mariners' graveyard. When I was last here several years ago major surf was rolling in under the lighthouse. I was aboard the Coast Guard buoy tender *Aspen* steaming offshore. Realizing there'd be no shelter on the leeward side of the head, the captain turned us back into the twenty-foot seas to ride out the storm through the night. I stayed in my rack for eleven hours and when I got up the next morning the seas had dropped to six to eight feet and there was a fan of brown water from weeks of heavy El Niño storms extending more than three miles out to sea.

I drive on through stands of Sitka spruce, pine, alder, and arrow-straight redwoods past Patrick's Point and Big Lagoon and Stone Lagoon, where 101 becomes the Redwood Highway and the wild outer banks of these fog-patched reaches of icy water look as distant and desolate as damnation, though also heartachingly beautiful. I startle two ravens feeding on a road-killed raccoon and they take flight in front of me like a couple of black tears in a nineteenth-century seascape.

Near Orrick in the Redwood National Park I pull over to watch a herd of wet and shaggy Roosevelt elk, maybe seventy or more of the big animals grazing in a soaking wet meadow.

Then around Hope Creek with the Irish band Planxty on the CD player I cross from Humboldt into Del Norte County. The size of Delaware, Del Norte (with a silent *e*) has a population comparable to that of the town of Eureka, including the three thousand inmates and guards at Pelican Bay State Prison.

I cross the Klamath River past the Yurok Tribal headquarters and half an hour later pull in at the Crescent Beach Motel in Crescent City. With no desire to stake a tent in the rain, chill, and darkness I instead luxuriate in a simple room with double bed, hot shower, and dial-up thermostat that I'm directed to through a breezeway that faces onto a wide, empty beach covered in driftwood and sand dollars.

The next day I head north of town with Grant Werschkull, executive director of the conservationist Smith River Alliance, the Smith being the last wild river up here. He takes me to the edge of Lake Earl, which was the mouth of the river about ten thousand years ago and with its outlet to the sea is still the largest coastal lagoon south of Alaska. Its shallow waters are full of trout and salmon and migratory birds, and it's surrounded by wetlands and grassy dunes and hummocks and is the site of another failed real-estate venture of the 1960s called Pacific Shores, where 1,500 lakefront lots were sold, mostly sight unseen, to people in Southern California and Hawaii with the promise of a golf course and shopping center to follow. However, no provision for water or sewage connections had been made and no permits granted. Then the Clean Water Act came into effect and sinking septic tanks into wetlands was no longer an option. Years went by and the landowners began to realize they were stuck with property they couldn't build on. In the 1970s California's Department of Fish and Game began buying up lots using park bond money. Today, some forty-five years later, Fish and Game has bought 51 percent of the parcels and has incorporated them into a spectacular eleven thousand-acre wildlife area. Five hundred acres of privately held lots remain. About 25 percent of these are in default or arrears on their property taxes. Patty McCleary, deputy director of the Smith River Alliance, tells me one of the group's roles is to act as an honest broker, to help facilitate continued public acquisition of the undevelopable land by identifying owners willing to sell.

"Some of the people I've talked to," she explains, "they were young people in Los Angeles in 1963 and their dream was that they were going to move to the coast and retire. And it's a hard decision to sell even after forty years, even if you're eighty and retired and live somewhere else because this was part of who you were that you owned property on the coast and many appreciate the coast and have visited here and love it and came around to understanding why this is so special a place and so were finally at peace with selling."

I convince Grant, lanky, friendly, and dressed for the weather in a fleece cap and green rain gear, to take a walk with me. We climb down some boulders by the Nautical Inn with its small water view restaurant onto Pelican State Beach below a low bluff with a few weatherworn beach houses painted in flaking blue and red. The beach itself is wide and flat with coarse dark sand below rolling forested hills and big offshore rock formations. It's been raining on and off and the gray skies are low and threatening. There's a big redwood stump where the edge of a forest once stood, a few yards up from the drumming surf where sandpipers are skittering along the foam line like nervous commuters. We stop by pieces of damp, twisted driftwood the size of coffee tables where a seagull is feeding on a dead orange sea star with eight-inch-long arms. The bird flaps away as we examine the big starfish, then returns after we walk on up the beach. Coils of fog are drifting through the conifers. Farther up there's a modern wooden building in the dunes with a slanted roof and lots of glass, and as we approach we can see a footpath through the saw grass and sand and walk up next to a parking lot and Sitka pine forest strip and climb some wide wooden steps onto the porch of the Crissey Field State Park welcome center in Oregon.

An hour later we recross the border, this time by car. There's a welcome sign going north and when we turn around a mile up the road and head back, we arrive at the triple-lane garagelike Smith River Agricultural Border Station, where we're asked if we're carrying any fruits or live plants and then are waved on through, being the only car in line.

Oregonians worry that folks visiting from California may stay on to live in Oregon and there's nothing they can do about it. Californians are happy to welcome southbound visitors, provided they don't bring apple bugs with them. California's border with Oregon feels loose and undefined and also a very long way from the international border fence at Playa Tijuana. While I understand that state borders are not national borders, I can't help feeling that there should be something more, because California feels more like a nation to me, a uniquely maritime nation unto itself.

RISING TIDES

*Those who live by the sea can hardly form
a single thought of which the sea would not be part.*

—HERMANN BROCH

I believe it's Californians' sense of entitlement to the coast and ocean, their understanding that it belongs to all of them—surfers, sailors, fishermen, the maritime industry, the tourist industry, the navy, the tribes, and every single beachgoer—that makes protecting California's seas both so contentious and so effective. Because of their wide range of users, California's ocean and shoreline can never be dominated by a single industry or interest. In Massachusetts there's a feeling the ocean belongs to the fishermen, and as a result New England's waters have long been overfished and depleted. In Louisiana they know it belongs to the oil companies, and things like the BP oil blowout of 2010, the loss of their coastal wetlands, and the "cancer alley" that's grown up along the lower Mississippi where the refineries are located is the price they've had to pay. In Florida the real-estate industry so dominates ocean and coastal uses that when you encounter bits of undeveloped "old Florida" it's like finding a piece of paradise lost. In California, however, it's the people who continue to fight over and protect their golden shore and deep blue sea.

According to the California Ocean Protection Act of 2004:

California's coastal and ocean resources are critical to the state's environmental and economic security and integral to the state's high quality of life and culture. A healthy ocean is part of the state's legacy, and is necessary to support the state's human and wildlife populations. Each generation of Californians has an obligation to be good stewards of the ocean, to pass the legacy on to their children.

South to north or river to sea, SeaWorld, Big Sur, the Golden Gate, the Beach Boys or, *Beach Blanket Babylon,* California's ocean waters are historic, cultural, legal, and literary phenomena bonded to the very DNA of the state. Its passionate love affair with the ocean is ongoing, its pop-cultural references to it too vast to fully enumerate. *The Endless Summer* starts and ends in California. The original *Treasure Island* was filmed on Catalina, and *Sea Hunt,* in which Lloyd Bridges played underwater investigator Mike Nelson—inspiration for generations of divers and marine scientists—was largely shot in the waters off Catalina where actress Natalie Wood also drowned and a criminal investigation into her death was reopened forty-five years later. *SpongeBob SquarePants* was created by California marine biologist Stephen Hillenburg, *The Little Mermaid* and *Finding Nemo* were brought to life by California's Disney and Pixar studios. It's also worth noting it was Southern California's *Baywatch,* not Florida's *Flipper* or Oahu's *Hawaii Five-0,* that became the most watched television series on the planet, though not purely for reasons aquatic. Admittedly *The Undersea World of Jacques Cousteau* was produced but not based in California. Still, Jacques' son Jean-Michel today works and produces underwater documentaries in Santa Barbara while Hollywood director and deep-ocean explorer James Cameron lives by the beach in Malibu.

California's coastal culture also has great literary depth. A romp down the coast would have to include Brett Harte, Mark Twain, Jack London, Ambrose Bierce, Amy Tan, Frank Norris, Maxine Hong Kingston, Isabel Allende, William Saroyan and Lawrence Ferlinghetti in Northern California. On the road would be Jack Kerouac, of course. Heading south past San Jose you'd find Luis Valdez and Luis Lopez, then continue on to where Daniel Duane surfed Santa Cruz and John Steinbeck partied with Ed Ricketts in Monterey and Carmel. There you'd also find Upton Sinclair, Joseph Campbell, Mary Austin, Carey McWilliams, and poets George Sterling and Robinson Jeffers. Then you'd make the steep climb up to Henry Miller in his Big Sur redoubt followed by a long slide past journalistic rogue William Randolph Hearst's castle and Santa Barbara's T. C. Boyle to L.A. There you would find Raymond Chandler, Robert Stone, Joan Didion, Walter Mosley, Helen Hunt Jackson, and onetime San Francisco detective Dashiell Hammett writing for Hollywood and drinking in La Jolla with Lillian Hellman close to where Chandler made his final home by San Diego's Windansea. Plus, don't forget the observations of Max Miller on the waterfront and Richard Henry Dana Jr. sailing by.

By contrast John Muir lived in the Bay/Delta town of Martinez but preferred to write about the Sierra Mountain granite that Ansel Adams photographed. Smeaton Chase rode a horse up the coast and wrote about it more than ploddingly well, while Hunter Thompson went to work at the O'Farrell Street strip club run by San Francisco's Jim and Artie Mitchell, an extension of the Barbary Coast bars and brothels praised by Warren Hinckle, before things went bad and Jim shot Artie to death. Marc Reisner in Sausalito wrote more trenchantly about freshwater and shaky earth, noting the oddness that California's major coastal cities were built where the water wasn't but the fault lines were. Then there are the famous scribes of city and state like Herb Caen in *Don't Call it Frisco,* Mike Davis in L.A.,

Neil Morgan in San Diego, and state historian Kevin Starr everywhere taking notes. Those are just the ones I can think of.

It's a game you can play while sailing, biking, or hiking the coast using almost any category you can think of: famous California surfers or sailors or best watermen (Coronado Navy SEALs versus L.A. lifeguards versus Coast Guard rescue swimmers), Hollywood types old and new such as the Olympic gold medalist swimmer-turned-actor Johnny Weissmuller *(Tarzan)*, dedicated surfer Sean Penn, or director/explorer James Cameron of *The Abyss, Titanic,* and *Avatar* fame. Many of the strangely beautiful 3-D alien life-forms in *Avatar* can also be found in the depths of the seas that he's visited. There's coastal activist Pierce Brosnan and his wife Keely, Sigourney Weaver, January Jones, and of course longtime ocean advocate Ted Danson.

"I'm not an expert. I am an actor. My job is to stand next to the experts and focus attention on them," Danson claims. Still, he has a depth of knowledge well beyond the typical celebrity advocating for a cause. He didn't set out to be an activist, he tells me. He just wanted to take his little girls to the ocean on a nice day back in 1986 but when they arrived at Will Rogers State Beach in Pacific Palisades it was closed due to pollution. "It seemed so strange to look at this huge, vast beautiful ocean and think that we couldn't enjoy it in the way we did when I was a kid," he says. Soon the actor, then starring as barkeep Sam Malone on NBC's hit series *Cheers,* met environmental attorney Robert Sulnick, and the two cofounded the American Oceans Campaign, which in 2001 merged with the global marine conservation group Oceana, which works on a number of problems from industrial overfishing to climate change. "Still, it's not all doom and gloom," says the lanky, silver-haired Danson, now starring in CBS's *CSI* and in several films, including *Big Miracle* about a couple of California gray whales stranded in the Arctic. "It's an opportunity to make a difference in the world," Danson explains his activism. "You just need to get involved."

Also making a difference are California's many ocean entrepreneurs, which only makes sense given that California has the largest ocean economy of any state. According to the National Ocean Economics Program based out of the Monterey Institute of International Studies, the California coastal economy was responsible for supporting more than fourteen million jobs in 2010 while paying $768 billion in wages to those who depend on the sea for their livelihoods, including coastal tourism, recreation, fishing, and ports. Even in a recession it seems a healthy ocean can keep blue businesses afloat.

A few examples would have to include the surfing and diving Meistrell twins, Bill and Bob, who made their own wet suits out of neoprene insulation from the back of a refrigerator sixty years ago before going on to found the Body Glove company in their Southern California dive shop. There's Hobie Alter, who redefined surfboards with foam and fiberglass and supercharged sailing with his Hobie Cat sailboat; Jack O'Neill, who brought neoprene wet suits to surfing and lost an eye to an early board leash; Randy Repass who, rather than a computer startup like Apple, used his Sunnyvale garage to create West Marine, the boat-supply company with sales of more than $600 million a year; also Sunnyvale's James Gosling and his robotic Wave Gliders, wave and solar-powered autonomous vessels the size of surfboards that have begun sailing the seas as research platforms for the navy, the oil industry, and marine scientists. There's ocean engineer Graham Hawkes, who's working to help Virgin Air billionaire Richard Branson "fly" Hawkes's one-man submersible *Deep Flight Challenger* to the deepest part of the ocean as James Cameron did on March 25, 2012, in a high-tech elevator-shaped submersible, *Deepsea Challenger,* which he codesigned. This made Cameron the third person in history to travel seven miles down in the Mariana Trench to the lowest point on earth. The last two humans to make that journey were Don Walsh and Jacques Piccard, back in 1960 aboard the U.S. Navy's bathysphere *Trieste.* When I last saw the Hawkes vessel, which looks like a hybrid of a torpedo and fighter jet, at his Point Richmond workshop, they were about to replace its glass canopy at the front end (the driver has to lie down flat to pilot it) with a new dome made entirely of quartz, a block of which they planned to buy from the semiconductor industry for around $70,000. The cost of the vessel itself was running around $6 million at the time.

More recently, Hawkes took Branson for a ride in his *Super-Falcon* two-seater sub off Guadalupe Island in Baja, where the twenty-two-foot vehicle was followed around by curious white sharks almost as large, including one that briefly came into view and escorted them like a combat wingman.

Hawkes, raised in England where he first began building underwater robots, dive suits, and submersibles, told me his working-class Cockney accent made it hard for him to raise capital from wealthy class-conscious British investors. When he moved to California more than thirty years ago, however, he found a much more entrepreneurial spirit and willing investors. It's an ocean of opportunity, you might say.

California-born natives Greg MacGillivray and the late Jim Freeman only wanted to catch waves before they shot the classic surf film *Five Summer Stories* and went on to pioneer IMAX films that have generated more than $1 billion in revenue. It was after hearing Oakland-based oceanographer, entrepreneur, and explorer Sylvia Earle talk about our seas being at an environmental tipping point that MacGillivray, his wife, Barbara, and son Shaun decided they also needed to make a difference. Their company has now launched the five-year One World One Ocean marine conservation project in partnership with Coca-Cola and other major companies. The effort includes 3D IMAX films, a TV series, and a theatrical movie release.

Mark Holmes and his Green Wave Energy Corporation based in Newport Beach, along with building wind and solar systems, is looking to use one of several wave turbine technologies (a vertical fiberglass cylinder with a large propeller) to create carbon-free commercial energy offshore.

La Jolla–based biologist and entrepreneur J. Craig Venter, a pioneer in sequencing the human genome, has been working for years sampling and cataloging life in the ocean, sequencing the genomes of hundreds of marine microbes. Through the J. Craig Venter Institute, he's been looking at modifying microorganisms like these to create clean fuels. He's also entered into a $600-million-dollar collaboration with Exxon to develop the next generation of biofuels.

Many millions more are being invested in start-up companies and corporations seeking to create algae-based biofuels, including Lisa

Morgenthaler-Jones's LiveFuels, which "taps the power of natural aquatic life to produce renewable fuels from algae." That's the PETA-proof way of saying they feed algae to forage fish and then use fish oil for fuel rather than trying to process the algae directly, an effort that has had mixed results to date. Other fish-based California ocean entrepreneurs include sustainable seafood chef Dory Ford, restaurateur Kenny Belov, and seafood wholesaler Paul Johnson.

Wyland, the California artist and entrepreneur who goes by his last name, owns several dozen galleries of the same name selling his marine life paintings, drawings, and sculptures. There's also a brand of nontoxic Wyland paints, instructional videos, a PBS series, music, films, a Wyland Hotel on Waikiki, a nonprofit foundation, etc. His giant whale murals grace cityscapes in Paris and Beijing, as well as in San Francisco, San Diego, and Long Beach.

"I came to California to visit my aunt when I was fourteen and wanted to see the ocean," the former working-class kid from Detroit tells me. "I was three days in West Covina before she brought us to the beach here," he says, pointing from his deck on Laguna Beach. "I spotted two gray whales spouting two hundred yards in front of me, right there." I look, but only see a stand-up paddleboarder and some bikinied sunbathers. "It changed me. Ten years later I moved here and painted those same whales on this building." He grins. "It was the Fahrenheit Bookstore and I painted it right there. Go hang over the side," he suggests. I go to the edge of the deck and hang over to where I can see, mostly upside down, the life-sized gray whale and calf mural, now redone in tile. Later, after the bookstore closed, he bought the building and turned it into one of his galleries and a live/work studio.

If you wanted to, you could expand the list of California's ocean entrepreneurs to include business folks who just love the sea like Patagonia founder and surfer Yvon Chouinard or the management team at Pacific Life Insurance who, with their company logo of a leaping humpback, decided to become major supporters of whale conservation. Playing by these rules, of course, you'd quickly get into the tall kelp of California business legends such as David Packard of HP, who helped create a world-class aquarium and major research center on Monterey Bay, Intel cofounder Gordon Moore who with his wife, Betty, established a foundation that's become a key player in marine conservation and science, or Google executive chairman Eric Schmidt and his wife Wendy who put $60 million into a pair of oceangoing yachts, *Lone Ranger* and *Falkor,* retrofitting them for oceanographic research. (Wendy also funded a million-dollar X Prize to improve oil-spill cleanup technology.) And then there's Oracle founder and yacht collector, Larry Ellison, who won the America's Cup in 2010 and brought it to San Francisco in 2013.

But what's the purpose of the game at this point? I mean what coastal Californian doesn't love the sea? As for the small minority of the state's population in its forested mountains, sere desert, and agricultural central valley, I suspect they do, too.

Unfortunately, we may soon have more sea to love than we can handle. In the twentieth century sea level rose eight inches along the California coast. Moderate projections have it rising at least a foot by 2050 and three to five feet by the end of the century. The California Ocean Protection Council's five-year strategic plan for 2012 through 2017 states:

> *The changing climate is transforming California's coast and ocean in unprecedented ways. In general, sea level is rising, temperatures are increasing, and precipitation and runoff are becoming more variable. The ocean is becoming more acidic as it absorbs carbon dioxide from the atmosphere. Other critical drivers of ocean conditions and productivity, such as ocean currents and upwelling, are also likely to change. . . . These impacts will intensify over the coming decades and will pose a growing risk to the state.*

Whenever I hear predictions like that, I think of the El Niño winters of the early 1980s when I lived in a cliff house in San Diego and serial storms battered the house, the cliff, the neighborhood, and flooded beach homes, commercial properties, and waterfront structures up and down the coast. My roommate Charlie went to shoot the waves breaking over the O.B. pier for his TV station and was hit by the backwash of one, soaking and destroying his $40,000 Ikagami camera. O.B.'s main street, Newport Avenue, was awash with ocean water, foam, and cars covered in kelp that day.

My friend Jon wanted to sell his boat up in the Bay Area. After seven weekends of waiting out storms he decided to go for it on the eighth and talked me into going along on the first leg to Oceanside. We beat our way out of Mission Bay but eight hours later, under battering rains, had only been able to get as far as Del Mar. We were four miles off the flooding Del Mar River and the sea was mud brown from runoff with a ladder and a fifty-five-gallon drum floating by, at which point we decided to turn around. We were driven south at breakneck speed and soon were back at Mission Bay's jetty, where we had to time our takeoff and literally surfed the thirty-five-foot sloop *Annie* through the harbor entry and into the protected waters of the bay. The next morning we motored back out to the entry to see if things had calmed, but it was still closed out with eighteen- to twenty-foot seas. We were talking to the harbor patrol when a big power yacht came charging past us, trying to break through. A wave caught it full-on, taking out the pilothouse glass and pushing it sideways toward the seawall. The patrol boat powered up its lights and siren and went to its assistance. Those were bad years with lots of coastal damage and lives lost, and I don't look forward to an increasing number of them.

A recent report by the U.S. Geological Survey predicts that with changing patterns of rain and snow, including less snowpack and faster-melting snow in the Sierra Nevada, we will see more frequent and intense flooding and droughts across the state. "We have to really think about anticipated changes in the frequency of extreme events," warns U.S.G.S. scientist James Cloern, the study's lead author. "As global warming proceeds, we're going to experience combinations of environmental conditions unlike any we've seen in the past."

One response may be increased use of desalinization plants along the coast to help offset water losses in the mountains. As this water conversion technology improves, the California Ocean Protection Council is recommending rule changes to ensure that if desal plants do become part of the state's water supply portfolio they not use the once-through intake/outfall pipes discussed earlier that heat up adjacent waters, not allow large-scale trapping of marine organisms, not allow briny discharges of salt back into the ocean, and that they be low-energy and/or clean-energy users so that they not add significant new greenhouse gases to the atmosphere. OPC is hoping to minimize the law of unintended consequences with early precautionary rule-making even as the state tries to adapt to the disruptive consequences of our ongoing energy choices.

Rising tides under the Golden Gate Bridge are projected to directly impact more than a quarter million people and threaten more than $60 billion in infrastructure in the Bay/Delta region where both the San Francisco and Oakland airport are built on filled wetlands, as is the town house where I live, come to think of it.

Still, for the next few decades it's extreme storminess, waves, and king tides, not sea-level rise, that will have the most impact according to another U.S.G.S. scientist, Patrick Barnard, who testified in front of the Ocean Protection Council in Sacramento while it was formulating its strategic plan.

Dr. Barnard notes that with stronger winds linked to warming seas, ocean waves are getting bigger with an increase in the size of extreme waves in the Pacific Northwest of about ten feet in the last decade. Cowabunga! For more on killer waves, climate change, and what it means for surfers see Susan Casey's book *The Wave*.

Globally, ocean surface temperatures in the summer of 2009 were the warmest since record keeping began in 1880. Planetwide, nine of the ten hottest years on record have occurred since 2000. The tenth record breaker was 1998. The hottest decade on record was the one ending in 2009, although if trends continue, the one ending in 2019 will be even hotter.

Why all this isn't bigger news is explained by former *Wall Street Journal* editor Frank Allen who says, "Environmental stories don't break, they ooze."

"This is not something that people are worrying about right now, so there's only so much you can do till they do," says Sam Schuchat, executive director of the state-run California Coastal Conservancy and secretary of the Ocean Protection Council. "You would think about air pollution when it got to where you started coughing leaving your house and you'd think about water pollution when the Cuyahoga River caught fire (in Cleveland in 1969). That's when people got serious. Or with oil it took a disaster like the Santa Barbara spill. If it's an issue off in the future it's kind of like earthquake preparedness, only [with climate impacts] we don't even have the benefit of occasional 4.5 tremors to remind people that it's coming."

Still, the state of California, having learned to adjust and adapt to major earthquakes, mudslides, fires, and occasional civil unrest, remains ahead of the rest of the nation in preparing for the inevitable impacts of fossil-fuel-fired climate change.

More important, the state is addressing the cause of the problem with its Climate Action Plan to reduce greenhouse gas emissions. Renewable non-carbon energy reached 16 percent of the state's electric sales by the beginning of 2012 and is targeted to account for 33 percent of utility-generated electricity by 2020. At some point this may include offshore systems such as wind, wave, tidal power, and OTEC, ocean thermal energy conversion, which uses the temperature difference between deep cold water and surface water to generate power, although given today's regulatory bottlenecks any significant commercial production of offshore renewable energy is unlikely before 2020.

To date, over 90 percent of California's existing fossil fuel plants have been built for or converted to burning low-carbon natural gas, while in the United States as a whole carbon-heavy coal still produces 40 percent of the electricity generated, along with huge plumes of carbon dioxide, acid-rain-generating sulfur dioxide, and the neurotoxin mercury, which leaves the smokestacks of coal-fired plants, then rains out over the ocean and works its way back up the food web and onto our seafood platters. Clean coal, of course, is the most disingenuous advertising logo since low-tar cigarettes and, like cigarettes, also leads to lung disease.

With more than half of U.S. venture capital investment in clean technology now taking place in California and with energy conservation and efficiency programs that have seen the state's per capita energy consumption hold steady over thirty years as the rest of the nation's increased 40 percent, it's easy to make the argument that California, along with Germany, Denmark, and a few other nations (go Cook Islands), is helping move the world off its dependence on coal and petroleum, the leading energy developments of the sixteenth and nineteenth centuries. Still, given the existing buildup of greenhouse gases in the atmosphere and their impact on the ocean, adaptation to a changed climate is also going to be necessary.

That's why a number of local California governments and agencies have begun taking action. In 2012 the San Francisco Bay Conservation and Development Commission (BCDC), the first coastal planning agency in the world, amended the San Francisco Bay Plan to make sure projected sea-level rise is incorporated into any new project such as a planned $1.5-billion-dollar high-rise development and new home community on Treasure Island in the middle of the bay. After flooding in 2010 shut down the Great Highway in the Ocean Beach section of the city, San Francisco tried armoring the eroding shore with piles of boulders. The Army Corps of Engineers proposed pumping sand dredged from shipping channels onto the beach as a solution, while a city think tank on urban planning put forward a plan for shrinking the Great Highway from four to two lanes and rerouting part of it inland, seeing "planned retreat" as the best method to deal with sea-level rise. In the South Bay a major wetlands restoration project now under way is expected to reduce the impacts of sea-level rise and flooding both on low-income predominantly Hispanic towns such as Alviso, as well as low-lying, high-dollar value corporate campuses such as those of Yahoo! in Sunnyvale and Google in Mountain View.

In Newport Beach in Southern California, city planners are looking into raising seawalls in waterfront neighborhoods such as Balboa Island that are already prone to flooding and also requiring foundations on new beach properties be raised several feet—a modest start to be sure.

Governments in San Diego, Ventura, and Humboldt Bay are also involved in multi-stakeholder efforts to begin coastal planning for sea-level rise. As of 2012 about half the towns along the coast had begun developing climate adaptation policies. "It's not uncertainty about the science keeping them from acting," says Amber Mace, former OPC executive director. "It's lack of funding, lack of staff, and lack of support from outside." Tools the OPC can provide include high-resolution seafloor maps with improved intertidal and shoreline maps to follow. Plus, OPC can offer links to a range of scientists who are working to downscale projections of climate impacts from the two hundred-mile grid scales used by the U.N.'s Intergovernmental Panel on Climate Change, to the local level where zoning, beachfront management, and other land use decisions are made.

The Ocean Protection Council has also gotten other state agencies to incorporate sea-level rise and climate change into their planning profiles, as has Governor Brown and Republican Governor Schwarzenegger, before him. The California Coastal Commission that requires all waterfront communities have Local Coastal Plans (LCPs) will soon require they revise them to incorporate projected sea-level rise and extreme flooding. It's also likely state grants to coastal communities will soon require applicants have a climate change adaptation policy in place in order to receive funding.

With increased coastal flooding expected due to more extreme weather patterns, the state Water Resources Control Board has established tougher standards for storm water runoff from construction and highway sites, and the construction trade industry has fought back in court where one judge ruled the board overstepped the bounds of the federal Clean Water Act. Of course, most of California's environmental laws are tougher then those of the feds. The California Environmental Quality Act (CEQA), for example, requires greenhouse gas emissions be accounted for in planning permits, whereas the National Environmental Policy Act (NEPA) does not require climate impacts be reported on federal environmental impact statements.

On the Central Coast farmers and ranchers and the Monterey Bay National Marine Sanctuary have worked out a voluntary water-quality program to reduce runoff on the eleven watersheds feeding into the bay. With use of year-round native ground cover, creek side plantings, soil-moisture management, and other simple techniques, they've reduced sediment runoff into Monterey Bay by more than half a million tons.

In L.A. six years of lawsuits by the environmental group Los Angeles Waterkeeper finally got the city to upgrade its storm water program in 2004. In 2011 they were back in court and together with the Natural Resources Defense Council won a ruling that the county flood control district responsible for runoff management had to further clean up its act. In practice this will likely involve an upgraded storm water system that moves beyond debris traps in storm drains and at the L.A. River mouth to rainwater runoff treatment aimed at getting rid of pathogens, pesticides, pet poo, and other pollutants picked up on the city's hardened surfaces before they reach the ocean. Under present conditions health advisories recommend Southern California surfers and swimmers wait seventy-two hours after a storm before entering the ocean.

The California shore is the site of numerous other efforts to protect the seas, including salt marsh, sea grass, and estuary restoration projects up and down the coast where 95 percent of the state's historic wetlands have been lost to development. There's a collaborative effort between the Nature Conservancy and fishermen in Half Moon Bay and other Central Coast harbors to keep the industry and the fisheries sustainable using an online tracking system called ECatch as well as a statewide sustainable seafood consumer education campaign that started with the Monterey Bay Aquarium back in 2000. The newly established MPA Monitoring Enterprise will evaluate and nurture California's newly created network of underwater parks along with many other marine science monitoring collaborations. There are marine debris initiatives, including a proposed state ban on single-use plastic bags, similar to ones already passed in San Francisco, Los Angeles, and dozens of other coastal towns. There are proposed and underway dam removals to restore sand for beaches downstream and habitat for salmon and steelhead upstream. There's even an America's Cup Healthy Ocean Project that's supposed to extend the worldwide sports event on San Francisco Bay to the protection of the waters on which it races. San Francisco Bay, of course, has long been to sailing what Indianapolis is to car racing.

"These are consistently the toughest inshore sailing conditions in the world," says Joan Garret, one of the media directors at the Saint Francis Yacht Club, "and it has created hardy sailors here with disdain for the stink of diesel engines, plus we have our environmental concerns in San Francisco. Down in Newport Beach and Southern California it's a whole other world where they like their powerboats."

No doubt if California were ever to become an independent nation it would quickly face the threat of civil war between north and south. Still, north or south, the California coast was created by some of the planet's most elemental forces, including uplift and erosion, earthquakes and tsunamis. If the Paleo-Indians of California could adjust to a post–Ice Age sea-level rise of several feet a century its modern people can adjust to four or five feet in the next century, even if we're thirty-seven million more numerous. Of course, it makes sense to act sooner rather than when we're thigh-deep in our flooded living rooms or—should the Greenland ice shelf melt—twenty feet underwater.

It's also worth remembering that in the last century civilization survived a major existential threat—the possibility of nuclear annihilation. There's no reason we can't deal with climate change and other challenges such as population growth.

What's frustrating is we know what the solutions are. If you stop killing sharks, tuna, and sea turtles they tend to come back; if you pay reasonable taxes to repair old sewer lines and improve water treatment plants and storm drains, you don't end up swimming in your own waste and bacteria; and when women are educated and empowered they choose to have fewer children. The challenge today is not in identifying solutions but in creating the political will to enact them.

Certainly if there's anyplace on the globe where there's been the convergence of scientific knowledge and inquiry, entrepreneurial spirit and a public willingness to lead the world in new directions, it's in California, Teddy Roosevelt's "West of the West."

If crisis is opportunity, then with our present-day economic morass, political gridlock, and vast and salty environmental threats, California has rarely had such a historic opportunity. People everywhere still look to California to see where the future will take us. They expect Californians to protect and restore the things they love and value and set an example, if no longer of "a shining city on a hill," then at least of a nice place by the water.

I'm back on the urban coast of San Diego at Charlie's house in Ocean Beach. It's Saturday night around midnight under a full summer moon when we notice dozens of lights on the beach down by the pier. The grunion are running, something that happens only in Southern California and Baja. Since Charlie's nine-year-old son, Joe, is up late, we decide to head down to the beach. I expect we'll locate the spawning fish—that come ashore to lay their eggs in the sand—by following the squealing voices of little kids chasing them along the shoreline.

As we get closer, however, I see there are at least as many adults as kids at the water's edge, most with serious predatory intent, their white plastic collection buckets planted high up on the beach, the line stretching for half a mile. Many of them are Southeast Asians originally from Vietnam, Cambodia, and Laos who arrived in California shortly after the United States lost its war in Indochina.

I talk to Mathew Khammao, a thick-set young guy around twenty with a fuzz of a beard who has just caught a fish in the wet sand. He says he's down here with his younger cousin showing him how to catch grunion. He's from San Diego but his parents are from Laos, "Laos Laotian not [tribal] Hmong," he explains.

"And you're keeping them to eat?"

"They're good fried whole or dried out."

"What do they taste like?"

"Like dried fish."

This is the second night of the run but the first they've come down to O.B., he tells me. There are hundreds of other folks here, many rushing into the water, more older teens and adults than children, with headlamps and flashlights sweeping the low breaking surf. A few are carrying plastic scoops and colanders—illegal since the Department of Fish and Game requires anyone over sixteen to have a fishing license and use only their hands, but I don't see any wardens around to enforce the rules. One tall guy in his twenties holding a flashlight in his mouth is running up and down the wet sand grabbing more of the slippery six-inch thin silver fish than anyone else. He's like a halfback sweeping his light from the breaking waves and across the beach looking for the reflection of egg-laying fish and then running at hard angles to catch them with both hands. "Cambodia rules!" he shouts after running twenty feet up the beach and grabbing two fish at once.

Joe is now running back and forth in the water with less success except at getting himself soaking wet diving into the shallows with knees and elbows. "Dad, one just bounced off my leg," he shouts excitedly.

"Look up on the sand," Charlie encourages him.

Another small kid, a girl, catches one and runs up to show it to her mom sitting in a beach chair who says, "That's great honey. Go put it in the bucket."

I talk to an older Asian man with a thick accent and a plastic bucket containing about two dozen grunion. He says they'll go in a "small fish stew." His friend comes over and they begin talking with their backs to me.

Suddenly, coming up the beach is a UFO of flashing lights, red, white, and blue, like a mother ship six feet off the ground with an escort of UFO fighters shifting positions close to the sand, really strange and inexplicable looking. As they come even with us we see it's a bare-chested guy in silk shorts wearing a strobing headband jogging with five Chihuahuas wearing similar flashing LED collars. Only in O.B., I think.

After about thirty minutes and several more salty soakings Joe finally succeeds in catching a grunion two handed, shows his silver fish off to us proudly, and then tosses it back into the waves.

It strikes me that grunion hunting has changed from what I remember years ago as being family oriented, hugely fun, and slightly romantic in that it always takes place two to six nights after a full moon on a high tide. Tonight it seems more like a frenzy of avaricious people looking to grab free bits of meat and as much as they can, as if they've just opened the doors for a holiday sale at Walmart. I'm thinking we could use more culturally appropriate marine education or at least more Fish and Game wardens.

The next day I go bodysurfing in O.B.'s seventy-degree summer-warmed waters before heading home, and it feels like a perfect beach day, like things haven't really changed that much.

Every epic tale, somewhere close to its end, should include a scene of homecoming and of a battle won.

I became aware of one of my own city's natural treasures only in 2009: 422 acres of spectacular San Francisco Bay–facing green space and submerged eel grass meadows that the city council planned to sell off for a megacasino development. Point Molate, located just north of the Richmond Bridge to Marin, contains a historic wine port (with a brick castle) that later became a navy fuel oil depot before the navy sold it to the city for a dollar in 2003. Moving from alcohol to petroleum to gambling might make sense in terms of a continuity of human addictions, but otherwise I didn't get it. As a friend who works on Bay Area watershed restoration noted, "Point Molate is the most beautiful part of the bay no one's ever heard of."

The headland is an example of the resiliency of nature left unpaved, rapidly reclaiming its terrestrial area as hilly coastal grassland and range-managed by mule deer and wild turkey with colossal toyons—Christmas berry shrubs—the size of live oaks. There are also live oaks, federally protected Suisun Marsh aster, native Molate blue fescue—a unique local bunchgrass horticulturists have bred for landscaping—coyote brush, wild mint, Dutchman's pipe vine, and its rarely seen companion, the pipevine swallowtail butterfly. "This is the most beautiful area imaginable for grassland geeks," Lech Naumovich, a red-bearded botanist said happily as he showed me around. Just offshore by an old wharf, acres of submerged aquatic plants acted as a nursery and sanctuary for bay fish and marine wildlife.

After hiking around the headlands I was convinced this could be the third emerald jewel of bay-facing green parks along with the Presidio of San Francisco and Fort Baker in Marin. In Fort Baker, along with a Coast Guard Station, marina, and the Bay Area Discovery Museum, you have the Cavallo Point Lodge, a small resort that was built on an existing historic site within the park but that didn't require loss of public ownership, paving over a major watershed, or installing four thousand slot machines in order to provide jobs and recreation for its community.

Unfortunately Point Molate, with its million-dollar views of the bay and Mount Tamalpais, had generated a more predictable plan tailor-made for a poor, predominantly African American and Hispanic community with high unemployment and a municipal history of corruption—transferring the land's title to Upstream LLC, a private consortium put together by a Berkeley developer who was working with a small band of Pomo Indians from Mendocino that he hoped would become California's next gaming tribe. Upstream had paid the city $15 million nonrefundable dollars toward a possible $50 million purchase price, promising to build the greenest most eco-sustainable billion-dollar casino, high-rise hotel, and parking structure this side of Las Vegas. They also promised tens of millions more dollars from imagined future gambling revenues to the city, county, environmental critics, and others. Along with the city land transfer, Secretary of the Interior Ken Salazar and the Bureau of Indian Affairs would have to agree to convert Point Molate into reservation land for the gambling proposal to advance.

The majority on the city council seemed to think Upstream's promise of service jobs for maids and security guards was the best they could hope to provide their low-income constituents. However, in my own conversations with a range of folks around Richmond, I found no indication there was any strong support for the casino plan. More typical were fears of increased crime, traffic, and gambling addiction. So after almost thirty years as a journalist I decided it was time to fight city hall. I wasn't alone; there was a well-established volunteer group called Citizens for a Sustainable Point Molate (CFSPM) that I worked with. There was the city's Green Party mayor, Gayle McLaughlin, who also opposed the plan. Plus, there was the Richmond Progressive Alliance, another active player in the city of one hundred thousand that thought Richmond could attract better jobs in renewable energy and green tech.

Going to city council meetings turned out to be better than watching cage fighting on TV, as the council argued loudly over the project with little respect for one anothers' opinions. One of the most vocal defenders of Upstream was Nat Bates, a longtime councilmember. When I suggested he recuse himself from voting on Point Molate because Upsteam developer Jim Levine was one of three financial sponsors of his weekly broadcast cable show, he demanded the city attorney publically repeat an opinion he'd solicited that this was not a conflict of interest. The Contra Costa County Buildings Trade Council also regularly turned out for the meetings handing out green T-shirts reading "Support the resort at Point Molate," even though most of their members didn't live in Richmond. "Remember, don't call it a casino, call it a destination resort," I heard one of their leaders coaching a member. "You put a casino out there and you'll manufacture money," a pro-casino speaker promised. Charles Smith, a member of Citizens for a Sustainable Point Molate and recently retired from AFSCME, the public employees union, wasn't impressed. "These construction guys would support building a concentration camp if it gave them a year's work," he griped to me as we sat in the audience one night. Even the gaming industry was beginning to feel the economic pinch of the recession, and after years of planning delays and promises unrealized, support for the megacasino shifted from five to two, to four to three council members. Finally they agreed to put a nonbinding referendum titled Measure U on the November 2010 election ballot that for the first time would let the citizens of Richmond vote on whether they supported a casino complex on their undeveloped waterfront.

The election marked a tidal shift in the ability of a poor community to determine the future of its own public shoreline and destiny and to respond to outside pressure. Also, never to be left out of local politics, was the Chevron Corporation, the city's major employer with a refinery just over the ridgeline from Point Molate that put $1 million behind three city council candidates who were not only supportive of Chevron but also pro-casino (though one who had voted for the casino while on the council opposed it in the election). Nat Bates, one of the Chevron-backed candidates, ran against Gail McLaughlin for the mayor's seat. From its inception Measure U was heavily fought over, with close to $1 million spent on the initiative both by the casino developer ($500,000) and local card rooms and smaller Indian gaming interests who didn't want the competition (more than $450,000). Plus, Chevron's $1 million was in play. Chevron money was used to dig up dirt on the mayor. It was announced that she had once declared bankruptcy and had been treated for depression. In a predominantly poor community with high unemployment and issues of health care access, I suspect this may have won her more sympathy than enmity.

Two weeks before the election a press conference was held on the headlands where Upstream, the Guidiville Band of Pomos, and three green groups announced an agreement to drop a longstanding environmental lawsuit in exchange for a promised $48 million payout from the slots to buy up additional shoreline for conservation (that would mostly be outside of Richmond). "When you have money, you draw money. It's a major shoreline protection agreement," claimed Robert Cheasty, president of Citizens for East Shore Parks, which was dropping its suit. The San Francisco Bay chapter of the Sierra Club and the local Audubon Society also endorsed the deal and added their names to a pro-casino flyer that went out to voters a few days later. Citizens for a Sustainable Point Molate claimed the agreement "threw Richmond under the gambling bus," and released a letter with the signatures of twenty other Bay Area environmental and marine groups opposed to the casino. When the people finally got their say they rejected the pro-casino Measure U by a vote of 57.5 percent to 42.5 percent. Mayor Gayle McLaughlin, despite being outspent by her opponent almost two to one, was reelected along with two anticasino candidates, fellow Richmond

Progressive Alliance member Jovanka Beckles, a children's mental health provider, and longtime city hall gadfly Corky Booze. None of the three Chevron-backed candidates won their races.

Five months later, after a raucous five-hour meeting in the city auditorium with more than three hundred mostly anticasino residents and hours of public testimony under a large hand-painted banner reading "Richmond voted no casino," the new council voted five to two to "discontinue" consideration of the casino plan. Secretary of the Interior Ken Salazar then put the final nail in the plan when the Bureau of Indian Affairs announced they could not approve Point Molate for a reservation site. The developer demanded his $15 million back in cash or property and later sued the city and Department of Interior, not seeming to realize that when you gamble you usually lose.

The Point Molate victory showed what a dynamic coalition of environmentalists and political progressives with deep roots in their community can achieve, but I think something more was also at play. From the beginning, when the casino had a big majority of council votes and looked to be a sure bet, I thought Point Molate could still be saved because there is a history, on the bay and along the shore, of preventing badly thought-out development schemes that might undermine the natural beauty, ecological integrity, and public access (or ownership) that have become a hallmark of much of California's coast and ocean. I felt Citizens for a Sustainable Point Molate and its leaders were walking the same paths of protest and organizing earlier trod by Save San Francisco Bay's founding mothers, by the Sierra Club of the 1970s that helped establish the Golden Gate National Recreation Area, and by many other activists who believed failure was not a viable option. When it comes to protecting public lands, watersheds, and the ocean, if you can't save them here you can't save them anywhere.

On Earth Day, 2012, seventy-five people participated in a cleanup at Point Molate Beach, the loveliest shoreline in the city, which has been closed to the public since 2004 due to budget cuts.

It's a warm day under a robin's egg blue sky as we collect a truckload of trash off this half-mile crescent of sand. CFSPM volunteers Joan, Pam, and Charles, Lech the botanist and his thirteen-month old daughter, Kiaya, are here, as are a number of families, a couple of kayakers, sailors from a nearby marina, dogs, photographers, a city councilman, and the mayor and her husband, who seem delighted with our work. Longtime resident Sally Amsbury says her family swam here thirty-five years ago. Community activist Andres Sotos tells me he came here as a teenager in the 1980s. "It was a makeout scene for us, isolated, a place we could come and have some fun." He grins with slightly wicked nostalgia. My friend Lincoln and I dig up a buried tire, pick up shotgun shells, a full Mercury sail and sail bag, and some oil boom that must be left over from the *Cosco Busan*. Another guy finds a complete marine toilet. Just offshore a sea lion cruises by. A pelican flies overhead. Andres and three other guys rig a rope sling to carry a three hundred-pound rusted pipe off the beach. After three hours the beach is clean. We gather on the grassy, tree-shaded bluff for food prepared by CJ's Barbecue & Fish, a local favorite. Small groups gather under the trees to look out across the bay. There's some talk about U.C. Berkeley's recent decision to open a major research lab at the other end of the city's waterfront on an old industrial field station near my house. It will work on clean energy and bring an initial eight hundred jobs to Richmond with more to follow. Things feel good, getting together with our neighbors, cleaning up our commons. We're expecting the city will reopen the beach shortly, (which it unanimously voted to do in July 2012) the first step to opening up all of Point Molate. Restoring this sometimes abused but still vibrant natural headland may take a long time, but that's okay because, to paraphrase one of my heroes, Peter Douglas, the bay is never saved, the bay is always being saved.

I head to Shelter Cove on the Lost Coast, turning west off 101 near the agricultural weed town of Garberville and through a foggy grove of sky-scraping redwoods that puts me in the presence of the sacred. Twenty mountainous miles later, I'm driving down into Shelter Cove, a finger of land jutting out into the Pacific. It's a flat bluff and hillside village below deeply forested mountains with 693 year-round residents, the only settlement of size left on the Lost Coast.

The random sprawl of its five hundred multistory vacation homes and smaller houses on the edge of the King Range wilderness is split by a three thousand-foot runway on the flats with tide pools, sea stacks, and rugged black-sand beaches on one side, rising forest on the other, and an unkempt nine-hole golf course at the south end of the airstrip, where a bunch of guys are drinking by their trucks when I arrive. One rusting pickup has a bumper sticker reading "Save Humboldt County—Keep pot illegal." You might think it's a moral statement, but actually it's a market statement. Lots of growers are worried prices will crater if the crop is legalized. Three deer graze just beyond the runway and two turkey vultures roost nearby on a low fence.

The cove itself is at the bottom of a steep boat ramp on a narrow strip of black volcanic sand next to an L-shaped pile of boulders that acts as a breakwater. More buzzards are circling overhead. The crescent cove is protected from northern storms but not those coming out of the south, as early sailors seeking refuge here soon discovered. Steep wooded cliffs march off to the south toward the Sinkyone Wilderness past No Pass and Dead Man's Gulch to Whale Gulch, where some thirty to fifty people still live in the high canyons that local rancher Bob McGee leased to the first back-to-the-land hippies of the 1960s.

That was already seventy-five years past Shelter Cove's primetime. In the late 1800s the town had a 960-foot steamship pier for loading tan bark from tan oaks before chemical treatment of leather came into fashion, also Durham cattle and Merino sheep from area ranches along with smoked salmon, deerskins, and abalone from local tide pools, creeks and the Mattole River to the north. Passengers from San Francisco would disembark to visit and put up at the Shelter Cove Hotel, destined to become "the greatest resort on the coast," according to the *Humboldt Times,* but times changed.

It was in the 1920s that engineers building the state coastal road decided the coast from northern Mendocino up through the King Range was too rugged for grading and swung California Highway 1 inland for more than sixty miles. Then the Depression came and people fled the steep mountain ranches and the black forest, which is what they called the elevated valleys whose canopy of trees were so thick they blacked out the sky. These steep ranges are the spawn of three tectonic plates that converge at the Mendocino Triple Junction—the Pacific, the North American, and the Juan de Fuca—pushing the mountains straight up out of the sea with King Peak at 4,088 feet the tallest coastal mountaintop in the United States south of Alaska.

Before World War II the young Machi brothers Mario, Tony, and Babe, came to Shelter Cove to fish each summer. As an army trooper during the war, Mario survived the Bataan Death March and two years as a Japanese POW in the Philippines by thinking about returning to fish here. In 1946 the brothers returned to develop Shelter Cove as a sportfishing resort and opened a marina. By the 1960s politically well-connected Southern California real-estate developers had discovered the cove and subdivided it into about five thousand tracts—at the time the biggest planned residential development in the state. They quickly began selling off the lots, often sight unseen. Half were on hillsides too steep to build on. Road access to more than a thousand were wiped out by winter rains. Not wanting potential buyers to realize how remote their "resort" was, connected to the outside world by a single twisting one-lane dirt road, they began flying them up from L.A. in twin-engine DC-3 aircraft. In 1971 one of the flights had trouble on takeoff and crashed into the ocean, killing seventeen people. Following passage of Proposition 20 the California Coastal Commission was created and helped put an end to reckless developments and real-estate scams along the coast. At Shelter Cove only about 10 percent of the five thousand planned lots were deemed fit for building on. Those lots are what make up today's village.

I call Joe Shepp, a building contractor with years of experience flying Northern California who's offered to show me around. Unfortunately, while it's clearing in Garberville where he keeps his plane, it's socked in down here by the water. We agree to see how the weather is tomorrow.

I head over to Black Sands Beach at the north end of town, past offshore pinnacles covered in cormorants and a few big orange sea stars. The waves are large and treacherous along the beach and on its steeply inclined slope, pounding over sea rocks and swooshing high up toward the bluffs with the rattle of beach stones caught in the surge. I go around a few bluffs between sets keeping a wary eye out for sleeper waves, as a number of people have died here. In 2000 a group of high school students from Canada were on the beach when one of their chaperones, a forty-five-year-old woman, was hit by a rogue wave. Two seventeen-year-old boys went into the water to try to rescue her. All three drowned. More recently in 2011 a twenty-nine-year-old visitor from Arkansas tried to go swimming here and drowned and his fifty-five-year-old mother nearly drowned trying to rescue him.

Toward sunset the low clouds part, revealing miles of rolling forest-covered escarpments to the north that remind me of Kodiak, Alaska. This beach is the end point for the twenty-four-mile-long Lost Coast Trail that starts on the Mattole River near Petrolia. It takes two to three days to complete the hike with lots of scrambling over boulders, across streams, up and down steep slopes, and along narrow beaches where you have to keep an eye on your tide charts to avoid getting trapped. In the course of hiking you've a good chance to see sea lions, harbor seals, whales, elk, deer, ospreys, bald eagles, skunks, raccoons, and perhaps a black bear or mountain lion paw prints in the dark sand.

The next day my luck turns. It's cleared up by noon with just a few scattered clouds as I watch Joe land his single-engine blue, red, and white Cessna 182 and taxi up next to me. I climb into the cramped cabin. Joe is about five-ten with a mustache and graying ponytail. Sixty-one he's been flying the Lost Coast for more than half his life and is one of only three pilots allowed to land at Big Flats, a private in-holding and world-class surfing break in the middle of the King Range National Conservation Area overseen by the Bureau of Land Management.

We take off into the wind and rise smoothly out over the water, turning south above town following the rising bluffs into the Sinkyone Wilderness, past the hillside settlement at Whale Gulch. Big white rolling waves are washing onto its volcanic black-sand beach littered with driftwood. From 1,800 feet up Joe calls the wave heights at between six and eight feet, which he's able to do because he's been surfing as long as he's been flying.

"This reminds me of Alaska," I tell him on the headphone mike I've pushed to my lips.

"Real estate's more here," he notes.

The standard forty acres of rural hillside land for growing marijuana in Humboldt now sells for around $250,000 even with the recession.

We pass over a few creeks and Bear Harbor and Mistake Point, which I bet does not have a happy story attached to it, and he points out Red Mountain in the interior before we turn around and head north. At Bear Creek the cliffs drop down to a milky channel that is blocked in by black sand. We pass over creek beds with chalky green opal-colored water, white surf, and grasses and scrub covering the eroded cliffs below the tree line and Joe tells me homeless folks were living on the creek outlets last summer, "a couple of hundred mostly younger people without jobs and growing marijuana and hiking into town for their few supplies and some had children. These are young people not making it in society and I hope they do all right." He then indicates a nice set of waves below and we fly back over the cove and are soon above Big Flat, which is a wide wedge of ground with a perfect point break like Rincon and Malibu below steep forty-five-degree slopes several thousand feet high. There are two small planes parked on a dirt strip near the private ranch house, half a dozen tents by the water, and half a dozen surfers in the water catching big clean sets. Joe tells me a good story about seeing two orcas breaching while taking off from the flats and a bad one about paddling out with his buddy and finding the body of a blond woman who'd disappeared two weeks earlier while abalone diving. Her body must have gotten stuck in an underwater crevice and another surge had dislodged it.

There are a number of small creek outlets along the coast below its steep cliffs and a hillside where the trees are all matchstick bare where there was a big lightning-strike fire. I can see what looks like a fine brown filament running across the mountainside that must be the hiking trail.

We fly past the wide sandy banks of the Mattole River where they've done successful salmon restoration work and where brown-colored black bears come to the riverbank to feed just like their bigger cousins up in Canada and Alaska. Then we fly over some big offshore rocks and the Petrolia-Ferndale road appears below us, running along the coast.

Joe tells me he's flown for LightHawk, the environmental volunteer air corps, and did some "granola drops" (aerial food supply) for Earth First! activists when they were occupying trees and blocking logging trucks in the now state-protected Headwater Forest Reserve, the redwood forest, back in the 1990s. He flew journalists and photographers over the giant redwood that the lovely and photogenic tree-sitter Julia Butterfly lived in for two years.

Up ahead beyond Humboldt Bay we can see a wall of gray, a weather front from the Arctic building up. We climb to 2,500 feet as turbulence begins to kick in and the coast flattens out below us. We pass over the wide wandering mouth and alluvial plain of the Eel River, "the mighty Eel." Joe grins and I'm impressed by all the cattle and dairy farms spread out around Ferndale. "This is a real farm dell where there's eighty to a hundred feet of river silt topsoil," he explains. We fly over Humboldt Bay and the harbor entry with its twin jetties and miles of breaking surf on either side, looking across the Samoa Peninsula toward the small city of Eureka before we bank around to head back over the mountains to Shelter Cove.

Turning south under spreading cloud cover broken by shafts of radiant sunlight, looking at the approaching wilderness cliffs and sea rocks contrasting starkly against the dazzling bright silver sea, I take a slow, cool breath and feel a sense of wonder and transcendence, that moment of connectedness you sometimes get being part of something larger than yourself. Looking out across the curve of the Pacific I'm reminded of all the connections that link those who go down to the sea and those who work and play upon its waters and those we remember lost to the sea and those who are redeemed by it and so feel compelled to give something back. Thanks to luck, history, and lots of good stewardship it seems to me at this moment that our sacred blue marble planet shines just a little brighter here along California's Golden Shore.

Acknowledgments

I'd like to thank my agent Kevan Lyon, editor Peter Joseph, Margaret Sutherland Brown, copy editor Frances Sayers, and others at Thomas Dunne Books, an imprint of St. Martin's Press, which is a division of Macmillan, all a part of the endangered ecosystem of publishing. Along with the many people mentioned and profiled in this book I'd also like to randomly acknowledge those who went out of their way to help get me around on and into the water including Grant Werschkull at the Smith River Alliance, Gerry McChesney with the U.S. Fish and Wildlife Service and Mary-Jane Schramm at NOAA who helped get me on the Farallones. For ship access I appreciate help provided by Cdr. Jason Salata at U.S. Naval Surface Forces, also Lt. Cdr. David McKinney and Chief John Lill and Sr. Chief Donnie Ryan aboard the USS *Makin Island.* U.S. Coast Guard Capt. Roger Laferriere formerly in charge of Sector Los Angeles was very helpful getting me around the San Pedro ports with additional thanks to Joe Nebelsky and his crew from USCG Auxiliary Los Angeles, also my escort Lt. Damien Ludwick and Jacobsen Pilot Service. Thanks to the Port of L.A. media master Phillip Sanfield and of course Executive Director Geraldine Knatz who we later presented with the Peter Benchley Ocean Award. Peter Olney and Craig Marillees of the ILWU (International Longshore and Warehouse Union) were and are most helpful friends as is Jon Christensen in San Diego, an inveterate sailor who's only gotten me shipwrecked once. Thanks also to Dave Schwartz who avoided getting us swamped. Thanks to Coast

Guard Sector San Diego for letting me go out with them. Thanks to Tim Molinaire and Scott Fielder for sharing water time in the surf and the kelp forests (though that's thanks enough). Also a shout out to the many marine science folks who gave me access to boats and labs including Dirk Rosen with MARE (Marine Applied Research & Exploration), Bruce Robison and Chris Scholin at MBARI (Monterey Bay Aquarium Research Institute), David Caron and Sean Conner at Wrigley, Steve Palumbi at Hopkins, Kenneth Coale at Moss Landing Marine Lab, Gary Cherr at the Bodega Marine Lab, and Paul Dayton at Scripps. Without knowing me, Joe Shepp was willing to give me a dramatic flyover of the lost coast. Many thanks. Also to Joan Garrett, Pam Stello, Charles Smith, and other members of Citizens for a Sustainable Point Molate for your commitment to saving a unique headlands in my homewaters of Richmond. And to Blue Frontier Campaign (www.bluefront.org) staff and board who let me wander off and get wet writing books about the ocean and coastal communities we're trying to protect. Thanks for your photos Jesse Altstatt, Kyle Thiermann (that's him in the curl), and the Ocean Institute and Monterey Bay Aquarium. And props to my good friend and video editor Ted Woerner who cut the book video that goes along with this lively tome. Finally, thanks to Anne Bolen in Alexandria, Virginia, who lent her critical editor's ear and some timely empathy as I was assembling this literary craft. You're in my heart on a further shore.

Recommended Reading

Arax, Mark. *West of the West: Dreamers, Believers, Builders, and Killers in the Golden State*. New York: Public Affairs, 2009.

Asbury, Herbert. *The Barbary Coast: An Informal History of the San Francisco Underworld*. New York: Basic Books 2008. First published 1933.

Bommelyn, Loren. *Tolowa People's Language*. Smith River, Calif.: Self-published, 2006.

Boyle, T. C. *When the Killing's Done*. New York: Viking, 2011.

California Coastal Commission. *California Coastal Resource Guide*. Berkeley: University of California Press, 1987.

Cannon, Lou. *President Reagan: The Role of a Lifetime*. New York: Simon and Schuster, 1991.

Casey, Susan. *The Devil's Teeth: A True Story of Obsession and Survival Among America's Great White Sharks*. New York: Henry Holt, 2005.

———. *The Wave: In Pursuit of the Rogues, Freaks, and Giants of the Ocean*. New York: Doubleday, 2010.

Chase, J. Smeaton. *California Coast Trails: A Horseback Ride from Mexico to Oregon*. Boston: Houghton Mifflin, 1913.

Dana, Richard Henry Jr. *Two Years Before the Mast: A Personal Narrative of Life at Sea*. New York: Barnes and Noble Classics, 2006. First published 1840.

Davis, Chuck. *California Reefs*. San Francisco: Chronicle Books, 1991.

Davis, Mike, Kelly Mayhew, and Jim Miller. *Under the Perfect Sun: The San Diego Tourists Never See*. New York: The New Press, 2003.

Doerper, John. *Coastal California*. New York: Random House, 2005.

Duane, Daniel. *Caught Inside: A Surfer's Year on the California Coast*. New York: North Point Press, 1996.

Eilperin, Juliet. *Demon Fish: Travels Through the Hidden World of Sharks*. New York: Pantheon Books, 2011.

Ellis, Richard, and John E. McCosker. *Great White Shark*. Palo Alto, Calif.: Stanford University Press, 1991.

Fagan, Brian M. *Before California: An Archaeologist Looks at Our Earliest Inhabitants*. Walnut Creek, Calif.: AltaMira Press, 2003.

Fish, Peter, ed. *California's Best: Two Centuries of Great Writing from the Golden State*. Helena Mont.: Farcountry Press, 2009.

Fradkin, Alex L., and Philip L. Fradkin. *The Left Coast: California on the Edge*. Berkeley: University of California Press, 2011.

Griffin, L. Martin. *Saving the Marin-Sonoma Coast: The Battles for Audubon Canyon Ranch, Point Reyes, & California's Russian River*. Healdsburg, Calif.: Sweetwater Springs Press, 1998.

Griggs, Gary, Kiki Patsch, and Lauret Savoy. *Living with the Changing California Coast*. Berkeley: University of California Press, 2005.

Hayes, Derek. *Historical Atlas of California*. Berkeley: University of California Press, 2007.

Heizer, Robert F., and Alan J. Almquist. *The Other Californians: Prejudice and Discrimination Under Spain, Mexico, and the United States to 1920*. Berkeley: University of California Press, 1971.

———., and Albert B. Elsasser. *The Natural World of the California Indians*. Berkeley: University of California Press, 1980.

Hellwarth, Ben. *Sealab: America's Forgotten Quest to Live and Work on the Ocean Floor*. New York: Simon and Schuster, 2012.

Helvarg, David. *Blue Frontier: Dispatches from America's Ocean Wilderness*. San Francisco: Sierra Club Books, 2006.

———. *Saved by the Sea: A Love Story with Fish*. New York: St. Martin's Press, 2010.

Holliday, J. S. *The World Rushed In: The California Gold Rush Experience*. Norman: University of Oklahoma Press, 2002.

Howarth, Stephen. *To Shining Sea: A History of the United States Navy 1775–1998*. Norman: University of Oklahoma Press, 1999.

Hundley Jr., Norris. *The Great Thirst: Californians and Water, 1770s–1990s.* Berkeley: University of California Press, 1992.

Jacobs, John. *A Rage for Justice: The Passion and Politics of Phillip Burton.* Berkeley: University of California Press, 1995.

Jeffers, Robinson. *The Selected Poetry of Robinson Jeffers.* Palo Alto, Calif.: Stanford University Press. 1966.

Jones, Ray, and Joe Lubow. *Disasters and Heroic Rescues: California.* Guilford, Conn.: Globe Pequot Press, 2006.

Kildow, Judith, and Charles S. Colgan. *California's Ocean Economy.* Sacramento, Calif.: California Resources Agency Report, 2005.

Kipling, Rudyard. *Captains Courageous.* West Berlin, N.J.: Townsend Press, 2007. First published 1896.

Labaree, Benjamin W., et al. *America and the Sea: A Maritime History.* Mystic, Conn.: Mystic Seaport Museum Publications, 1998.

Leet, William S., Christopher Dewees, Richard Klingbeil, and Eric Larson. *California's Living Marine Resources.* Sacramento: University of California Press, 2001.

Lichatowich, Jim. *Salmon Without Rivers: A History of the Pacific Salmon Crisis.* Washington, D.C.: Island Press, 1999.

Linder, Bruce. *San Diego's Navy.* Annapolis: Naval Institute Press, 2001.

London, Jack. *The Cruise of the Snark.* New York: Macmillan, 1911.

———. *Tales of the Fish Patrol.* Berkeley, Calif.: Heyday Books, 2005. First published 1905.

Love, Milton. *Certainly More Than You Want to Know About the Fishes of the Pacific Coast.* Santa Barbara, Calif.: Really Big Press, 2011.

McPhee, John. *Assembling California.* New York: Farrar, Straus and Giroux, 1993.

Miller, Max. *Harbor of the Sun: The Story of the Port of San Diego.* New York: Doubleday, 1940.

Misuraca, Karen. *The California Coast.* Stillwater, Minn.: Voyageur Press, 2001.

Motavalli, Jim, ed. *Feeling the Heat: Dispatches from the Frontlines of Climate Change.* New York: Routledge, 2004.

Nathanson, Andrew, Clayton Everline, and Mark Renneker. *Surf Survival: The Surfer's Health Handbook.* New York: Skyhorse Publishing, 2011.

Nunn, Kem. *The Dogs of Winter.* New York: Pocket Books, 1997.

Ocean Resources Management Program. *California's Ocean Resources.* Sacramento Calif.: State Printing Office, 1997.

Orbelian, George. *Essential Surfing.* San Francisco, Calif.: Orbelian Arts, 1982.

Paddison, Joshua, ed. *A World Transformed: Firsthand Accounts of California Before the Gold Rush.* Berkeley, Calif.: Heyday Books, 1999.

Palumbi, Stephen R., and Carolyn Sotka. *The Death and Life of Monterey Bay: A Story of Revival*. Washington, D.C.: Island Press, 2011.

Parent, Laurence, and Elinor DeWire. *Lighthouses: Sentinels of the American Coast*. Portland, Ore.: Graphic Arts Center, 2003.

Parker, Bruce. *The Power of the Sea: Tsunamis, Storm Surges, Rogue Waves, and Our Quest to Predict Disasters*. New York: Palgrave Macmillan, 2010.

Pew Oceans Commission. *America's Living Oceans: Charting a Course for Sea Change*. Arlington, Va.: Pew Oceans Commission, 2003.

Powell, David C. *A Fascination for Fish: Adventures of an Underwater Pioneer*. Berkeley: University of California Press, 2001.

Rayner, Richard. *The Associates: Four Capitalists Who Created California*. New York: W. W. Norton, 2008.

Reisner, Marc. *A Dangerous Place: California's Unsettling Fate*. New York: Penguin, 2003.

Ricketts, Edward F., Jack Calvin, and Joel W. Hedgpeth. Revised by David W. Phillips. *Between Pacific Tides*. 5th ed. Palo Alto, Calif.: Stanford University Press, 1985.

Riegert, Ray. *Hidden Coast of California*. 11th ed. Berkeley, Calif.: Ulysses Press, 2007.

Schmieder, Robert W. *Ecology of an Underwater Island*. Walnut Creek, Calif.: Cordell Expeditions, 1991.

Shanks, Ralph, and Wick York. *The U.S. Life-Saving Service: Heroes, Rescues and Architecture of the Early Coast Guard*. Edited by Lisa Woo Shanks. Novato, Calif.: Costano Books, 2004.

Sharpsteen, Bill. *The Docks*. Berkeley: University of California Press, 2011.

Sollen, Robert. *An Ocean of Oil: A Century of Political Struggle Over Petroleum Off the California Coast*. Juneau, Alaska: The Denali Press, 1998.

Starr, Kevin. *California: A History*. New York: The Modern Library, 2005.

———. *Embattled Dreams: California in War and Peace 1940–1950*. Oxford: Oxford University Press, 2002.

Steinbeck, John. *Cannery Row*. New York: Penguin, 1992. First published 1945.

———. *The Log from the Sea of Cortez*. New York: Penguin, 1995. First published 1941.

———. *Sweet Thursday*. New York: Penguin, 2008. First published 1954.

U.S. Commission on Ocean Policy. *Report of the U.S. Commission on Ocean Policy*. Washington, D.C.: Government Printing Office, 2004.

Warshaw, Matt. *The History of Surfing*. San Francisco, Calif.: Chronicle Books, 2010.

Wellock, Thomas Raymond. *Critical Masses: Opposition to Nuclear Power in California 1958–1978*. Madison: University of Wisconsin Press, 1998.

White, Peter. *The Farallon Islands: Sentinels of the Golden Gate*. San Francisco, Calif.: Scottwall Associates Publishers, 1995.

Winchester, Simon. *A Crack in the Edge of the World: The Great American Earthquake of 1906*. New York: Harper Collins, 2005.

Winslow, Don. *The Dawn Patrol*. New York: Vintage Books, 2008.

Index

dugout canoes, 19
Dunlop, John, 181

Earle, Sylvia, 69, 193, 297
Earth First!, 287
Eastham, Lt. Cdr. Will, 162
Eckart, Carl, 197–98
ecological collapse, 48, 59
eggers, 59
Eisenhower, Dwight, 149
El Niño Southern Oscillation, 192, 253, 299–300
elephant seals, 226, 233, 263–64
Elk, CA, 283
Elk Valley Indians, 26
Elliot, Ron, 231–32
Ellison, Larry, 299
Ely, Eugene, 143
Endangered Species Act, 30–31, 63
Endris, Todd, 221
energy. *See* alternative energy
English colonialism, 36
Environmental Protection Agency, 168
environmentalism
    militarism and, 149–50
    redwoods and, 271
erosion, 253
Eureka, CA, 287–88
exostosis (surfer's ear, swimmer's ear), 107

Fagan, Brian, 21
Farallon Islands, 17, 85, 232–35
Farallon Patrol, 230–31
Farr, Sam, 171, 182, 186–87
Farragut, David G., 140–41
Fielder, Scott, 79
Figueroa, José, death of, 48
fisheries management, traditional, 72, 74

fishing, 27–29. *See also* commercial fishing; overfishing; recreational fishing
    for grunion, 307–9
    for subsistence, 83–84
Fitzgerald Marine Reserve, 267
Flagg, Marco, 222
Fletcher, Bob, 72–75
Fletcher, Troy, 30, 33
flood events, 253, 300, 304
Foo, Mark, 2, 103, 105–6
Ford, Jeremy, 132
Fort Bragg, 44, 71, 268–72, 284–85
Fort Ord, 148, 184, 266
Fort Ross, 46–47
fossil fuels. *See also* alternative energy
    in California, 302–3
    weaning off, 155, 163
Fox, Adam, 231, 236–39
Franklin, Ben, 193–94
Fraser, Captain, Alexander, 58
Freeman, Jim, 297
Freeth, George, 91–93, 95
Fremont, John Charles, 54–55, 139–40
French, Leroy, 218
Friedman, Tom, 163
Frye, Donna, 108–9
Frye, Skip, 99, 108
Fujii, Ens. Everett, 272–75

Galapagos Islands, 77
Garamendi, John, 172
Garberville, CA, 286, 314–15
Garret, Joan, 306
Geffen, David, 258
genocide, 23–25
Ghost Forest, 66
Giddings, Al, 217–18
Gillespie, Archibald, 55, 140
global trade, 4